The Reasons for the Commandments in Jewish Thought

From the Bible to the Renaissance

The Reference Library of Jewish Intellectual History

The Reasons for the Commandments in Jewish Thought

From the Bible to the Renaissance

ISAAC HEINEMANN

Translated by Leonard Levin

Boston
2009

English Translation: Leonard Levin

This translation is based on the following edition:
טעמי המצוות בספרות ישראל — Ta'amei HaMitzvot BeSifrut Yisrael

Published in Hebrew, by (formerly) The Religious Division,
The Youth and Hechalutz Department, World Zionist Organization
(now The Department for Jewish Zionist Education, the Jewish Agency for Israel),
under the supervision of The Jewish Agency Press. Jerusalem 1953, and other editions.

www.jewishagency.org/education

ISBN 978-1-934843-53-6

Book design by Yuri Alexandrov

Published by Academic Studies Press in 2009
28 Montfern Avenue
Brighton, MA 02135, USA
press@academicstudiespress.com
www.academicstudiespress.com

Contents

The Reason for the Mitzvot xii
Author's Preface to First Edition (1942) xiii
Translator's Preface xv

Chapter 1
The Nature of the Question 1
Reasons not to engage in such an inquiry 1
Reasons Such Inquiry is Mandatory 3

Chapter 2
The Biblical View 5
The sources of correct behavior prior to Sinai: God's will and human conscience 5
Even "irrational" commands do not oppose objective morality 6
Conscience Is Important Even After Sinai 7
Types of Reasons in the Torah: Appeal to Authority 8
Understanding the Objective of a Mitzvah 9
Connection to Other Mitzvot or Principles 9
Emotional Reasons 10
Where The Torah is Silent Concerning Reasons 12
The Torah Is Reticent About the Religious Value of the Mitzvot 12
Investigation of the Reasons — Its Basis in the Torah 14

Chapter 3
The Views of the Rabbis 15
1. Irrational from the Individual's Perspective 15
2. Rational from the Lawmaker's Perspective 18
The reasons for the ***ḥukkim*** are hidden 19
The Torah Does Not Distinguish Between Rational and Irrational Mitzvot 21
Why did the Rabbis Distinguish Between Rational and Non-rational Commandments? 21
3. Methodological Questions 23
Is it fitting to seek out intellectual reasons for the mitzvot? 23
Is it permissible to derive halakhic conclusions from the reasons for the mitzvot? 24
4. The Reasons for the Mitzvot According to the Rabbis 25
Measure for Measure 26

Symbolic Reasons 26
The Mitzvot Influence Our Behavior 27
Expound Them and Receive Reward 28

Chapter 4
The Views of the Hellenistic Jews 34
Each Person a Supreme Authority on the Mitzvot's Value 34
Irrational Reasons Not Valued 35
The Greek Autonomous Ethic Influenced the Hellenists 36
National Conservatism as a Reason 37
"Do Not Separate From the Community!" 38
"Natural Law" vs. the Laws of the Legislators 38
The Method of the Extreme Hellenists 39
Philo's Method 40
The Torah's Laws Similar to the Laws of the Universe 40
Ethical Explanations 41
Josephus on Theocracy 42
Philo's Social Explanation 43
Utilitarian Reasons 44
Motivations of the Hellenists and the Rabbis 44
Pros and Cons of the Hellenistic explanation 45
Did Greek Culture Impoverish their Jewish culture? 46

Chapter 5
Views of the Medieval Philosophers 47
General Introduction 47
Three Medieval "Schools" and Their Interaction 47
Disagreements among the Schools 48

Chapter 6
Saadia Gaon 51
The Different Tasks of Human Reason 51
Intellect can help explain the mitzvot 52
The Rational and "Hortative" (***Shim'iyot***) Mitzvot 52
Many Hortative Commandments Have Plausible Reasons 53
The Virtues of Saadia's Method 54
The Drawbacks of Saadia's Method 55
Saadia favors utilitarian reasons 55

Chapter 7
Baḥya ben Joseph Ibn Pakudah 57
The purpose of ***Duties of the Heart*** 57
The Heart — Source for Performing the Mitzvot 58
The Levels of Mitzvah Performers 58
The Propadeutic Value of the Written Torah 59
The Value of the Torah for the Educated Also 60
The Commandments of the Limbs Attest to the Commandments of the Heart 60
Religiosity of the Heart and Fulfillment of the Commandments 62
How does Baḥya's outlook differ from Saadia's? 62

Chapter 8
Rabbi Judah Halevi 65
Purpose of the Kuzari 65
The Mitzvot Seek to Train Us for Coming Closer to God 65
Mitzvot Necessary to Arrive at the Top Rank 66
To reach God, perform the divine commands! 66
Halevi's Approach is Not Magical.......... 67
Our Reason Cannot Understand All the Mitzvot 68
History Testifies to their Value 69
Life of Body and Life of Soul Parallel 69
Psychological Explanations 70
God of Religion vs. the Metaphysical God 72
The Emotional Experience 73
The "Practical-Religious" Value in Halevi 73
Halevi's Personality 74

Chapter 9
Abraham Ibn Ezra.......... 76
The Value of Knowing the Reasons 76
Utilitarian and Ethical Reasons. 77
Symbolic Reasons 77
Secret Relations Between Mitzvot and the Forces of Nature 78
Mystical Arithmetic 79
Astrological Explanations and Their Limitation.......... 79
The Arrangement of the Temple and Its Affairs.......... 81
Toward an Understanding of the Esoteric Explanations 82
Mitzvot that seek to preserve racial purity 82
Ibn Ezra's Common Cause with the Jewish Hellenists 83
Ibn Ezra — Mystic of Science 83

Chapter 10
Abraham Ibn Daud 85
Both the "rational" and "hortative" mitzvot are eternal 85
The mitzvot as acknowledgment of our gratitude.......... 86
Interpreting the Ten Commandments 86
Ranking the "hortative" mitzvot 87
In praise of Abraham for not second-guessing God 88
"Weakness" of the hortative mitzvot: Ibn Daud's relation to Saadia and the modern rationalists 88
Why Ibn Daud Preferred the Rational to the Hortative Mitzvot.......... 90
Why, if all mitzvot are valid, do they differ in rank? 91
Similarities and differences in Baḥya's and Ibn Daud's rankings 92
Ibn Daud, Halevi and Ibn Ezra 93

Chapter 11
Maimonides 95
The Different Points of View in His Various Books 95
1. Is it possible and permitted to explain the mitzvot? 95
Permitted to explain the mitzvot, but not to reject them 96

Those who forbid us to consider the reasons for the mitzvot have erred 97
Caution is required in investigating the reasons for the mitzvot 98
Impossible to Explain All the Details 99
2. The Foundations of Maimonides' Explanation 100
The Torah's Intention: Perfection of Soul and Perfection of Body 100
Three Assumptions for Explaining the Narratives and Precepts of the Torah (With Consideration for Non-Intellectuals Also) 101
Examples for the Above Principle 103
Joy in the mitzvot that Maimonides showed in his life and works, vs. what he says in certain places 104
Tensions with regard to actions 104
Tensions with Regard to Feeling 105
The relation between theoretical and practical man 107
3. The explanation of the Commandments 107
Explanations that Maimonides rejects 108
Casual supports (***asmakhta***) 108
Utilitarian Reasons 109
Some of the Moral Explanations are Social 109
(1) Commemorating historical facts. 110
(2) Cosmological explanations 111
(3) Inculcating the Fear of Heaven 111
(4) Distancing Us from Idol Worship 111
The Sacrifices: Weaning Us from Idolatry 113
His Proofs 113
Maimonides, Ibn Daud and Modern Rationalists 114
Summary 116
More Than Just Intellectualism 116
A Comprehensive, Many-Sided Approach 116
Three Kinds of "Believers," Two in Error 117
Advantage of all the mitzvot 118
Why is only the Torah called a divine law? 118

Chapter 12
Gersonides. 120
Comprehensive Explanation for All Narratives and Mitzvot 120
Hygienic Reasons 121
Many mitzvot act on our moral qualities 121
The reasons for the mitzvah of the Sabbath 122
Gersonides' critique of Maimonides on the sacrifices 123
The Reasons for the Implements of the Sanctuary 125
Reasons for the Priesthood 126

Chapter 13
Ḥasdai Crescas 127
Defense of the Torah against Christian attacks 127
The generation of the wilderness was not spiritually inferior 127
Original Sin; salvation through circumcision and the Akedah 128
How are we redeemed through these two commandments? 129
The salvific power of all the mitzvot 129

The love of God is the pivot of faith 130
Why so many mitzvot? 131
Primary purposes 131
Intermediate purposes 131
Our Eternal Lives Are Not Dependent on the Acquisition of Correct Opinions 132
Rather: The Ultimate Purpose of the Mitzvot of the Torah is Love and Fear of God 133
How Does the Torah Educate Toward Love of God? 134
The Reasons for Various Mitzvot 134

Chapter 14
Joseph Albo 141
The Reasons for the Sacrifices and Sabbath 141
The Three Kinds of Laws and Their Value 141
Everything Goes According to the Heart's Intention 142
Judaism Surpasses Christianity in Its Appreciation of the Heart's Intention .. 143
Practical value realized from keeping the mitzvot 143
Levels of Feeling Connected to Fulfillment of the Commandments 144
The Relationship Between Religious Emotion and Fulfillment of the Mitzvot 145
Not by Intellectual Understanding but Rather by Reverence for God Do We Earn the World to Come 146
What is the difference between Crescas and Albo? 147
The Value of Albo's Method 148

Chapter 15
Don Isaac Abravanel 149
Categories of the Torah's Commandments 149
There is an Intrinsic Value to the Mitzvot of the Torah 149
There is No Uniform Purpose for All of the Mitzvot of the Torah 150
Abravanel Objects to Utilitarian Reasons for the Mitzvot 151
Abravanel is Sparing with Social Reasons for the Torah's Mitzvot 151
Abravanel's Method of Interpreting the Mitzvot 152
The Reasons for the Sacrifices 152
The Reasons for the Shofar 154
The Pedagogic Value of the Mitzvot 155
Ethical-Religious Explanations of the Torah's Commandments 156
The Religious Influence of the Mitzvot 157
All the Mitzvot Speak to Us in Allusions and Symbols 157

Chapter 16
Summary of the Medieval Thinkers 159
The Difference Between the Hellenistic and Medieval Thinkers' Explanation of the Mitzvot 159
Balance of Autonomous and Heteronomous Reasons 159
The Creator's Wisdom is Recognized in His Mitzvot 161
We Must Observe the Mitzvot Even If Their Reasons are Hidden From Us .. 162
The Love of God, Not Pursuit of Happiness, Enables Us to Fulfill the Creator's Mitzvot 163
The Individualistic Direction in Explanation of the Mitzvot 163

Chapter 17
Principal Conclusions 165
(A) A Systematic Arrangement of the Answers to the Problem 166
The Differences Between the Two Types of Reasons 166
The Apologetic Factor 167
The Theoretical Factor 168
The Practical Factor 169
Different Views Concerning the Reasons for the Commandments 169
Consequences of the Mitzvot 171
(B) What Can We Learn from the Classic Jewish Thinkers' Explanation of the Reasons for the Mitzvot? 176
The Subjective Factor 176
The Value of the Explanations 178
The Apologetic Method 179
The Sociological Method 180

Abbreviations 184
Notes 185
Glossary 197

Index 200

Dedicated to the memory of my father
Rabbi Israel son of Rabbi Meir Yefet
Scholar, teacher and composer
Who heard and made heard
The harmony of our religious life.

As Torah was given to those who left Egypt, so it is given again in every generation. It is not an inheritance and does not come automatically. It is incumbent on every generation to receive it and uphold it, to ponder it and explain it to itself according to its measure of understanding. An era passes and an era comes, but the Torah remains forever. To what does this apply? To its mitzvot and halakhot, but the explanation of its ideas and the reasons for its mitzvot are renewed every day, taking off one form and putting on another.

Because of the passing and changing times, the people of Israel were removed from one land to another, from one climate to another, they forgot one language and learned another language, they left the circle of one culture and entered the circle of another culture, but their Torah remained with them and they kept its mitzvot and halakhot in hand. All the generations learned the same Torah, and all the dispersed communities observed the same mitzvot. However, the ideas of Philo and his colleagues are not the same as the manner of explanation of the circles of Sefarad, nor were the ideas of the Sages of the Aggadah the same as the ideas of the teachers of Hasidism. There are seventy facets to the Torah; the facets that are revealed to one generation are not revealed to a different generation.

This comprehensive and basic book opens to the educator and to every Jew who studies it the gates of the palace of Jewish thought in all its chambers, its periods, its climates, and its methods. Many matters of the inwardness of Torah and of its truth will become clear and evident to the reader, yet he will understand that what remains stored is still greater than the visible, for the hidden things belong to the Lord our God but the revealed are for us and our children, to do all the words of this Torah.

I. H.

Author's Preface to First Edition (1942)

This book had its origins in my lectures on the aggadah and on the Jewish thinkers of the Hellenistic and medieval periods that I gave at the Jewish Theological Seminary in Breslau. I attempted to impress on my students the value of the explanations of the Torah by our predecessors, and my labors were not in vain. My students vied with me in researching this area. While I was discussing Philo's outlook, they shed light on their views concerning Baḥya and Maimonides, and together we completed in German a book in which were translated the most important excerpts in which the Jewish philosophers spoke of the reasons for the mitzvot. The book was prepared for publication by the Schocken house in Berlin, but because of the Holocaust that overtook the Jews of Germany it was not published.

When I was privileged to come to Israel and to join the laborers in the Torah that goes forth from Zion, I consulted with Rabbi Y. L. Fishman and the late Dr. Abraham Obadiah about the publication of my research. They informed me that among the educational circles of the religious youth there was occasionally felt the need to survey the explanations of the mitzvot, and they invited me to compose this book for the curricular needs of these educators.

The first purpose of this book is *historical*. It seeks to describe the answers that were given to our question in ancient times and by the medieval philosophers, to explain them on the basis of the responders' personalities, taking into account the factors of their ages. For the benefit of those who deal in depth with the problem I specified the sources in which the philosophers discussed our question, as well as the modern researches in these topics. One should add to them two articles that I wrote, which have been printed in the meantime and which should appear shortly: one on the collection "Rabbi Saadia Gaon," which is being published by the Mosad Ha-Rav Kook, and one in the journal *Kneset* (on Rabbi Judah Halevi).

However the purpose of this book is not only historical. I tried to demonstrate that the ideas of our predecessors on the question of religion in general and on the reasons for the mitzvot in particular are based not only on the scientific ideas of their time, but also on the Jewish experience that is common to the ancients and the moderns, and therefore they have a value that endures over time. Therefore I emphasized the essential and timeless value of our predecessors' views within the historical narrative and have also devoted a separate chapter to this at the end of the book.

Without sacrificing its scholarly value, I have tried to give the book a popular presentation insofar as the serious theoretical topic discussed in it permits. I have retranslated or explained in contemporary language the primary citations I have brought from these thinkers. I limited myself to what the topic absolutely requires. I have spoken only of the *reasons* for the mitzvot and have not entered, for example, into their classification or the question of their abrogation. I did not collect all the views scattered in our literature but only the most important answers that were given to our question, and I rested content with a selection of examples that show the method of the thinkers. As for movements outside Judaism that our thinkers opposed or from which they derived benefit, I have treated them only briefly. I have mostly ignored the controversial literature.

The index was prepared by my daughter, Hannah Amreich.

The religions section of the Department of Youth and Pioneering of the World Zionist Organization and the Mossad ha-Rav Kook made possible the publication of this book despite these hard times. In addition I have been assisted by Zvi Harkavy, Isaac Werfel, and Dr. M. A. Kurz in the editing of this book, the first that I have managed to write for the Hebrew reader. They and Mr. Harkavi polished its style and adapted it to the needs of the readers. My friend, Dr. Ephraim Urbach, also assisted me on the first chapters. I express my heartfelt thanks to all of them.

Translator's Preface

It is over sixty years since Isaac Heinemann wrote his monumental work *Ta'amei Ha-Mitzvot,* based on his lectures at the Jewish Theological Seminary of Breslau in the 1930s. Yet barriers of language and cultural frame-of-reference have denied this work the influence it rightly should have had in Jewish thought. There are echoes of his approach in the method and writings of Abraham J. Heschel and Seymour Siegel, but the contemporary discussion of halakhic authority still has much to learn from his analytical approach and his scholarship on this topic.

Isaac Heinemann (1876–1957) was a leading humanistic and Judaic scholar who enriched his generation's understanding of Hellenistic and rabbinic Jewish thought in his important studies on Philo and the Aggadah of the rabbis, and his many years of teaching in Europe and in Israel. His *Darkhei Ha-Aggadah* ("The Ways of the Aggadah") still stands as a leading appreciation of the relation of form and message in rabbinic non-legal literature. The current volume turns to the legal thought of the rabbis as understood by many generations of pre-modern Jewish thinkers. It addresses a central topic that is vital to the substance of Jewish religious life in all its forms, under whatever denominational label (or lack thereof) it may be practiced.

Heinemann represented a traditionalism that did not align itself strictly with the modern party lines of Jewry. He taught at one of the institutions of European Conservative Judaism final and had his work published in Israel by the youth movement of Mizraḥi, representing modern Orthodoxy. Volume II of his work treats with equal respect the thought of Moses Mendelssohn, Samson Raphael Hirsch, Zechariah Frankel, and Franz Rosenzweig. The line that he drew was between those who did and did not accept the binding character of the body of traditional halakha as a whole, putting him at odds with Abraham Geiger, Hermann Cohen, and Reform Judaism generally, but this was an opposition born of principle, not simply party affiliation.

The relationship of his position to that of Mordecai Kaplan (to take the leading theorist of a positive approach to Jewish observance on the basis of its being non-revealed sancta of the Jewish people rather than the revealed explicit will of God) is more complex. Both Heinemann and Kaplan appreciated the insights of Max Kadushin into the practical-ethical orientation of rabbinic thought. Heinemann nowhere mentions Kaplan but condemns by implication all who disbelieve the revealed status of the mitzvot. At the same time, Heinemann is very appreciative of the Hellenistic thinkers Philo and Josephus, who (he remarks with wonderment) called Moses the legislator of the Torah, by analogy with Solon and other famous legislators of different nations in the Hellenistic world. Heinemann correctly appreciates that the difference between the Hellenistic thinkers and the rabbis on this point can be traced to their different placement in the Hellenistic multicultural milieu. The same difference led Philo and Josephus to stress the autonomous-based reasons for observing the mitzvot, in contrast to the heteronomous emphasis of the rabbis. It may be a stretch to call Philo and Josephus Kaplanians before their time. But it is not at all far-fetched to find in the range of positions sketched by Heinemann ample precedents to illuminate and inform the diversity of positions in contemporary Jewish thought on the rationale of Jewish observance.

But to appreciate Heinemann, we must understand him starting from his own presuppositions. Heinemann was a supernaturalist. God gave commands to the people of Israel, some more "rational" (the *mishpatim*), others apparently less amenable to reason (the *ḥukkim*). If by "autonomy" we mean the self-legislation by human beings based on human reason, then human beings can agree with the binding character of the *mishpatim* from a standpoint of autonomy, whereas they can only accept the validity of the *ḥukkim* from a heteronomous acceptance of the "yoke" of divine authority. But this is only the start of the game, for the real challenge of the intellectual enterprise called *ta'amei ha-mitzvot* ("the reasons for the commandments") is to reveal how the *ḥukkim* also can be explained rationally, in whole or in part.

The divine origin of the *ḥukkim* is an assumption that is basic to the thought-system of the rabbis and the medieval philosophers whose views are the principal subject matter of this volume. If reasons can be offered for the *ḥukkim*, these are reasons that obtain from the divine point of view: they are God's reasons. But the fact that we are able to intuit and analyze them is based on the fact that reason is a common feature of God and humanity, a part (maybe the central part, along with moral consciousness) of our being created in the divine image. So they are human reasons as well.

Are they "necessary and sufficient" reasons? Perhaps not. Perhaps only in the case of the *mishpatim* is the connection between reason and the law so necessary and direct. Even if rational, there is an aspect of contingency that clings to the *ḥukkim*, even when rationally understood. Part of this contingency is historical. A good many of the mitzvot are rooted in ancient history, whether the pre-history of the creation of the world or the proto-history of the creation of the nation of Israel out of the crucible of the Exodus and conquest. The Exodus need not have happened in the first place (in fact, some claim it did not happen, or did not happen as reported — but we need not enter that controversy here). But having happened (or the memory having been implanted in the Jewish people of its occurrence — whether wholly historical or not, that memory still remains formative of Jewish identity), it becomes a necessary ingredient in the definition of Israel as a nation and Judaism as a historical religion. In that sense it is "necessary" in the sense that what is done cannot be undone, and the future must be built upon the foundation of the memory of the past. And the action of Jews as Jews must be a response to the remembered historical reality that has brought them to this point.

Another part of the contingency is historical on a different level. The prohibition of pork and meat-milk mixtures has no explicit reference to events in Jewish history (and the prohibition of the sciatic nerve has reference only to a mythical event). Nevertheless, the very fact of the prohibition itself is a part of Jewish history — that, and the fact that Jews have suffered ostracism, persecution, and death for their obedience to this prohibition, so that it has become a proverbial marker of Jewish identity. Still, the complex of dietary laws has also been one of the richest lodes of speculation over the inherent rationality of the mitzvot. Are they for medical reasons? To inculcate moderation of the appetites? Astrological? Ethical-symbolic (milk symbolizing the maternal love of the mother animal for its young)? Pedagogic? Every thinker and every generation comes up with different reasons, and has its own preferred taste for liking certain explanations and rejecting others.

Maimonides was of two minds about the perfect rationality of behavioral norms, whether ethical or ritual. On the one hand, he did not regard ethical inquiry (or the related enterprise of finding reasons for commanded behaviors in general) as on the same intellectual level as physics and metaphysics. Physics and metaphysics achieved objective truth; ethics ("the knowledge of good and evil") was more on the level of opinion, and Adam made a bad bargain in rejecting the former in order to gain the latter. Such is Maimonides' reading of the Eden narrative, as narrated in Chapter 2 of Book I of the *Guide of the Perplexed*. There may have been an element of tongue-in-cheek to this interpretation; nevertheless, it accords with his rejecting Saadia's doctrine that there are "rational commandments." Moses may have been the wisest legislator of all (according to the more radical esoteric interpretation of Maimonides' theory of prophecy in the *Guide*), yet even the wisest legislation has an element of improvisation and concession to historical circumstance (as in Maimonides' famous explanation that the Torah's commandment of sacrifices was a concession to the ritual custom of the ancient world).

On the other hand, in Part III of the *Guide* Maimonides made the most thoroughgoing effort in all of history (at least up to that time) to find a basis in reason for all of the mitzvot of the Torah. God does nothing purposeless, nothing in vain. Hence, all the mitzvot must have a rational purpose; it is only a shortcoming of our own reason and ingenuity if we fail to find it.

And find it they did — for centuries, in many different ways. Heinemann is at his best in giving as full an inventory as he can of the various reasons given by the medievals for the traditional mitzvot. He categorizes them in different ways in different parts of his book. At the outset, he finds four kinds of reasons: scientific, apologetic, theoretical-religious, and practical-religious. In hindsight, he discovers an additional threefold classification: intellectual, practical, and emotional. Either way, there are different kinds of reasons because there are different kinds of human beings in a religious community. Some are driven by the desire to understand, some by emotional involvement, some by the joy of practical participation. It is the nature of religious observances to be complex and multi-faceted, to satisfy different people in different ways. Thus all these categories of reason will have some validity in explaining the value of the religious observance for different kinds of people.

But at this point, Heinemann's analysis, which was started on the assumption that the mitzvot are to be taken as divinely revealed, becomes relevant as well to people who are not wholly comfortable with that assumption. Divine reason and human reason have after all a common aspect; what is rational to God is rational to human beings as well. Thus, divine reasons may be able to work equally well when reclassified as human reasons, even when the divine origin of the mitzvot is doubted. On a theory of human authorship, the speculative answers that the medievals offered as to the reasons God commanded the mitzvot can serve us at least in part as a suggestion of the reasons human beings devised the mitzvot, or why the mitzvot work in the context of a religious community.

At this point we may take Heinemann's methodology a step further. He allowed a pluralism of approaches among the intellectualists, emotivists, and pragmatists in the theorization of the reasons of the mitzvot, but stopped short of granting parity as between supernaturalists and humanists. However, the reality in today's Jewish community (and by extension, in the Western community comprising religious believers and secularists) is that from this point forward, we are never going to get a total consensus around one religious outlook. Traditionalists, believing that God commanded the mitzvot of the Torah, and religious humanists, ascribing the Torah to human authorship, are going to have to live together in community and come to accommodation with each other. How, then, will they be able to achieve this?

The dual divine-human aspect of the "reasons of the mitzvot" may help bridge this gap between supernaturalists and naturalists in today's Jewish community. A community is, after all, united by practice more than by belief. Different members can attach different meanings to common observances, and (following the Talmudic paradigm) intellectual disagreements can be framed within a common rubric so long as the differing parties accord each other legitimacy and are united by common commitments and concerns. There is certainly plenty of diversity and disagreement among the thinkers Heinemann presents in this study; he may forgive us if we extend his tolerance for diversity one step beyond the point where he was willing to apply it.

Still, one may demur: Can there be a mitzvah for a naturalist? If the Torah is conceived by some as humanly authored, what is their notion of "commanded"? Here, too, we can learn from Heinemann. He shows us how in the Bible itself, some mitzvot are heteronomous whereas others are autonomous. Cain is condemned for murdering Abel, although there was no utterance from God "You shall not kill" until after the Flood. "The blood of your brother's blood cries up from the ground." Some imperatives are so obvious that they do not need to be spelled out or ascribed to a specific author. When Moses realizes he stands on holy ground, he takes off his shoes. When the sailors of Jonah's ship perceive the storm, they cry out to God. And when a Jew sees a tradition — laden with the wisdom of the ages and testifying to the glory of God — in need of maintenance and perpetuation, he steps in and commits himself to it. The Jew, face to face with the tradition and feeling responsible to the situation, feels responsible to God in that situation — this is one meaning of "being commanded," which Rosenzweig (who was no fundamentalist) especially taught us to appreciate.

The Torah confronts us as a black box. It has a label on it: "Ingredients: xx% of divine authorship, yy% of human authorship" — only the numbers are rubbed out and illegible. Some of us maximize the divine factor, others the human factor. This is a disagreement over the unknown and unknowable. We are responsible in any case to do what we conceive as our duty to God, based on the best knowledge available, which is incomplete.

The study of the "reasons of the mitzvot" gives us clarity to guide us in this murky enterprise. Our God-given reason is the best instrument we have for understanding the Torah and for arriving at knowledge of right and wrong — and these two must correlate positively, for it is as a guide to right and wrong that we turn to the Torah in the first place. Fortunately, we are not unaided in our search; many have gone before us in a similar quest. It is to aid us in that search that Heinemann has provided this guide to the thinkers of Judaism on the "reasons of the commandments."

Leonard Levin
New York, November, 2007

Acknowledgments

This translation is a revision of a draft prepared jointly by the members of my class in "Reasons for the Mitzvot," Cecelia Beyer, Loren Chachkes, Daniel Dorsch, Philip Ohriner, Ita Paskind, and Jeremy Ruberg, in the theological seminar of the Rabbinical School of the Jewish Theological Seminary of America (New York) in Fall, 2006. The six students all participated with great enthusiasm and each contributed his or her weekly installment on the chapter or thinker of the week, which I then revised to improve accuracy while leaving the style of each author intact in the original draft. For the penultimate draft I took on with mixed feelings the role of the Redactor, overriding the stylistic diversity of the original in favor of greater uniformity, but the original character peeks through in places. Thus the ordinary reader will probably view this as a unified work, while those more skilled in "Higher Criticism" may be able to parse out the J,E,P,D composite character of the text. Some of the collaborators may feel slighted at my considerable (but not complete) overlaying of their individual voices, but I am grateful to all of them for providing the groundwork of the first draft that made my task in preparing this version so much easier. I am also grateful to Judy Cohen for performing the final copy-editing on the English text of this work, and to Laura Shelley for preparing the indexes.

A Note on Notes

There are three kinds of notes to this book. Notes have been placed at the bottom of the page when they add materially to the argument made in the adjacent text and may be of interest to the general reader; these are subdivided into Heinemann's original notes (generally marked "IH") and my own amplifications to (and occasionally dissent from) his arguments (marked "LL"). Any unmarked notes at the bottom of the text are Heinemann's. Additionally, there are notes primarily of interest to the scholar, making reference to the primary and secondary sources documenting Heinemann's claims; these have been relegated to the end of the volume.

L. L.

The Reasons for the Commandments in Jewish Thought

From the Bible to the Renaissance

Chapter 1
The Nature of the Question

What led thinkers to delve into the reasons for the commandments? Some will say scientific curiosity. This answer is no doubt sufficient to explain why we ask about the nature of the practices of various peoples, for instance the custom in India to burn widows on the pyre and the like. But when an investigator is dealing with his own religious practices that he accepts as commanded, the question takes on not just a theoretical but an existential cast. First, such a thinker will ask the reasons he must perform these commandments that are required of him and not just the reasons for the commandments themselves. There are two basic motivations in us for performing the commandments: (1) the belief in the *authority* of the legislator, and (2) the belief in the *value* of the commandments. Inquiry into the value of the mitzvot has a point of contact with scientific inquiry into their reasons. If, for example, certain practices have a social value, we may assume that whoever legislated them did so for that reason. Indeed we must not ignore the profound difference between these two modes of inquiry. The purely scientific investigator will not differentiate between worthy and unworthy reasons; his question is purely psychological. But whoever is interested also in performing this practice will ask specifically about the value of the reasons and their justification. More especially, whoever seeks to defend his ancestral customs will strive to contradict the arguments of those who attribute unworthy reasons to them (for instance, that the sacrifices were instituted in order to feed the gods) and to highlight those reasons that demonstrate the justice and wisdom of the legislator.

Reasons not to engage in such an inquiry

It was not just a scientific need that sparked our thinkers to investigate the reasons for the mitzvot, but rather religious-national needs. Because recognizing the value of the mitzvot would be likely to strengthen practical and theoretical commitment to religious life, one might have assumed that those who valued the mitzvot would give their blessing to such inquiries. But this was not the case. There were to be found in our people — and not only there — thinkers who were opposed in principle to any inquiry into the reasons for laws. We cannot understand the factors that operated on those who tried to explain the mitzvot unless we are also familiar with the rationale of those who opposed such explanations.

Non-Jewish thinkers have already questioned the view that knowing the reasons for the laws is an incentive for complying with them. Seneca wrote, citing a famous Greek philosopher: "I condemn Plato because, not content with specifying the laws, he added general principles. The law should be like a voice addressing us from heaven! It should command, not discuss! Tell me what I must do! It is not for me to learn, but to obey." (Letters 38, 94)

This view agrees with the saying of Rabbi Isaac (BT *Sanhedrin* 21b): "Why were the reasons for the Torah not revealed? Because when the reasons for two laws were revealed, this caused the greatest of men to stumble."*

Thus the sages of the Land of Israel did not publicize the reasons for their decrees until after twelve months had passed, in case someone might not agree with the reason and thus disparage the decree.[1] Such sayings are indeed directed at those obligated by the mitzvot, but their logic applies to their interpreters as well. Whoever imagines that he can strengthen discipline by offering reasons is in fact weakening it, because he makes the observance of the law dependent to some extent on the assent of the individual addressed by it.

Such concerns apply to all "commandments," including laws of human origin, but additional compunctions are aroused regarding the mitzvot attributed to divine revelation. Maimonides (*Guide* III, 31) testifies that in many people's view divine commandments characteristically have no apparent reason, in contrast to human enactments, whose reason is obvious. Even if divine commandments are there for a reason, what business is it of ours to know it? The author of the *Tur,* (YD 181) in rejecting Maimonides' view on the prohibition of removing one's beard and the reason for it, writes, "We do not need to seek the reason for the mitzvot, for it is the King's decree that is binding on us even if we do not know their reason." The simple Jew who overrides his own will in favor of the will of his Creator is more worthy in his view than the philosophizer who seeks reasons that agree with his own opinion. What value is to be gained by investigating the reasons for the mitzvot? Even if there were some useful outcome, are we able to stand in judgment

* The "greatest of men" alluded to here is Solomon. The laws are those regulating the conduct of the king in Deuteronomy 17:14–17. He should not keep many horses lest he turn the people back to Egypt; he should not have many wives lest his heart go astray. Solomon thought that, knowing the reasons stated, he could be lenient concerning the laws themselves, but he was wrong — he entered into an Egyptian alliance, and his many wives turned his heart astray. (LL)

over our Creator's intentions? "Will you plumb the mind of God, or discern the purpose of the Almighty?"

Such arguments that inhibit the inquiry for reasons for the mitzvot[2] were familiar and obvious to everyone. Nevertheless, many of our people's leaders regarded such inquiry as not only permitted but obligatory. They were also able to base their views on important religious considerations.

Reasons Such Inquiry is Mandatory

The first reason is the apologetic. The nations among whom Jews have dwelt, from rabbinic times to our own day, criticized the mitzvot whose reason was not apparent to everyone. Our holy laws were depicted by our accusers as baseless and senseless or even based on ugly and despicable reasons such as avarice and misanthropy. They view their observance as rote imitation that does not inspire in us any feelings of love or devotion to God toward which other religions (in their view) are directed. These attacks and indictments found some echo among the less faithful of the Jewish people. The rabbis already testify that not only the gentiles but also "Satan" — the evil urge within us — "refutes some of the mitzvot"; and who is there who fears God and loves the mitzvot who will not make an effort to silence our accusers and bring to light a verdict justifying the Torah by clarifying and explaining its mitzvot?

The second reason is based on the "rational" part of the Jewish religion. To be sure, the Creator's thoughts are higher than our thoughts "as heavens are higher than earth" (Isaiah 55:9), and therefore we should not be surprised if God's Torah contains mitzvot whose reason is hidden from us. We cannot hope to be able to exhaust the whole depth of our Torah's reasons. But on the other hand, the Torah's conception of God is completely different from that of ancient idolatrous religions. The latter would not recognize any connection between the will of the gods and ethical law. We believe in a righteous and merciful God who desires His creatures' goodness. We will impugn God's honor if we view His commandments as the orders of a tyrant who imposes the yoke of His will on His subjects only to demonstrate His power. One should assume that He desires His creatures' welfare, and therefore He imparted to them just and useful commandments. Just as it is incumbent on us to find the "finger of God" in the wonders of nature and in the events of our lives, even though unsolvable mysteries and riddles will remain, so too we will not be guilty of "questioning God's attributes" if we attempt to recognize to the best of our ability the wisdom and justice in God's mitzvot. We should call this factor "theoretical-religious." In the philosophers' outlook it merges with the purely scientific reason that we mentioned at the beginning of this chapter.

There is a third reason in addition: the "practical-religious." Obedience to a mitzvah does not contradict the view that the commanded individual has his own autonomy and acts according to his understanding of it. On the contrary: any commander wants captains who understand his intentions, so that they can carry out his orders in accord with their proper meaning and purpose. Such an understanding is even more important in the case of religious commands that are liable to have an effect on our ideas and our virtues. In many of its commandments the Torah itself has expounded the beneficences of the Creator that they call to mind, and the feelings of kindness that they arouse in us (for instance, the mitzvah of Peah — the "corner of the field"). The educational value of the mitzvot will be diminished if we fulfill them only to discharge our obligation and earn our future reward; it will be enhanced to the extent that the intentions of the Torah, both explicit and hidden, will find an echo in our souls.

Surveying these reasons will enable us to understand and expound the explanation of the mitzvot by our great teachers.

Chapter 2
The Biblical View

The sages of Israel in all ages availed themselves of the allusions found in the Torah as the basis for their opinions. Therefore we must ask: To what extent did the Torah determine the position of its interpreters, and how much room for discretion did it leave them? In order to answer this question, we begin by explicating the plain sense of the Torah from the standpoint of the belief in its literary unity and integrity, a belief that was shared by the thinkers whose methods we deal with in this book.

The first question is: Is the obedience that God demands from all persons rational or irrational, that is to say, is a person commanded only by those commandments that were received from the Creator in a supernatural manner or also by those commandments that originate from one's conscience?

We remarked above that the Jewish religion is not purely rational nor is it purely irrational. Perhaps we can appreciate this composite aspect more clearly if we consider specifically those commandments that are incumbent upon people not under the Torah's jurisdiction, namely the patriarchs and non-Jews.

The sources of correct behavior prior to Sinai: God's will and human conscience

On the one hand, God charges them with commandments, some of which are temporary (such as the prohibition against eating from the tree of knowledge and the command for Abraham to leave his homeland) and others binding in perpetuity (such as the prohibition of murder and the commandment of circumcision). On the other hand, God penalizes people for sins concerning which only conscience has admonished them, for the Creator has not yet declared against them. For example, God punishes Cain for his brother's murder, though only in the age of Noah was murder explicitly forbidden. The generation of the flood was punished because "they corrupted their ways." Sodom and Gomorrah were burned in fire because their inhabitants were "very evil and wicked before the Lord." Onan was sentenced to death because he did not assist in continuing his brother's seed. The gentiles in the days of Amos the prophet were condemned for their cruelties and lack of faith. The people of Nineveh were condemned to the "upheaval" of their city until they repented from their evil ways through full repentance. However, Ruth the Moabite received her reward for remaining faithful to the house of her late husband.

There are thus two sources for human duties: explicit commandments of the Creator and the voice of one's conscience. The source for the latter we will call "rational," not as opposed to "emotional," but in the sense referred to by Kant when he speaks of "practical reason." Thus not by arbitrary caprice, but rather through our reliable deliberation and pure feeling do we determine by precise examination what is good and what is bad. But the first-named source, namely God's command, is at first sight entirely irrational: a person is obligated to uphold the divine commandment even when it seems to him to contradict morality (as in the case of Abraham, who sent away Ishmael and Hagar even though he originally opposed this demand of Sarah's, and who was even willing to sacrifice his son). All the more so must he adhere to God's commandment even when he cannot find sufficient reason for it (for example, when Abraham left his father's house for an unknown land).

Even "irrational" commands do not oppose objective morality

But when we scrutinize this matter, we can see many characteristic features. First, not only does the content of the commandments never contradict morality in an objective sense, but the contradictions are only in human perception. A case in point is when God said to Abraham, "Do not fear for the boy and your maid-servant . . ." In other words, not only for "your son" but also for Hagar, who is now only your servant, no longer your concubine — hinting that God will keep an eye on both of them. And the rest of the story supports this. Therefore truthfully, there is no cruelty in the commandment. For the same reason, Scripture prefaces the story of the Binding of Isaac with the statement, "God tested Abraham," even though by doing so, it spoils the dramatic suspense. The reader knows from the start that God desires only to prove Abraham worthy but never intended for Abraham to execute the commandment.

Second, even though God demands that we be obedient to His commandments simply because of their divine origin, this does not mean that they do not also have a reason comprehensible to our minds. For the commandments that were given in perpetuity, Scripture adds reasons: Murder is forbidden for "man was created in God's image." Circumcision will be "a sign of the covenant between Me and you." As for the commandments that were dictated for a specified time, although an explicit reason is not given, the commentators were right in saying that the prohibition of the tree of knowledge was for the betterment of mankind because the loss incurred by this "knowledge" was far greater than the gain. When God commanded Abraham to leave his homeland and to banish Ishmael, these commandments sprang from God's desire to establish Isaac's progeny in the holy land. The same applies in similar cases.

The first source of human obligation, God's will, is thus not entirely irrational, but a mixed case. More precisely, the mitzvot that God announced before the giving of the Torah are in a certain sense irrational from the human perspective because a person must perform them whether he knows their basis or not. But they are rational from the perspective of the blessed Law-giver because they have a religious, moral, or useful reason. There is a disclaimer to this rule: on the one hand, one can point out that the prohibition against murder is surely comprehensible by a human being and rational from his perspective, and therefore was in effect prior to being explicitly announced. On the other hand, we must stress that the reason for the commandment is not in all instances a "sufficient reason" in the philosophical sense. Nevertheless, this rule is generally valid and wholly appropriate to the conception of God in the Holy Scriptures: He is a living God, not an idea that took on divine form; He acts by His will, but this will of His does not issue from caprice.[1] Rather, just as He is a righteous judge, so is He a righteous legislator.

Thus from surveying the pre-Sinaitic laws that apply to all humanity, one can learn something about the mitzvot in the Torah in the narrow sense, that is, the 613 mitzvot that were given to Israel.

Conscience Is Important Even After Sinai

Perhaps some will argue that there is no similarity between religious life before and after the giving of the Torah with respect to its sources and reasons. Does not the Torah determine the course of our lives in all its details, seemingly without leaving conscience any room for discretion? Indeed, we do not usually find in the Torah narratives that people are punished if they have not transgressed God's word; but on the other hand, we are hard put to find any explicit order that Moses and Aaron transgressed by the waters of Meribah, or that Aaron and Miriam disobeyed when they "spoke ill" of Moses. Even though the Torah attempts through the mitzvot to endorse the voice of conscience and to restrict our free discretion, nevertheless the opinion that a person within Israel is only responsible for what is explicitly written in the text is mistaken, and all of the great teachers of our people opposed this idea. The prophets denounced every abhorrent deed and its underlying causes, even if these were not mentioned in the Torah. They said, "unchastity, wine, and intoxicants seize the heart" (Hosea 4:11), even though the Torah does not explicitly forbid either intoxication or sexual indulgence as such. They severely condemned those who say, "When will the New Moon be over, so that we may sell grain? — and the Sabbath, so that we may set forth wheat?" (Amos 8:5), even though it is not explicitly forbidden to sell after the Sabbath is over. Even if the Torah warns against "hardening one's heart" (Deuteronomy 15:7), does it also command us to "break every yoke" as the prophet demands? (Isaiah 58:6). Perhaps this was one of the goals of the prophets, and not the least of them, to denounce their compatriots for not paying heed to those requirements of behavior that were not explicitly indicated in the Torah or sanctified by custom, and nevertheless imagined themselves to be perfectly righteous. The example of the prophets has been emulated by the leading preachers in every generation until today, emphasizing the "obligations of the heart" and moral improvement, in order to complement and elaborate the chapter-headings that the Torah provides in accordance with the holy and pure feelings of their hearts.

Because the Torah comes not to quiet the voice of our conscience but rather to amplify it, every person who stood and swore at Sinai has at his disposal two sources for his religious life: one that is entirely "rational" and a second that is more "composite." It is our task here to investigate the "compositeness" of the second and to verify whether the principle that we established above about the fusion of rational and irrational elements in the commands incumbent on general humanity also applies to those that are specific to the people of Israel. This question can be resolved by looking at the reasons that the Torah has added to its mitzvot, whether explicitly or by way of allusion.

Types of Reasons in the Torah: Appeal to Authority

The first type includes those that the term "reason" does not quite fit, except in its broader sense, because these emphasize not the value of the mitzvah, but only the authority of their divine legislator, and that God can be counted on to give good reward to those who do His will and to punish the rebellious. The Torah offers this kind of reason both for religious and moral commandments. In both cases one can find the signature phrase "I am the Lord"; furthermore, the conclusion "you shall fear God" is appended only to ethical commandments (Leviticus 19:14 and 32; 25:17, 31 and 43). We must fulfill these mitzvot too because the Creator commanded us to do so.

Understanding the Objective of a Mitzvah

Reasons of the second kind, where the Torah endeavors to explain the goal behind the mitzvah, are also supplied both for moral and religious commandments. There are mitzvot that it is impossible to fulfill without considering their goals. This is obvious in the case of the city of refuge. But also in connection with the mitzvah of leaving dropped or forgotten sheaves of wheat, or leaving the corners of one's field, the Torah adds the goal (for example Leviticus 19:10): "For the poor and stranger you should leave them." There was a widespread practice to leave a number of sheaves for demons, so that they shouldn't harm the owners, and thus the Torah took pains that we should be aware of the true ethical reason for this rule.

From here we move on to commandments where the Torah at least wants us to know the reason. We need to know the historical reasons for the laws of Passover and to announce them to our children (see for example, Exodus 12:26). The commandment of sukkah is given: "In order that your generations may know that I housed the children of Israel in booths" (Leviticus 23: 43). The mitzvah of the garment-fringe (*tzitzit*) is commanded "so that you may remember and perform all of My commandments" (Numbers 15:40), which is not possible for one who does not think about the reasons for the mitzvah, and this logically applies to tefillin (Exodus 13:9). The mitzvah of Sabbath is also likely to remind us of the covenant "between God and the children of Israel" (Exodus 31:17), and to serve as a symbol for this covenant only if one knows its relation to the Sabbath of the days of Creation, which is set forth in the Ten Commandments.

Connection to Other Mitzvot or Principles

There are mitzvot the reasons for which are based on other mitzvot or on general logical or religious principles. The King "may not take many horses, so that he not return the nation to Egypt, etc." "He may not take many wives, so that they do not turn his heart" (Deuteronomy 17:16ff.). It is forbidden for the Israelites to enact a treaty with the prior inhabitants of the Land of Israel or even to have mercy on the Seven Nations, in order that they will not influence them to do evil (Exodus 34:12, Deuteronomy 20:17, and more). The priests may not ascend by stairs to the altar in order to avoid indecent display of the body (Exodus 20:25).

The Torah offers a logical principle in order to explain the exoneration of the young betrothed woman who is raped (Deuteronomy 22:26). The meaning is: just as one does not blame a murdered person and all other victims of violence, so too one does not blame this woman who has been raped. The Torah relies upon a historical fact in declaring, "Do not pervert the judgment of the stranger, or of the orphan, nor take a widow's garment as a pledge. Rather, remember that you were a slave in Egypt, and the Lord your God redeemed you there; because of this I command you to do this thing" (Deuteronomy 24:17f.). That is to say, logic dictates: "I, who redeemed you, may act with you as a master who commands his servants." Perhaps it is also possible to explain in this manner the reason: "for all the firstborn are Mine, because on the day that I struck all the firstborn in the land of Egypt I consecrated to Myself all the firstborn in Israel, both man and animal" (Numbers 3:13). The text draws another conclusion from this fact when it declares, "For [the Israelites] are My slaves, whom I brought out of the land of Egypt; they shall not be sold as slaves" (Leviticus 25:42), and similarly, "The earth is the Lord's and all its fullness" (Psalms 24:1) and therefore, "The land shall not be sold in perpetuity; for the land is Mine" (Leviticus 25:23).

We may remark that these logical principles are all ethical or religious and are not merely utilitarian. There is not even one verse in the Torah that is only in the vein of "sound practical advice." Some reasons seem utilitarian on the surface, such as: "all of Israel will hear and see," "so that your slave and maidservant may rest the same as you," or "you shall make a parapet for your roof, that you should not bring any blood upon your house, if any man falls from there." But in the last analysis these are all ethical.[2] Also, when the Torah warns us about sins that are related to "defiling" or "polluting" the land — "so that the land shall not vomit you out" (Leviticus 20:22) — these explanations are no different from those that contain within them assurances ("so that your days may be lengthened" etc.), which do not diminish the ethical character of these commandments.

Emotional Reasons

More important are the emotional explanations. The Torah was not given to the ministering angels or to philosophers, but to a lively, emotional people. Therefore, the Torah turns in her explanation of her commandments not to the mind alone, but also especially to feelings, by arousing in the heart feelings of affection or revulsion. Sometimes the Torah is content to add a few phrases with emotional overtones such as "he has broken faith with her" (Exodus 21:8) (in order to denigrate a man who casts off his maidservant), or "since you had your will with her" [literally: "humiliated her"] (Deuteronomy 21:14). But not infrequently the Torah also adds complete verses, for example: "so that your slave and maidservant may rest like yourself," "You must remember that you were a slave in the land of Egypt," "A stranger you must not oppress," "You know the life of a stranger for you were strangers in the land of Egypt" (Exodus 23:9). This connection between our historical experiences and the rights of strangers and slaves is not logical in itself. The Torah is confident that the remembrance of the affliction and the oppression will arouse in us feelings of sympathy and compassion for people who are our brothers in sorrow. The Torah is also confident that "composite" emotions are rooted in the heart of her readers — that is to say, emotions that are not ethical alone, but that express a religious and perhaps also an aesthetic aspect. For example: the concept of "abomination" is indeed predicated not only on evil actions (in Proverbs) but also on the forbidden sexual relationships (Leviticus 18:26 et al.) and dietary prohibitions (Deuteronomy 14:3). The ethical teaching of the concepts of "impurity" and "purity" is quite rare, but when the Torah proclaims "do not defile yourselves in all these matters" (Leviticus 18:24 in connection to the sins of forbidden sexual relationships) it is confident that the feeling of revulsion towards impurity will have its effect on the listeners. Among these concepts is found that of "holiness," whose scope is clarified by the fact that the Torah prefaced the quintessence of its precepts by the injunction, "You shall be holy" (Leviticus 19). The first verse already attests to the fact that this portion will embrace ethical commands (such as honoring parents) as well as religious commands (such as the Sabbath), whereas the text will go on to enumerate the principle "love your neighbor as yourself" alongside the prohibitions of mixed species. The same is the case throughout the entire Torah. The commandments that have a relation to this concept of "holiness" distinguish the "holy people" mentioned in Exodus 22:30, among whom are included the priests, whom the Lord "sanctifies" (Leviticus 21:8); then there is the "holy day" (the Sabbath), which God "sanctified" (Genesis 2:3), concerning which the Israelites are bidden, "remember it to keep it holy" (Exodus 20:8), as well as the Sanctuary (which in the prophetic books and psalms is called "His holy mountain" and "His holy habitation"). The Torah is certain that its call to sanctity will find a ready echo in its readers' hearts. There are even "commandments" that the Torah does not command categorically but only conditionally, in the event that people will want to take them on themselves. This is clear in the matter of vows (including the Nazirite vow), to which the Torah does not ascribe any exaggerated value ("if you refrain from vowing, you incur no guilt" — Deuteronomy 23:23). The Torah's rules concerning vows come only to guide a person's religious inclination. The same applies to optional sacrifices, and more broadly to the whole service in the Temple, to which the pious Jew yearns "as the hart pants after the water brooks" (Psalm 42:2). It is very important that not only ethical mitzvot but also religious mitzvot are based on the individual's initiative and the rhythm of his emotions.

We have cited selected verses demonstrating the fit between the divine command and human emotion on the principle of "less is more."[3] Those familiar with the Torah can add other examples as they wish. Our citation is sufficient to illustrate the ways in which the Torah itself implicitly explains its own commandments.

Where The Torah is Silent Concerning Reasons

Even though the Torah was generous in giving reasons for its commands, nevertheless its general tendency is rather consistent with the verdict of the Greek philosopher that we cited earlier: "The Lawmaker should command, not discuss!" The Torah does not speak in the language of a commander in need of his subjects' approval. "Sufficient" reasons are very rare in the philosophical sense; perhaps only in the matter of the rape of the betrothed young woman does the law come down with logical certainty from the reason that the Torah adds. In most cases, indeed, the reason reveals the rationale for the law, for example the mitzvot that have an historical basis; but, of course, we should not ask why the Torah selected for the remembrance of the Exodus from Egypt the symbols that were established and not others (for instance that we should sit with our waists girded and our sticks in our hands, and so forth). Additionally, we should not ask why such prominent symbols as these were not fixed for the remembrance of the giving of the Torah. In general, the Torah tends not to give reasons for the details of mitzvot and their minutiae (like the sacrifices). Among the mitzvot there are several whose reasons we can only suppose, but we can never know with certainty (e.g., the order of the ritual on Yom Kippur, the ritual for the purification of a person impure because of contact with a corpse, and the one afflicted with leprosy). Specifically, the obscurity and the secrecy that rest on them imbue them with a character of "exaltation and awe."

The Torah Is Reticent About the Religious Value of the Mitzvot

Nevertheless, the matter is completely different regarding the general principles of the mitzvot. Certainly, the Torah does not speak at length about the compatibility between the command of the Creator and human logic and will, but only by intimation. By the same token the Torah also does not speak at length about the inner lives of its characters and does not indicate its opinion of their deeds except "by way of the narrator's arrangement of the events."[4] In the ancient world, the author and the listener in general were not used to lengthy discussions of what was undetectable to their senses; rather they came to their conclusions not from words but from facts that they saw or heard. The Torah is also satisfied with providing facts and with giving subtle hints about reasons for human life as well as about the intention of the Creator. Just as the Torah does not go on at length in praise of the Creator or His Providence, but is rather satisfied with several priceless epigrams (for example: "Shall not the Judge of all the earth do justice?"), so too does it not go on at length about the ethical value of the mitzvot or about the relationship between them and our conscience; it only declares that "the thing is close to you in your mouth and in your heart to do it" (Deut. 30:14). The nations of the world will also recognize Israel as "a wise and discerning people" "or what great nation has laws and rules as perfect as all this Teaching?" (Deut. 4:6–7). Just as the stance of the Lord that stands out from the stories in the Torah is uniform, and only based on this uniformity is it possible to understand the process of the events the Torah tells of, so too we must understand the generalities of its mitzvot not from the aspect of "jot upon jot . . . here a trifle, there a trifle" or based upon other different reasons, but rather on the foundation of its uniform goal: to educate the Israelite nation to be a holy nation whose heart is pure with its God.

From all of this we learn that the generalization that we fixed with regard to the mitzvot that were given to all human beings is valid also with regard to the 613 commandments in the Torah.

Observance of the mitzvot that proceeded explicitly from the divine utterance, "is irrational from the point of view of the human actor." Even if we do not understand their reasoning, we are obligated to uphold them; and if we do understand them, we must intend not only to uphold the mitzvot of our conscience, but also to do the express will of our Maker with a full heart and to arrange the entire process of our lives according to His mitzvot.

Indeed, the will of the Creator — even though it is impossible for a mortal to penetrate to the depths of its secrecy — is certainly not "irrational." This Master, the yoke of whose kingship we accept upon ourselves, is not like a tyrant who takes satisfaction from prevailing over his constituents and by burdening them, but is rather like a father who instructs his children for their own benefit. Certainly on the basis of the rules that emphasize God's power and sovereignty — such as "for the land is Mine," "the children of Israel are My servants" — the Torah commands mitzvot that are for the benefit of human beings in general and specifically for the benefit of the poor and oppressed.[5] Not only do we recognize the educational goal that the Torah intends to achieve by its ethical and religious mitzvot through the reasons that the Torah adds either explicitly or implicitly — to raise us up to the level of a "holy nation" — but we also feel how appropriate it is for the good inclination of our heart.

There are found in the Torah, then, important beginnings for the explanation of the mitzvot; only on the basis of these beginnings is it possible to understand the development of the problem with which we are dealing.

Investigation of the Reasons – Its Basis in the Torah

Indeed, the Torah informs us that the performance of mitzvot does not depend at all on the understanding of them. Therefore, all of its commentators who uphold it emphasized unanimously the value of the "authoritative" reasons. This principle gives some support to those who claim that there is no benefit in investigating the reasons for the mitzvot. Nevertheless, those who disagree support themselves explicitly on the fact that the Torah itself begins the practice of explaining its mitzvot, and its manner of explanation serves as an outstanding example for its commentators who uphold it, each in his own way.

Explanations of the mitzvot in the Torah are appropriate for the practical-religious and theoretical-religious factors. The Torah deepened the feelings of piety and morality by way of adding reasons. All Jewish philosophers — those closely tied to science and those not — followed it and added ethical/moral, religious, and historical reasons to those already in the Torah. Additionally, the theoretical aspiration to clarify that we have "righteous laws and statutes" is common to all the scholars of our nation, but is particularly prominent among the methods of the philosophers. Among them, the scientific factor and the will to prove the compatibility between the best of the ethical methods of the scholars of the nations of the world and our Torah grew. The Torah, then, did not bind the hands of those who uphold it; rather, the opposite is true: it awakened their activity. Over the course of time, the great scholars of Israel have found new viewpoints caused by the times, like apologetics, but the foundation of the investigation into the reasons for the mitzvot was based in none other than our Torah.

Chapter 3
The Views of the Rabbis

Even though the Tannaim and Amoraim only intended to clarify the Torah, nevertheless they were not satisfied just to reveal what was already included in the plain sense of the text. They themselves commented on their explanations through their midrash of the verse "my word . . . like a hammer that breaks the rock in pieces?" (Jeremiah 23:29, BT *Sanhedrin* 34a, BT *Shabbat* 88b) in order to point out that one verse leads to numerous meanings. Perhaps it is possible to go in the footsteps of an expression that is in the Talmud and compare it to electric sparks that ignite and travel between two poles, that flow as one as if they aspire to unite in one connected current. Thus the spirit of the expounder yearns for the Torah and the Torah says "interpret me"; only one who knows and understands the dipolar character of their explanation, that is to say the influence of Jewish experience on the Scripture's fully-articulated content, will plumb the full depths of their views on the nature of mitzvot and on their reasons.[1]

1. Irrational from the Individual's Perspective

The performance of mitzvot is irrational from the perspective of the performer because the obligation to observe them is not dependent on his intellectual assent. This principle is not spelled out in the Torah. It was not the rabbis' way to formulate abstract concepts like these. But many of their statements confirm that they were keenly and precisely aware of the Torah's view on this matter.

We should first state that the rabbis distinguished between an act that was commanded and an act that is within a person's discretion. This distinction also has Halakhic value (BT *Rosh Hashanah* 28a). "Ravah said . . . mitzvot were not given to us for the sake of *hana'ah*" (enjoyment or benefit — see Rashi). That is to say, the benefit that its observance realizes for us is different in principle from the benefit that we seek for the sake of our needs. Thus, "one who vows to have no enjoyment from a fountain may take a ritual bath in it in the rainy season" for in that case he will not have any bodily pleasure, "but he may not do it in the summer time." This dictum in effect expresses just the difference between one who does an act according to his inclination and one who does an act categorically in order to fulfill an obligation — a difference known according to the method of Kant. But other expressions indicate with clarity the heteronomic character of the mitzvot. It is not just that we do not have permission to "to judge against our creator" and to be "overly righteous" (*Ecclesiastes Rabbah* 7:16) — that is to say too merciful (like King Saul, who had pity on some of the nation of Amalek) — rather, even when we fulfill the mitzvot with a full heart, it is incumbent upon us to recognize the distinction between our will and the commandments of the Creator. In *Sifra Vayikra* 20:22: Rabbi Eleazar ben Azariah said: "From where do we know that man should not say, 'I do not wish to eat non-kosher meat,' 'I do not wish to indulge in forbidden sex,' but rather 'I wish, and what can I do since my Heavenly Father decreed on me thus?' The Torah teaches, 'I have separated you from the nations to be Mine.' Thus we find that he separates himself from sin and accepts the yoke of the kingdom of heaven." This opinion is also expressed in the well-known phrase: "God held Mount Sinai over our ancestors like a funnel and said to them: 'If you accept the Torah upon you, it will be good, and if not this will be your grave'" (BT *Shabbat* 88a).

All of these expressions prove the deep difference between the Torah of the rabbis and Kant's outlook, according to which one should rely on "practical reason" alone. If there is some exaggeration in the Aggadah cited above, in any event the heteronomic idea is obvious here, and it is not the view of a lone individual. Regarding the heteronomic idea we have also a naïve, uncoached witness whose faithfulness all acknowledge: the use of language. Many times Israel is compared to slaves "who serve their master" (or their king or their Lord). In this expression there is no shame like the translation of "slave" in many languages, but rather honor. Were not also Moses and Job called "servants of God"?[2] Therefore the rabbis say, "don't read the word חרות (Exodus 32:16) as '*ḥarut* = engraved [on the tablets]' but rather as '*ḥerut* (freedom).'" They also had the audacity to say that every judge who judges a judgment that is scrupulously true "is considered a partner with God," and that "all who keep the Sabbath are as if they 'made' Sabbath").[3] But all this freedom and independence is based, of course, on the obedience of the fulfiller. Also the word "yoke" — as in the "throwing-off of the yoke" in the Yom Kippur confessional prayer *al ḥet*, the "yoke of the kingdom of heaven," "yoke of mitzvot" (BT *Berakhot* 13a), "yoke of Torah" (Mishnah *Avot* 3:5), "your necks were brought in a yoke (of wisdom)" (Ecclesiasticus of Ben Sira 51:26) — this word does not have a sense of torment or burden; its meaning is rather that we do this out of obligation that we receive with willingness and heartfelt desire. From here it is good to say that "Rabbi [Judah the Patriarch] received upon himself the yoke of the kingdom of heaven" (BT *Berakhot* 13b) in the sense of: "He recited the Shema," specifically the first paragraph — in which the love of God is written. But even though the expression does not express painful servitude, it expresses servitude nevertheless. Therefore, we can say that in the thought of the rabbis the fulfillment of the mitzvot is based on the personal connection — a connection of both love and fear — that exists between us and our Father in Heaven.

There is another lone view that differs considerably from the conception common to most of the Jewish sages (BT *Kiddushin* 31a). It is told of a non-Jew who gave up great profit in order that he would not awaken the slumber of his elderly father. Afterward, a red heifer was born in his herd, and he sold it for the same sum that he had lost by heeding the commandment "honor your father." "Rabbi Hanina said: If this was [the outcome] for one who acts without being commanded (Rashi comments: God gives him his reward), then for one who acts because he is commanded, how much the more so! — as Rabbi Hanina said: 'Greater is the one who is commanded and acts than one who is not commanded and acts.'" Rabbi Joseph (the blind) said: "Originally, I thought that if anyone would tell me that the halakha agrees with Rabbi Judah, that a blind person was exempt from commandments, I would make a banquet for the rabbis, seeing that I am not obliged yet to fulfill them; now, however, that I have heard Rabbi Hanina's dictum: Greater is the one, etc., to the contrary, if anyone should tell me that the halakha does not agree with Rabbi Judah, I would make a banquet for the rabbis."[4] The Talmud cites the dictum of Rabbi Meir: "A non-Jew who studies the Torah is comparable to a high priest," and adds, "They do not receive a reward as one who acts out of being commanded, but rather, as one who acts without being commanded, as was said by the great Rabbi Hanina etc."[5]

We may draw the inference:

(1) In speaking of "one who is commanded", Rabbi Hanina refers only to one who is explicitly commanded by God, not one who merely listens to the voice of his conscience, even though the latter (for example, the gentile who gave up his wealth in order to fulfill the commandment of "honoring his father") did not follow after the inclination of his heart, but acted in accord with the "categorical imperative" of Kant. This linguistic usage was well understood and there was no need at all to explain it.

(2) Also, Rabbi Hanina and his colleagues were not unaware that according to the Torah there are good acts that are commanded only by our conscience, and these actions are desired by God. The rabbis' view is thus very different from that of the Church, according to which only deeds based on the correct faith bring reward, whereas the rest are regarded even as "cautionary sins." There is thus no inconsistency in the fact that the righteous gentiles such as the people of Nineveh are held up as a model,

or that they defined five mitzvot that are "entrusted to the heart."[6] The heteronomy of the commandments should not be understood to mean that autonomous commands do not exist, but rather that the heteronomous ones are very important, in contradiction to Kant's view, and in Rabbi Hanina's view heteronomous obedience is even more important than heeding the voice of conscience.

(3) This view does not follow necessarily from the rabbinic outlook. Indeed, before he knew of the abovementioned saying, R. Joseph held that in fact the fulfillment of the uncommanded good deed was more praiseworthy. This view is quite understandable — do we not hold that whoever takes additional demands on himself, spending increased time in Torah study, prayer, and all types of beneficent acts (of course, without neglecting his other obligations), is to be praised? And truly some of the rabbis were generous in their praise of converts, who certainly were not "commanded" to take on the yoke of commandments. For example, see: *Tanḥuma Ekev* § 3: "'And if you hearken (obey)...' What is written prior to this passage? 'Not because you are more numerous than all the nations' and not because you do more mitzvot than them; because the nations do more uncommanded mitzvot than you and they give credit to My name more than you."[7] There is no basis, therefore, for claiming that Rabbi Hanina represents the general view of the rabbis, but it is very characteristic that when R. Joseph heard this, he agreed with it immediately. It is also worth mentioning that we find no one who differed with this explicitly. And this is not opposed to the admiration accorded to the stringently pious person, for his actions are based on his Creator's desire, not on his private reckoning. Precisely the circumstance that our actions conform to God's explicitly stated desire gives them religious worth. This distinction applies not only to Jews; in speaking of the nations of the world the rabbis distinguish between "thirty commandments that they assumed willingly"[8] and the seven commandments that God commanded them, for which they are subject to punishment.[9]

2. Rational from the Lawmaker's Perspective[1]

From our faith in the Creator's perfection, it follows that His commandments are not the orders of a tyrant, but rather that they were given for the benefit of His creatures. The rabbis explicitly express this view. The saying of Rabbi Hananiah ben Akashya is well known: "God wanted to make Israel meritorious, therefore He gave them much Torah and many commandments" — and the saying of Rab: "The mitzvot were only given in order to purify humankind through them. Because what does the Holy and Blessed One care if one slaughters from the neck or from the nape?" (*Genesis Rabbah* 44:1).[11] The verse "the way of God is pure [*tzerufah*]" (Psalms 18:31), upon which this saying was based, proves that for Rab the connection between the conception of God and the value of the commandments was obvious.[12]

This principle is articulated especially in connection with the non-ethical mitzvot such as the dietary prohibitions (*Tanḥuma Buber Shemini* 8:12; *Leviticus Rabbah* 13:3) and circumcision (*Tanḥuma Buber Tazria* 7). In their explanation of the sacrifices, too, the rabbis emphasized that God is not dependent on His creatures' worship of Him. As for the ethical commandments, the Yom Kippur prayer says, "and if a person is righteous, what can he give You?"

But isolated sayings appear to contradict this view. In line with the assumption that the maintenance of the world is dependent on the performance of the commandments, God says to his angels, "If Israel had not accepted the Torah, there would be no dwelling-place either for Me or for you" (*Pesikta Rabbati* 20). Therefore, "happy am I and happy are you when you fulfill all of these conditions that I stipulated with you" (*Leviticus Rabbah* 35:2). These expressions that speak of the Shekhinah "in human language" (that is to say, in expressions appropriate for mortals) speak mythically. They express their ideas in an artistic form and are not meant to be taken literally.[13] It is sufficient here to remark that in any case they do not negate the rule that we established, that the fulfillment of the commandments has intrinsic value, that is to say, value based on their content and their character, and not only on the fact that God commanded us to do them.

But on the other hand: from our recognition of this inner value, it does not follow (as we saw above) that the value of each commandment is recognizable to our dim eyes. On the contrary, whoever emphasizes the supernal source of the commandments, who defines "commanded-ness" as only fulfilling the explicit will of his Creator and not as listening to the voice of conscience, certainly tends to the view that the Torah surpasses human understanding; that is to say it is not for us to delve into its secret reasons with the resources of our conscience and our logic. Such a person is proud of possessing commandments whose wisdom is "hidden from the eyes of all the living" (Job 28:21). Indeed the rabbis emphasized that there are classes of commandments whose reason is impossible to fathom.

The reasons for the ***ḥukkim*** *are hidden*

We learn in *Sifra* (on Leviticus 18:4 § 140):

> "My commandments (*mishpatai*) shall you do . . ." — this refers to matters in the Torah that had they not been written, reason would have dictated that we should write them, such as [the prohibitions of] stealing, the forbidden

> sexual relationships, idol worship, blasphemy, and murder . . . "and My statutes (*ḥukkotai*) you shall observe" — these are commandments concerning which the evil inclination, as well as idol worshippers, argue against — such as [the prohibitions of] eating pork, wearing linen and wool together, the release of the levirate wife, purification of the leper, the red heifer, and the scapegoat ritual. The verse teaches: "I am the Lord" — I have laid down the law and you are not permitted to question it.[14]

Recognizing the irrational character of these commandments did not stop the rabbis from responding to the criticisms that non-Jews and their Jewish fellow travelers directed at many of the commandments that refer to the relationship between human beings and God. However, most of their replies are apologetic and do not reveal the true views of their authors.

A non-Jew argued to R. Johanan ben Zakkai that the ceremony of the red heifer smacks of witchcraft. R. Johanan ben Zakkai replied that the non-Jews would expel a "frenetic spirit" by smoke and incense. "Similarly this spirit is an impure spirit. We sprinkle waters of impurity on it and it flees." After the non-Jew had gone, R. Johanan ben Zakkai's students said to him, "Master, you deflected him with a reed (i.e., you gave him a pro forma answer), but what would you say to us?" R. Johanan ben Zakkai said to them: "By your lives, the dead body does not defile, nor do the waters purify, but it is the decree of God. God said: 'I have laid down a law and have made a decree and people are not permitted to stand in judgment over my decree,' as is written in the Torah, 'This is the statute (*ḥukkat*) of the Torah.'"[15]

In order to understand the answer of R. Johanan ben Zakkai, it must be mentioned that the belief in frenetic spirits was very common in that period, even among educated people. Therefore, the practices to which R. Johanan ben Zakkai equates the red heifer did not seem to them to be superstition. Thus, the answer defending the Torah against the charge of witchcraft had a certain justification. However, his students were also justified in their complaint that their teacher only answered the question at the level of the questioner. For one cannot (from a Jewish standpoint) justify the commandments of the Torah on the basis of pagan practices whose value is dubious. Therefore, he replied to them that the laws of impurity and purity only have their basis in the will of the Lawgiver. That is to say, indeed they are not witchcraft, but we cannot find a rational explanation for them, so we should rest content with the fact that God commands them.[16]

Because the reasons for the "irrational" commandments are hidden from us, we should not conclude that they do not have any reasons at all! We find in *Pesikta de-Rav Kahana* § 4:

> God said to Moses, "I will reveal to you the meaning of the law, but for others it will be a *ḥok*." "On that day it will be a light of honor and *kipa'on*" — the written text has יקפאון [instead of וקפאון], meaning that those things that are hidden from you are destined to be revealed to you in the light of the world to come. Thus it is written: "And I will bring the blind on a path they do not know" (Isaiah 42:16). Rav Aḥa said, "Things that were not revealed to Moses were revealed to R. Akiva."[17]

The Torah Does Not Distinguish Between Rational and Irrational Mitzvot

However, both the distinction between the commandments whose reasons are revealed and those whose reasons are concealed, as well as the view of those who say that the *ḥukkim* are more objectionable to the evil inclination than the commandments that are amenable to rational explanation — neither of these two conceptions is found explicitly in the Bible. Both in the Ten Commandments and in the Holiness Code, the Torah lists rational and non-rational commandments together, and to each of them it supplies authoritative explanations (such as "I am the Lord"), as well as logical explanations (such as "You shall be a holy people to Me"). The opinion of the rabbis, that the evil inclination is particularly opposed to the non-rational commandments, is not in keeping with the human reality of biblical times. On the contrary, the prophets protested against the idol worship and violent acts of their contemporaries; as for Israel's neighbor-nations, they also had their own "irrational" commandments and they did not mock our irrational commandments, just as the Torah does not disparage the Egyptians whose custom did not allow them to break bread with foreigners. Therefore, how and on what basis did the rabbis arrive at this distinction and their explanation for it?

Why did the Rabbis Distinguish Between Rational and Non-rational Commandments?

Although this division proposed by the rabbis does not have an explicit source in the Torah, it does have a basis in the dual origin of our obligations that we elaborated above. The Torah recognizes our reason and conscience as legitimate sources for the proper conduct of life in God's eyes. Thus the rational commandments are doubly grounded, and so they are more firmly fixed in our hearts than those that have only the single ground of the explicit will of the Creator. The attack of the evil inclination and the pagans against those commandments that reason is not able either to justify or to contradict can only be explained by means of an assumption — that reason *alone* is permitted to decide our actions. This assumption was remote from the outlook of people of the biblical period. They dwelt amidst their own kin and were inclined to hold firmly to the customs of their ancestors in the same way that they held onto their ancestors' language. However, during the Hellenistic period (from the time of Alexander the Great onward), a great wave of assimilation and religious intermingling engulfed everyone living in the Mediterranean world. Together with this flood grew ideas of individualism and humanitarianism that indeed did not annul the national ideology but weakened it to a marked degree. Hellenizing intellectuals, who hauled their ancestral traditions for judgment before the courts of modern ideology, arose in all of these nations. Some of them abandoned their ancestral customs, and some of them justified them with explanations based in reason. Not just Jew-haters, but also those who found flaws in idolatry and felt a sense of unity with the teaching of monotheism and therefore entered into friendly relations with our people, accused the Jews for not abandoning their statutes that were lacking in rational justification, and they attributed to these commandments incorrect reasons, like superstition and misanthropy.[18] This way of thinking influenced the Jewish people. The spirit of individualism itself found an echo among them, in particular after they stopped being a people dwelling alone. The national framework weakened, and willy-nilly they became more like their surroundings in their language and in their way of life. In the biblical period the son's question, "What is this to you" (Exodus 12:26) has the sense of "Ask your father and he will tell you" and not the sense of a complaint. Someone of the Hellenistic period would emphasize "to *you*," as in the explanation of the "wicked son" in the Haggadah, as an "I" against a national "you" (while his father in his well-known response includes himself in the "I" that encompasses the whole nation of Israel). The comment, "inasmuch as he has excluded himself from the community, he has become a heretic" is not intended literally, but comes only to explain the verse. The individualistic spirit is only considered heretical when it leads to rejection of the yoke of mitzvot. However, this statement proves that the Sages recognized with clarity the danger that individualism caused the observance of those mitzvot that constitute Jewish uniqueness. Indeed, this danger first came into being in their age. The wicked people of Biblical times were generally not led astray by their reason, but by the desire to be "like all the nations that surrounded them," and they adopted from the Egyptians and Canaanites just such customs as reason would reject. This (national) assimilation did not cease completely, of course, in the later period and the Sages described it properly when they said, "You did not act as the right-minded, but as the corrupt amongst them" (BT *Sanhedrin* 39b). However, from the days of the Mishnah onward another danger from individualism was added to the first danger.

3. Methodological Questions

Is it fitting to seek out intellectual reasons for the mitzvot?

In the light of our explanation so far, we can understand the answer of the Sages to the two methodological questions: (1) the theoretical question: Is it fitting to seek out intellectual reasons for the mitzvot; and (2) the practical question: Is it permitted to derive conclusions for halakha from cases like these?

In the Talmud *Berakhot* 32b they discussed the first question: On the reason for the law of the Mishnah "The one who prays, 'Your mercies extend to the bird's nest' . . . should be silenced," two Amoraim disagree. One justifies the ruling of the Mishnah by saying that "he is casting jealousy on the work of creation"; his colleague reasons that "he makes the attributes of the Holy Blessed One into mercies when they are really decrees."[19] Also in the Jerusalem Talmud (*Berakhot* 9:3) we find a difference of opinion. One says "that he is like one who criticizes the attributes of the Holy Blessed One: Your mercies extend to this bird's nest but to that man (me) they did not extend!" — and the other says "that he gives a limit to the attributes of the Holy Blessed One: May Your mercies extend to this bird's nest (and no further)"; according to a third opinion "they do not well who take God's attributes to be mercies; and those translators among the people of Israel who interpolate: 'Just as I am merciful in heaven, so should you be merciful on earth: do not take the mother ox or sheep and its young as a sacrifice in the same day' — they do not well, for they take God's attributes to be mercies."

This criticism is aimed at Targum Pseudo-Jonathan, who translated Lev. 22:28 in this manner. The statement in *Leviticus Rabbah* 27:11 is appropriate for this translation: "It is written: A righteous person knows the soul of his animal, and this is like the Holy Blessed One in whose Torah it is written: 'Do not take the mother from her children' . . . Another interpretation: A righteous person knows the soul of his animal, and this is like the Holy Blessed One in whose Torah is written: '[When] an ox, a lamb, or a goat [is born] etc. [it shall remain at least seven days with its mother before being available for a sacrifice].'" Perhaps these exegetes are the ones who explore the "reasons of the Torah" that were singled out for praise in BT *Pesaḥim* 119a (Maimonides correctly notes that these passages indicate methodological differences). Indeed, the view of those who attribute a humanitarian reasoning to these two mitzvot needs no explanation. Rashi (BT *Berakhot* 32b) explained the view of their opponents: "God did not act on the basis of mercy, but rather to impose His legal decrees on Israel, to impress on them that they are God's servants and the keepers of God's mitzvot, decrees and statutes, even those things that an adversary or a pagan could argue over, saying: What need is there for this commandment?" It is not for us to judge how far-fetched a position these sages took, in light of the fact that the Torah itself "has made mercy out of God's attributes" by writing "for I am merciful" (Exodus 22:26). When the Sages forbade forcing a woman to submit to a levirate marriage with a disfigured brother-in-law (Yevamot 4a), they based themselves on the juxtaposition of "do not muzzle the ox" with the law of the levir (Deuteronomy 25:4–10) — a far-fetched argument, but for a humanitarian purpose, and we find nobody who opposed them. It is enough, then, to note that the above-mentioned opponents of giving rational reasons were more restrictive than their colleagues about the permissibility of finding intellectual reasons for the Torah's mitzvot. One should not be astonished that they utilized the most polite version "the translators did not do well . . ." They knew and they admitted that the intention of their opponents to make the mitzvot appear more reasonable (and by this to counter the attacks of the doubters) was appropriate, but they feared that through this the heteronomic characteristic of the performance of mitzvot would be slighted, and if so, the gain achieved by such explanations would be outweighed by its loss.

Is it permissible to derive halakhic conclusions from the reasons for the mitzvot?

Regarding the "practical" question: It is known that the Torah was not made available to rational explanation without certain reservations: "We do not punish based on logical deduction"; there are mitzvot that are considered innovations such as the forbidding of mixing milk and meat (BT *Ḥullin* 108a) and the punishing of scheming witnesses (BT *Sanhedrin* 27a), or that are considered "decrees of the text" such as the command of leaving the forgotten part of the field (according to one opinion — BT *Bava Metzia* 11a). But precisely the exceptions shed light on the general rule. Had all of the mitzvot in the Torah been just "decrees of the text," one mitzvah could not teach about another and the Sages never would have been able to understand one issue from another, to expand and to limit the force of the mitzvot just as was done with all of halakhic literature.[20] The Sages agree, then, with the opinion that there is a "rational" basis — that is to say a foundation that is given to our intellectual understanding — for most of the mitzvot of the Torah. This matter is confirmed when we look into the disagreement over the question of whether "we interpret the Torah's reasons." We learn in BT *Bava Metzia* 115a: "A widow, whether she is poor or wealthy — we do not take a pledge from her, according to Rabbi Judah. Rabbi Simeon says: We take a pledge from a wealthy [widow], and not from a poor [widow], for you are obligated to return the pledge to her and you bring her into disrepute among her neighbors." What are they actually disagreeing about? Even Rabbi Judah does not forbid investigating the reasons for the mitzvot. He is opposed only to the fact that we would be reducing the force of the mitzvot through this investigation, and indeed, it is doubtful whether the reason that R. Simeon attributes to this mitzvah is correct. Another limitation of Rabbi Judah is recognizable from *Sanhedrin* (Mishnah 2:4, BT 21a) — there, Rabbi Judah permits a king to have many wives "as long as they would not lead his heart astray"; R. Simeon forbids him to have many wives in any case, and even one if she would lead his heart astray. According to the Gemara's explanation, R. Judah understands the text "his heart should not stray" as an explanation of the previous prohibition. He also interprets, then, the reason that the text itself offers in explication of the law. If R. Simeon had claimed: "If so, the text should have said just 'he should not have too many wives' and remain silent, but I [R. Judah] say: What is the reason he should not have too many wives? So that his heart does not stray." Precisely because in his opinion it is incumbent upon the commentator to explain the reasons for the mitzvot and to derive conclusions for halakha, R. Simeon understands the verse "he should not stray" not as providing a reason for the previous, but as a new mitzvah. Therefore it is forbidden (1) to have many wives "even like Abigail"; and (2) to marry even one woman who is liable to make the king's heart stray. Here, too, R. Simeon's conception does not seem to agree with the plain meaning of the text. R. Judah does not show, then, an extreme tendency for irrationality when he opposes this procedure of basing the halakha on dubious conjectures.[21]

The differences of opinion that we dealt with in this chapter demonstrate, indeed, that the Sages paid attention also to methodological questions that are connected to the clarification of the mitzvot, but the value of these arguments is very limited. They are mentioned only in connection with two or three mitzvot. The opinion of the Sages on the question of reasons for the mitzvot is prominent only in their great project of expounding the Torah.

4. The Reasons for the Mitzvot According to the Rabbis

The rabbis found in the will of the Creator decisive arguments to adhere to His commandments. The faith in the irrational foundations for upholding the mitzvot — in the will of the Creator and His reward — served as the cornerstone of the rabbis' religious life. Just as all of the attacks, coming from the evil inclination and from the nations of the world, were powerless to upset their faith, so, too, could the finest explanations not add anything to their joy in accepting the burden of the mitzvot. Therefore, one should apparently be surprised at the fact that they invested so much in the investigation of the reasons for the mitzvot. Only after we have surveyed their investigation will we be able to fathom their reasons.

Measure for Measure

There are a few mitzvot that one is able to explain without prejudging the question of their influence on people, on the basis of the major principle "measure for measure."[22] Some of them serve as atonement for specified sins, like the three famous mitzvot that were given to women because (1) Eve spilled Adam's "blood"; (2) she brought about the curse of him who was the "challah" of the world; and (3) she extinguished his soul, which is likened to "a candle" (*Genesis Rabbah* 17:8).* And the majority of them were given to reward the righteous. For the merit of Abraham that he did not take of the spoils "so much as a thread or a shoelace," his sons merited the mitzvot of the garment-fringe and levirate marriage (*ibid.* 43:9; and one can also find other examples); because he compared himself to dust and ashes, they merited the commandment of the red heifer; the sons of Aaron were given the upper arm symbolizing the hand of Phinehas, the cheeks symbolizing his prayer, and the stomach symbolizing the stomach of the Midianite woman (BT *Ḥullin* 134b).

Symbolic Reasons

This explanation provides us with a transition into the symbolic explanations, which are quite numerous.[23] It is sufficient here to point out some of the explanations pertaining to the Four Species that are found in *Leviticus Rabbah* 30:9: "The product of the *hadar* tree — this is Abraham whom the Holy and Blessed One endowed (*hidder*) with a ripe old age. Branches (*kappot*) of palm trees — this is Isaac who was tied up (*kaffut*) and bound on the altar. Boughs of leafy trees — this is Jacob; just as the myrtle is decorated with leaves, so too was Jacob decorated with many sons. Willows of the brook — this is Joseph; just as the willow withers first before the other of the three species, so too did Joseph die before his brothers." Or (*ibid.* 12): "The fruit of the *hadar* tree (i.e., the citron,

* The three mitzvot, of course, are menstrual purity, challah, and lighting Sabbath candles. (LL)

which has taste and fragrance) alludes to those who study Torah and perform good deeds. Branches of date-palm trees (the date has taste but no fragrance) alludes to those who study Torah and do not perform good deeds. Boughs of leafy trees (the myrtle has fragrance but no taste) alludes to those who perform good deeds but do not study Torah. Willows of the brook (with neither fragrance nor taste) alludes to those who do not study Torah nor do they perform good deeds. The Holy and Blessed One said, 'They should be bound together in one bundle and atone one for each other's deficiencies.'" The former explanation rests content with pointing out the parallels, whereas the latter also has a moral resonance, like other homilies that we shall mention later.

The Mitzvot Influence Our Behavior

Most often, the mitzvot were accounted for by demonstrating the influence of their performance or non-performance on our lives. This influence is not only spiritual. Some of our rabbis, such as Rabbi Ḥisda, believed in the mystical power that comes from doing mitzvot: "From the time of the destruction of the Temple the power of the rain and the wind was diminished."[24] They attributed this mystical power to the law of circumcision: it imposes the fear of Israel upon "all earthly creatures, humans, beasts, animals, birds, and creeping-things" including even the Leviathan, which flees before the sight of the circumcision (*Tanḥuma Tzav* § 14, 42; *Pirkei de-Rabbi Eliezer* § 10). Our rabbis also acknowledge that some of the mitzvot have reasons that are more *utilitarian* than moral. Some of these details can be understood according to the principle that "the Torah protects the property of Israel."[25] The Torah restricts marital relations between husband and his wife "in order that she will be as dear to her husband as on the day of her wedding" (BT *Niddah* 31b). The Torah imposes an oath on one who concedes in part to a plaintiff's claim, as "a man does not lie brazenly before his creditor" (BT *Ketubot* 18b). The rabbis explained in great detail the utility of the mitzvah to assist one's enemy whose donkey collapsed: "He started talking to himself, saying 'So-and-so was my friend and I did not know it!' The two of them went to an inn and ate and drank. What caused the two of them to reconcile? The fact that one of them saw this [law] in the Torah [and obeyed it]!" (*Tanḥuma Mishpatim* 1). Indeed, the last example shows the influence of the Torah only on our behavior and not on our inner disposition. But if we pay attention to the great value that the rabbis attributed to peacemaking, it is similar to the following examples that point out the *educational* influence of the mitzvot. The modern Jewish scholar Samson Raphael Hirsch justly remarked that the calendar has the same place in Judaism as the catechism of dogmas in Christianity. The calendar (that is to say the series of mitzvot that follow the yearly cycle) serves also as a description of Jewish history. According to the Torah itself, the Sabbath comes to remind one of creation, while the Torah commands the father to tell his son of the miracles to which the symbols of Passover allude. But the rabbis added further to this commandment when they said that whoever does not explain these symbols has not fulfilled his obligation. They explicitly taught the historical value of the holiday of Shavuot, on which, according to the Book of Jubilees (6:17), all of the covenants mentioned in the Torah were enacted. For all the festival and fast days, they found historical reasons, which the liturgical poets would describe at length. Even the prohibition of linen-wool mixtures was given (according to *Tanḥuma Bereshit*) because "it would go against reason to mix the offering of the sinner (Cain) and the offering of the guiltless (Abel)."

Expound Them and Receive Reward

Ethical-religious influence proceeds from the mitzvot, according to the rabbis, whether in their observance or in the mere act of expounding them.

There are commandments that were given — according to the Rabbis — not for the purpose of being observed, but rather in the name of "explaining them in order to receive a reward."* One of them is the commandment regarding the rebellious son, that "never existed and never will exist" (BT *Sanhedrin* 71a). Indeed, how nicely did they explain this commandment by connecting it with previous mitzvot in the Torah: He who marries a women only for her beauty will in the future grow to hate her, and she will give birth to a rebellious son!

The Midrash (*Tanḥuma Ki Tetzei* 1) adds another homily based on the textual sequence of the mitzvot (Deuteronomy 22): Whoever observes the commandment of sending away the mother bird from the nest will merit a new house, a vineyard, an ox and donkey, fine clothes, and finally a wife and children. Such explanations are quite common. The section about the Nazirite is adjoined to the section about the adulterous woman, as "whoever sees the adulterous woman in her disgrace will vow to abstain from wine" that brings one to sin (BT *Sotah* 2a). These examples show us that the rabbis paid attention not only to the decrees of the Torah, but also

* It is surprising that Heinemann does not perceive that by deeming them such, the rabbis radically exercised their own autonomy — in effect relegating these rules (offensive to the modern ethical sensibility and probably to that of the rabbis) from "active" to "theoretical" status! But this action of the rabbis illustrates another principle of Heinemann — that when the rabbis acted in unusual fashion, they were extremely coy about their reasons for doing so. (LL)

to the factual situations that cause them (e.g., not about the reasons for the laws of the Nazirite and suspected adulteress alone, but also about the factual conditions that make for marital jealousy and ascetic practices). They sought not only to give reasons for the commandments, but also to find a reason for everything written in the Torah, including the order of its topics and their mutual connections in general. Therefore they described at length the affliction of leprosy itself and the sins that caused it, more than just the laws of leprosy.

Indeed, inquiry into the laws themselves enlightens us in matters of religion and ethics. Precisely in it we can see the bipolar character of the midrash that we expounded above: between our conscience and the mitzvot pass sparks of ideas; the former explains the latter, and the latter confirm and clarify the former. Thus the sages asked *(Mekhilta Mishpatim* 15): "Why did the Torah see fit to impose a more severe penalty on the *gannav* than on the *gazlan*? Rabban Johanan ben Zakkai said: The *gazlan* (who robs directly from the person in his presence) accords equal respect to the servant (mankind) and to his master (God), whereas the *gannav* (who steals in secret) accords greater respect to the servant than to his master . . . and treats the supernal Eye as if it does not see." Also (*ibid.* 2): "Why was the ear, of all limbs, considered deserving of being pierced? Rabban Johanan ben Zakkai spoke of it as a kind of stringency: The ear that heard 'You shall not steal' but went and stole, is especially deserving of piercing, of all his limbs." (See also *Tosefta Bava Kama* 7:5: "Because it heard at Sinai, 'For the people of Israel are My slaves — only Mine' and it cast off the yoke of Heaven to take on the yoke of human mortals.") Also (*Mekhilta, loc cit.* 12): "See how beloved was labor to Him who by His word brought the world into being: The ox that labors is [if stolen] recompensed fivefold, whereas the sheep that does not labor is recompensed only fourfold. Rabban Johanan ben Zakkai said: The Holy and Blessed One has consideration for people's dignity: the ox, that walks on its own legs, is recompensed fivefold, whereas the sheep, that is carried on the shepherd's shoulders, is recompensed fourfold."

Just as the author of that first homily derives a moral from the laboring animal that applies to human labor, so similarly in other places the rabbis draw analogies between humans and lower beings to point a moral. On the basis of the fact that only domesticated and not wild animals are brought as sacrifices, they interpreted the verse, "God desires the *nirdaf* (i.e., the persecuted)" as referring to the righteous and the people of Israel (*Ecclesiastes Rabbah* on Ecclesiastes 3:15). From the verse, "Seal [the wood of the Tabernacle's ark] inside and outside" (Exodus 25:11), Rava deduced: "Any scholar whose inner [moral] character does not match his outer, is no scholar" (BT *Yoma* 72b).

Such analogies not infrequently take on an *a fortiori* form. Many examples are recorded in the *Sifra* to Leviticus 20:16, for instance: "If, of an animal by which harm came to a human being, the text says, 'let it be stoned,' then in the case of a person who caused his friend to be diverted from the way of life to the way of death, how much more so should the All-Present cause him to pass away from the world!" Also in the case of other mitzvot they emphasized the ethical and social reasons: "Why did the Torah stipulate that the property of the righteous [in the idolatrous city] should be destroyed? What led them to settle in that city? Their property! Therefore their property should be destroyed" (BT *Sanhedrin* 112a). "For the sake of four things the Torah commanded to leave the corner specifically at the edge of the field: [as a precaution against] the robbing of the poor, wasting the time of the poor, suspicion, and the injunction 'you shall not finish off' [harvesting your field]" (BT *Shabbat* 23a — see the full passage for elaboration). It is well to remark that these last two utterances were both attributed to R. Simeon, whose tendency to interpret the reasons for the mitzvot is already familiar to us.

Not only does the "study" have a moral influence on us, but also the "deed" (i.e., the actual fulfillment of the mitzvot). It is a major principle of the Sages that one mitzvah leads to another, and one sin leads to another (Mishnah *Avot* 4:2). Thus they said that "sin constricts a person's heart" (BT *Yoma* 39a), whereas "whoever has tefillin on his head and arm, fringes on his garment and a mezuzah at his door-opening is well-fortified against sinning."[26] In the view of some of our rabbis, the Sabbath was given especially for the purpose of learning Torah (*Pesikta Rabbati* 23 end, p. 121a).*

When we survey the Sages' explanations of the mitzvot, it is surprising that ethical reasons are relatively rare. It did not occur to them that circumcision and dietary laws are likely to restrain our carnal urges, as the philosophers would explain. This fact would seem to stand in contradiction to those famous sayings according to which the whole Torah has only an ethical purpose. This ethical purpose is apparently evidenced by the saying of Rab that we mentioned above ("the mitzvot were given only in order to purify mankind") and Hillel's famous response according

* We do not wish to deal at length with the reasons of "rabbinic mitzvot." It is well known that in his introduction to his Commentary on the Mishnah Maimonides drew a distinction between protective enactments ("*gezerot*"), enacted as a "fence around the Torah" and to discourage sin, and positive enactments ("*takkanot*"). The reasons for the latter could be historical (e.g., Hanukkah), religious (e.g., the institution of the prayer liturgy), or utilitarian. Stein discussed the rabbinic enactments instituted "for the sake of repairing the social world (*mipenei tikkun olam*)" and "for the sake of peaceful relations" (*mipenei darkhei shalom*) in his article in Wohlgemuth's *Jeshurun* Vol. 268 (1924), pp. 11ff., but there were, of course, other utilitarian reasons as well. (IH)

to which the whole Torah is only a "commentary" on the command "to love your neighbor as yourself."* It agrees also with the expression that God "sanctified us by His commandments" — for there is no sanctity that does not include ethical good — as well as with the saying that the Torah starts with, ends with, and includes in its center deeds of lovingkindness. *(Tanḥuma Buber Vayera* 4)** If so, how can we explain that although the vast majority of the Sages believed in the religious-ethical purpose of our Torah, nevertheless they made hardly any attempt to find ethical reasons for the mitzvot? It is impossible to regard so many sayings as mere hyperbole,*** nor can we dismiss them as the views of lone individuals to whom many were opposed. It is indeed possible that not all the interpretations of the mitzvot were preserved for posterity. But the fact that the ethical explanations are so infrequent proves at least that they were not regarded as very important by the rabbis' audience or by the editors of the Talmud and the Midrash.

Some may wish to explain this contradiction on the basis of the manner of the rabbis' intellectual style and method of inquiry: it was not their custom to prove some abstract principle through interpretations that are themselves only conjectural. Whoever did such a thing was perhaps regarding them as building a house without a foundation. But in any case, their lack of moralistic interpretations highlights the profound difference between the rabbis and the later rationalists. The latter tried to find, insofar as possible, a sufficient reason not only for the mitzvot themselves, but also for their observance. The proof that there could be a rational reason even for those mitzvot that seemed to be arbitrary dictates of the Torah enabled them, if not to annul entirely the heteronomic aspect of our obedience, then at least to soften somewhat the harshness of that heteronomy. Such an intention never occurred to the rabbis. They were convinced that the mitzvot had ethical reasons. Their faith in this was based both on the recognition that it was precisely its ethical content that differentiated our

---

* Hillel is literally quoted as saying, "What is hateful to you, do not do to your fellow." But there is really no material difference between the positive and negative formulations of the Golden Rule; here I agree with G. Kittel, *Probleme des Spätjudentums* (1926), p. 109. (IH)

** The well-known sayings in which the rabbis discuss whether the "major principle" at the heart of the Torah is "Love your neighbor as yourself" or "This is the book of the generations of humanity: in God's image God created the human being" (see *Genesis Rabbah* 24:7 and the commentary *Minḥat Yehudah ad loc.*) prove simply that many of the specific mitzvot (not all) are included in these verses. (IH)

*** Several mitzvot, such as the garment-fringe and the Sukkah, are declared to be "equal to all the mitzvot. (*Sifri* Numbers § 115: "If one observes the garment-fringe, he is considered to have fulfilled all the mitzvot.") There are similar sayings about deeds of lovingkindness (Wohlgemuth 45ff.). (IH)

Torah from the religions and laws of the pagans, and on the Jewish belief in a righteous and compassionate God. The rabbis could be compared to a child who is convinced that his parent would not command him anything that was not for his benefit and edification. If the child succeeded in recognizing the reason for some of those commands, fine and good, but he feels no need to seek out the reasons for those commands in a systematic way, and he does not mind if it is also incumbent on him to fulfill certain commands whose reasons escape him. Thus the Sages did not try to find an ethical reason for all the commandments in the Torah, especially not for the majority of those that they called *ḥukkim* — positive laws in the narrow sense. Their purpose in explaining the mitzvot was twofold: (1) to demonstrate the value of the Torah to the people in order to endear it to them, and (2) to reinforce its educational effect. These objectives are recognizable in their entire religious-educational enterprise. The first is prominent in their interpretation of the Torah's narratives: here too they derived lessons from juxtapositions in the text and interpreted the episodes under the aspect of "measure for measure." They explained the motives of the Biblical heroes not in simplistic psychological terms but in a way for us to appreciate God's justice and to draw moral lessons from the deeds of our predecessors.[27] The second is based on their faith that "whoever has more wisdom but fewer deeds, his wisdom does not endure" (Mishnah *Avot* 3:12). It is possible, indeed, to educate a person more through exemplary deeds than through abstract principles (in the manner of the philosophers). But a deed does not operate of its own accord unless we make a connection with the wisdom embodied in the deed. Just as the rabbis associated ethical teachings with some of the mitzvot so that they could have a positive effect on our character, so through their enactments they put into practice the religious-ethical potential of the Torah. Perhaps it is no coincidence that the same rabbi who said, "the mitzvot were given only to purify mankind" also instituted the prayers of Rosh Hashanah (such as "*uvekhen ten paḥdekha*" — "therefore instill the fear of You . . .") that are so heart-moving and motivate the throng of worshippers to that repentance for which the Days of Awe were intended. Above all else, the rabbis endeavored not to prove the ethical value of the mitzvot but to facilitate their ethical effectiveness in reality.

Of the "factors" that we defined in Chapter One, the "scientific" factor operated only rarely. (The question, "Why did the Torah say . . . ?" is found only in connection with questions of physiology: see *Niddah* 31b.) We must also not overrate the apologetic factor: they responded to Jewish dissenters by reasserting authority while answering pagans with pro-forma replies. The "theoretical religious" factor is prominent in their general doctrine that there is an ethical purpose for the entire Torah. But this did not motivate them to investigate the reasons for the mitzvot systematically. Nearly all their explanations are rooted in the "practical religious" factor; they succeeded in building a bridge between the perpetual commandments, incumbent on every Jew, and the warm, lively emotion that is renewed in every generation in each individual. The rabbis were not theoreticians or prophets, but they were unequalled in Jewish history as popular educators.

Chapter 4
The Views of the Hellenistic Jews

Our inquiry in this chapter does not embrace all Jews who were influenced by the culture of Greece, but rather only that specific circle of people who attempted to integrate their traditional religion with Greek learning. They knew (in complete contrast to the earlier Hellenists of the Hasmonean period) the true character of Greek philosophy, and in particular they knew that the famous philosophers disbelieved in the gods of Homer and acknowledged the unity of God and the value of ethical life. When they read in the books of Plato that it is incumbent on us "to be like God as much as possible by doing what is good," they recognized that this objective is very similar to the objective of the Jewish faith. And precisely since the social reality in the Hellenistic period was completely contradictory to any religious and traditional ideals, the Jews saw in these philosophers the true partners of the Judaism that was also fighting idolatry, violence, and the life of hedonistic indulgence. Not *despite* faithfulness to the tradition of their ancestors did they admire Greek science, but rather, precisely because of it, as science was also apt, according to their opinion, to confirm and to deepen, by way of logic, the essential principles of our religion. They did not refrain, of course, from directing criticism against certain individual doctrines of the scholars of Greece, but they believed in the fundamental agreement between Torah and science to the point that they regarded Plato and Pythagoras as the students of their master Moses. Therefore, they dedicated their energies to demonstrating in detail the correlation that exists between Judaism and Greek science. In this way, they came to a new formulation of our question, the question of the reasons for the mitzvot.

Each Person a Supreme Authority on the Mitzvot's Value

Philosophy taught that the value of the mitzvot is not determined by routine and custom, and not by individual thought, but rather only by human reason, formed by methodological investigation. The outcome of such a procedure obligates each one who takes upon himself the name of "enlightened." For all of the laws in the world, including the laws of Judaism, this assumption offered both danger and hope: any law that did not stand up to examination in the court of science would necessarily suffer depreciation, even in the eyes of its adherents, whereas any law that was confirmed by reason should properly find admirers, even among the nations that did not know of it before. The value of the explanation of the mitzvot would thus be much greater in the eyes of the Hellenistic Jews than for the rabbis, whose faith was strong and who did not attach much importance to the performance of the mitzvot of the Torah by gentiles.

Thus we do not find any Hellenistic Jewish writer who did not pay attention to our problem. Philo wrote three works (one of which is four books in length) on the mitzvot of the Torah.* Their essential function is to explain all of the laws according to their plain sense and significance. Josephus dealt with the mitzvot and their reasons in brief, but it was his intention to write a full book devoted to the description of the mitzvot and their explanation.[1] Also, in the Letter of Aristeas and in the Fourth Book of the Maccabees** are found allusions to the reasons for the mitzvot. Some of these books were indeed addressed to Greek readers, but they were intended also for the Jews. The apologetic literature in our days (the European and the American) is also read more by Jews than by Christians, and it also has succeeded in bolstering the self-esteem of many Jews who were led into self-doubt by the attacks of anti-Semitism. Indeed, the midrashic defense is not identical to the Hellenistic defense. The rabbis were able to deflect the non-Jewish attacker "with a reed " [i.e., with a pro-forma response], while instructing their students to submit to the will of the Creator, whereas Philo was not in a position to "speak to the Jews as a Jew and to the Greeks as a Greek." In addressing both audiences simultaneously, he was forced to find sufficient reasons for the performance of the mitzvot in general and more specifically for their value. For not only did the Jews agree with the Greeks regarding the authority of science as an expert judge for all faiths, but also the criteria by which the Greeks evaluated laws and practices influenced the Jewish students to a noticeable extent. Because of this, the Hellenistic Jews came to an explanation of the mitzvot that seems superficially similar to that of the rabbis, but is actually quite different.

Irrational Reasons Not Valued

This difference is demonstrated by the fact that for the Hellenists, the irrational reasons were far less important than the rational reasons. A major pillar of the rabbis' outlook was their yearning to abrogate their own will

* *On the Decalogue*, *On the Special Commandments* (in 4 volumes), *On the Virtues*.

** These may be found in Charlesworth's edition of *The Old Testament Pseudepigrapha*, Volume 2.

in favor of God's will. And yet the Hellenists, even though they believed in a revealed Torah and in reward and punishment,[2] did not emphasize this, but rather tended to call Moses "the Lawmaker." This was not mere imprecision on their part. Philo writes in the introduction to his book *Life of Moses*: "I wish to describe Moses, whom some have called by the name of lawmaker: Jews and others thought of him as the transmitter of our Torah." Philo thus does not completely reject the idea that Moses himself gave the Torah. Josephus, even though he believes in the Sinaitic revelation, writes: "Moses was not a fraud or a deceiver, but rather he was similar to Minos (the king of the Cretes) and to other well-known lawmakers according to the Greeks: they attributed their laws to Cebes and Apollo, whether because they believed it to be so, or because they hoped that by presenting the matter that way it would become easier for them to persuade the community."[3] These two Hellenistic writers indeed mention the faith in revealed Torah as a reason for obedience,[4] but more as the accepted view of the community than as their own. This view of the Hellenistic writers is singular in the history of the Jewish idea.* Indeed, we find deniers of the belief in a divine Torah, in particular in the days of Philo and in our own time, but all those who believed in it considered "Torah from Heaven" a cornerstone of the religious faith of Israel and a strong basis for performance of its mitzvot.

The Greek Autonomous Ethic Influenced the Hellenists

Why did the Hellenists disregard what was central in their co-religionists' view? The Jewish Hellenists, of course, did not expect that the Greeks would give more credence to Moses' claim to divine revelation than to similar claims of other Greek or Asiatic legislators.[5] There is another reason for the position of the Hellenists, one that stems from their world-view. The rabbis emphasized the heteronomic character of the performance of the mitzvot, and were actually proud of themselves for taking on the yoke of the kingdom of heaven. They served their Creator as servants who serve their master; they even tended to prefer the one who acts out of commandedness over the one who acts because of his conscience. However, the doctrine of Greek ethics — which was most definitely autonomous — influenced the Hellenists.** Whereas the rabbis, in their defense of Phi-

* However, it has become a common view of non-Orthodox Jews in modern times. That is one reason the views of the Hellenistic writers described here are amazingly relevant to contemporary Jewish discussion of theology and observance. (LL)

** We have cited the rabbis' maxim: "Read not *ḥarut* but *ḥerut*, for the free person is one who engages in Torah (*Avot* 6:2). Philo, on the other hand, wrote an entire treatise on the Stoic doctrine that the true free man is the sage who listens to his conscience! See the discussion on "one who acts out of commandedness" in the previous chapter. (IH)

nehas' zealous intervention, resorted to the theory that he acted only on the basis of a halakhic precedent that had "been forgotten," Philo teaches that the Levites killed "of their own will" those who were guilty of the worship of the golden calf and he neglects to discuss Moses' command.[6] The doctrine that the Torah came from God is important in the eyes of the Hellenists, not quite directly, but in a roundabout way; that is to say: to the extent that it guarantees the agreement of the mitzvot with the voice of our conscience and rational ethics. One can prove this agreement in detail. In their opinion, the entire value of the Torah depends on this proof.* The doctrine of the Torah's supernal origin may be supportive to this argument, but not decisive.

National Conservatism as a Reason

On the other hand, the Hellenistic Jews established other irrational reasons for the performance of mitzvot, in accordance with the world-views of most of the Greek circles. Socrates, Plato, Aristotle, and most of the leaders of the Stoics were not cosmopolitan. In spite of the criticism that they directed against the laws and religions of the world, including those of the Greeks themselves, they felt themselves to be part of their nation and birthplace, and they respected whoever remained faithful to the customs of their ancestors, as long as they were not offensive to reason. The important thinker who founded, it appears, the "humanistic" ideal, was the same who taught that each nation is obligated, in spite of its commitment to humanity at large, to hold on to its traditional characteristics and its special customs.[7] Most Greeks admired the people of the East because they remained faithful to their ancient culture, as opposed to the innovative Greeks. Jewish Hellenists utilized these ideas in order to justify and even to praise their fidelity to their ancestors' religion and their laws. "All human beings keep their customs, especially the nation of Israel," wrote Philo.[8] In his wish to justify his nation's rejection of the king's ritual, he claimed before the Emperor (Caligula): "Love of the birthplace and adoration of its laws are rooted in every person; there is no need to instruct you about this, seeing as how you also love your birthplace very much and greatly honor you ancestors' traditions." He, like Josephus, emphasizes the antiquity of the Torah, specifically in relation to Greek laws: "There is no honor for an Emperor for disgracing ancient ordinances";[9] they each praise their nation for having not changed the customs of their ancestors. Maccabees IV adds

* Josephus writes: "Which of these it was who made the best laws, and which had the greatest reason to believe that God was their author, it will be easy, upon comparing those laws themselves together, to determine" (*Against Apion* II, 163).

the important point that "God certainly permitted for us foods that would agree with our souls" (5:26).

"Do Not Separate From the Community!"

There is yet another irrational reason: enlightened people do not have the right to separate themselves from the community — they must be agreeable in the eyes of others.[10] This reason assumes that there is a difference regarding appreciation of the mitzvot between the educated elite and the masses. Therefore, this reason is not found among the rabbis. However, the historical reason was not acceptable to them even though it is hinted at in Scripture[11] and even though the rabbis valued custom very much and spoke, it seems, with compassion for the non-Jews who "are in possession of their ancestors' custom."[12] They believed in only one form of the heteronomic idea: theonomy. The rest of the heteronomic reasons — which suited the non-Jewish religions as well and in some sense were made to justify those who upheld them — did not find favor in their eyes.

"Natural Law" vs. the Laws of the Legislators

The rational reasons for the performance of the mitzvot advanced by the Hellenstic Jews were also grounded on the assumptions of Greek thought, perhaps even more so than the irrational ones. The Greeks differentiated between two types of "laws": (1) "natural" or "unwritten" law, which is equal for all human beings, and (2) legislators' law, which is only a human invention. The vast majority of Greek philosophers taught that natural law rules not only in the life of humans, but in the entire world, and through it the world becomes the "cosmos," that is to say, a beautiful and set order. However, they were divided over the value of the laws that were invented by people. The extremists rejected all of the subtleties of human beings with a severity that rivals even the doctrine of Rousseau, but the moderates justified these laws by making them agree with true natural law. In their opinion, special laws were there only to "explain" natural law — just as, according to Hillel the Elder, the entire Torah is only an explanation of the mitzvot related to justice. Because of this, the moderates also rejected all of the mitzvot that do not "imbibe strength from natural law," especially several of the ritual actions, in which they did not see much intrinsic value. Indeed, they participated in traditional ritual, but just out of that conservatism that we clarified, "only because the state commands the ritual, and not because of the view that, God forbid, the spirit of the gods derives pleasure from it" (Seneca).

All of these assumptions are echoed in Jewish circles. Philo's book *On Joseph* testifies to this clearly. Joseph is the politician whose name suits him, for all of the laws of the state are only a human "addition"* to the "divine" natural law. Philo also differentiated, then, between Divine and human mitzvot, in a completely different way than did the rabbis. The Divine character of true law is not recognizable on the basis of historical tradition, except when it is brought into line with the law of nature — an agreement to which our intellect bears witness.

The Method of the Extreme Hellenists

But is it possible to prove a similarity between the natural law and the 613 commandments? On this question the Jewish Hellenists were of differing views — even those who believed in the absolute value of the Torah of Moses — just as their Greek teachers were divided concerning their own laws. There were radical Jews who interpreted all of the Torah allegorically, the stories as well as the commandments. The Torah did not mean to command the circumcision of the flesh, but rather the circumcision of the heart. The Passover sacrifice does not recall the deed of the Lord "that He passed over the houses of the children of Israel in Egypt" (indeed the story itself should not be explained according to its simple meaning; more accurately, it has an allegorical meaning), but rather it awakens us to "pass over" our desires, and so forth. Indeed, allegorical explanations of the commandments are also found in the Talmudic and Midrashic literature (consider for example in *Tanḥuma Buber Kedoshim* 14, on the verse, "and you shall declare its first fruits as *orlah* (forbidden)" (Leviticus 19:23); the verse speaks not of a fruit-tree but of a male baby whose father sanctifies him to the Torah when he is four years old). But it never occurred to the rabbis that interpretations like these should override the observance of the commandment in its plain sense.[13] It is interesting to point out that the Hellenists apart from Philo, and in particular Josephus, did not find it worthwhile even to mention the allegorical explanations of the commandments.[14] Even Philo, though he certainly did not reject the allegorical method, not only did he oppose their practical conclusions and hold onto Sabbath, circumcision, and the food prohibitions, he also struggled to find a scientific explanation for all of the commandments of the Torah. The three of his works that we mentioned are the first attempt to reply in a methodical and scientific way to the question of "the reasons for the commandments."

---

* A play on Joseph's name, which means "may he add." (LL)

Philo's Method

Philo's point of departure is the Greek premise that initially there was only the unwritten natural law. This law was modeled by the Patriarchs in their exemplary lives. Afterwards the Torah comes to interpret and to specify the natural law, first by way of the Ten Commandments and afterwards by the way of the "Special Commandments" that are, in Philo's thought, only the details of the Ten Commandments. This approach is both historical and philosophical. It explains the evolutionary development of the Israelite religion and also justifies the content of the commandments. Another approach of Philo categorizes the commandments within the rubric of the virtues according to the Greek ethical doctrine. The first approach is the basis of the bulk of Philo's writings on Jewish law, comprising *The Decalogue* and *The Special Commandments* (in four volumes). The two views are combined and interwoven (and this was the cause of annoying repetitions in his work), but they are not contradictory because natural law is the moral law.

It was Philo's goal to explain all of the commandments. Even the commandment of honoring parents he explains at great length (*Special Commandments* II, 226), discovering no fewer than five reasons for it. If he seems to us to be splitting hairs, we should recall that such rhetorical extravagances were sweet to the palate of his Greek and Hellenistic readers.

The basic goal of these Jewish-Hellenistic writers was to offer explanations for the commandments, or at least to explain their value in new ways. Therefore they make efforts to prove:

1. The commandments of the Torah conform to the laws of the universe, in accordance with the Greek assumptions;
2. They have an educational influence on those who fulfill them;
3. They cause great benefit to the individuals and to the community.

The Torah's Laws Similar to the Laws of the Universe

The Torah celebrates the cosmos. For Philo and Josephus the Temple symbolizes the world and its divisions, whereas for the rabbis its order corresponds to the Heavenly Temple.[15] The Torah's choice of dates for festivals gives prominence not only to the new moon, but also to the full moon and the equinoxes (Philo, *On the Special Commandments* II, 155 on Passover and Sukkot). It goes without saying that the prohibitions of animal hybrids (*ibid.* III, 48) and vineyard graftings (Josephus, *Antiquities* IV, 228) are regarded as natural laws. In addition, the use of water and ash in the purification ritual of the red heifer is in keeping with the Greeks' theory of the four elements.[16] Moreover, in the Hellenistic reading the Torah is appreciative of the powers upon which the order of the world is based. Particularly in the view of the Pythagorean school, these powers are the numbers. This method made a definite impression on the rabbis as well. They justified the appreciation of the number "7" in the Torah by the significance that it has in nature, but whereas the Midrash (Leviticus Rabbah 29:11) relies on Biblical verses and alludes also to the sevenfold periods in Jewish history, Philo only mentions natural phenomena.[17]

This distinction between the rabbis' preference to explain nature on the basis of religion and the Hellenists' method to justify religion because of its correspondence to nature* is clearly prominent in Philo's outlook, according to which ethical powers are discernible in natural processes.[18] "Equality is, as the naturalists taught, the father of Justice, and everything in heaven and earth was arranged by this Equality in accordance with inviolable laws. The evenings and the days are equal in duration; in the cycle of the moon equality dominates, because in the measure that she increases, so in equal measure does she diminish, in quantity and in magnitude." In Philo's view, equality governs also in the jurisprudence of the Torah: "It deprecates the legislators who imposed on the guilty penalties dissimilar to their deeds, for example financial penalty for assaults . . . rather it commands that the guilty should suffer exactly as they did to others, that is to say they should suffer penalization in their property, if they caused damage to the property of their peer, but in their body, if they damaged the body of their peer."[19] He departs, therefore, from the method of the rabbis not only in his interpreting "eye for an eye" literally,** but also in holding that the cosmic order*** is the basis for ordering human life!

Ethical Explanations

This idea that nature and its study teach us about justice and equity brings us to the second kind of explanations: the ethical. The Hellenists were not satisfied with refuting the accusations of their opponents, who claimed that the Torah imbued its followers with misanthropy (an objective that Josephus set for himself in his book *Against Apion*). They also turned the tables on their attackers: they sought to prove that Judaism is based on

* The mystics, from *Sefer Yetzirah* onward, take an intermediate position. (IH)

** It is unlikely that Philo departed deliberately on this point from the law of his day. More likely, either the Alexandrian Jewish community was unaware of this aspect of rabbinic law, or the rabbinic law itself adopted the monetary interpretation of *lex talionis* at a later date. (LL)

*** Philo's view is comparable to that of the rabbis in teaching that the stars, by showing perfect obedience to the will of their Creator, set an example for humanity. (IH)

justice and teaches justice. From the days of Plato onwards there arose many philosophers in Greece who depicted ideal political laws, in which social and moral justice ruled instead of indulgence, violence, and domination, which were continually on the increase, especially in the Hellenistic period. Many of these schemes took on utopian forms. And along came the Jews, who taught that the ideal and social law is not in our imagination and not in heaven but rather is revealed to us in the Torah of Moses. According to the Fourth Book of the Maccabees (5:23) "The Torah teaches us prudence and self-restraint, that we should rule over all pleasures and cravings; it educates us to endure with patience and with a desiring heart every suffering and misfortune; it guides us towards justice, so that we should travel on the straight path in all our ways; and it teaches us piety thus: that we revere only the living and enduring God." The author is in fact alluding here to the four cardinal virtues that the teachers of Greek ethics ordained, only in place of the Greek virtue of wisdom it substitutes piety. This change, even though it is symptomatic, is not in open opposition to the Greek idea. Many of the Greek thinkers also valued piety, and some went so far as to teach that it ought to be the basis of the laws of the state.[20]

Josephus on Theocracy

On this basis, it is possible to understand the conception of Josephus, who emphasized these two points of view, the ethical and the religious. He also established that "we have admirable laws from the aspect of piety, brotherly love, philanthropy, justice, industry, and courage."[21] We have already established that in the view of the Hellenists the divine origin of the Torah does not prove its value, but rather the opposite: on the basis of the analysis of the laws one can determine which lawgiver is the best and therefore credible in his claim to a divine connection. Therefore Josephus compares the Torah to the laws of the Greeks, the philosophers and the statesmen[22]; it is not a "monarchy," or an "oligarchy," or a "democracy" — rather, if it is possible to say, a "theocracy." With respect to the conception of the one God, the one who demands that we lead moral lives, indeed there is no difference between the Jews and the great Greek philosophers. However, they shared their wisdom only with a certain few people, whereas Moses combined study and action, and not only persuaded his contemporaries to accept his words, but also implanted in the hearts of their children and remote descendants an unshakable faith in God. He did not regard piety as a part of morality, but rather regarded the other virtues (justice, prudence, courage, fraternal love between all citizens) as a part of piety. Whereas other lawgivers guided the community either through intellectual instruction or by instituting behavioral norms, he combined both ways. He did not leave room for the keepers of his commandments to determine even small matters by their own discretion, in particular concerning dietary practices and the times of rest; and on the other hand, he commanded us to listen to the reading of the Torah not once or twice, but weekly on every Sabbath.* As a result of this, the Jews are united in their view of God, their ritual practices, and their ethical virtues. But our laws are very strict. Sexual relations are forbidden except in order to procreate; it is completely forbidden to expose newborn infants to die (as the Greeks did). Many transgressions are punishable by death.[23] Despite this, Jews are commanded to honor their parents, to treat the poor kindly, to show mercy to enemies and even to animals. Even though Josephus did not explain the particular mitzvot at length, it is still possible through his list to see in fact how the Torah guides its followers to a life of morality and piety through the laws specific to Judaism.

Philo's Social Explanation

Even more than Josephus, Philo emphasizes the ethical and social character of the Torah's commandments. In a few places he proves at length that the commandments lead to all good virtues (*The Special Commandments,* I, 314),[24] in particular to subduing desire (IV, 97–135), to the love of justice (IV 136–202), to courage (*On the Virtues,* 1–50), and to similar virtues (51–174). For example: the commandment to fast on Yom Kippur, which occurs precisely during the harvest season when everything is available to us, teaches us to control our impulses [*The Special Commandments* II, 195] and the same applies to the dietary prohibitions [IV, 100, etc.]. Concerning relations between a man and a woman Philo denounces any sexual relation that is not for the purpose of procreation, and on the basis of this reason he explains the abstinence from relations between a man and his wife at certain times [III, 32ff.]. In order to prove the social objective,[25] he relies, of course, on the prohibition of charging interest [II, 74], on the commandment of the Jubilee year [II, 110], and on the prohibition against performing work on the Sabbath [II, 66]. With regard to justice, he claims that the Torah is not only concerned about the well-being of slaves [II, 79ff], but also animals and even trees [*On the Virtues* 125–160], in contrast to the majority of Greek teachers of morality who did not recognize any obligations aside from those towards human beings. Specifically, he interprets the prohibitions of (1) sacrificing the mother and young on the same day, (2) eating meat and milk together, and (3) yoking an ox and donkey together in this manner. Also, the majority of the historical reasons that Philo cites reinforce his social

* Philo, too, emphasizes the value of the Sabbath (*On the Special Commandments* II, 62 et al.).

message. Very rarely he attaches historic-national value to the holidays (he associates the giving of the Torah with the New Year — see II, 188), but he sees many of the commandments as reminders of the lives of the ancients, the ancestors of all humanity.[26] The Sabbath, for example, hearkens back to the era of mankind before the use of fire, and the prohibition to "kindle a fire on Sabbath" depreciates in some sense the culture that is based on the use of fire. The identification of matzah as "poor man's bread" is truly intended to praise the simple food of the ancients, whose lives, unspoiled by class differences and indulgence, should be held up as a model for us.[27]

Philo frequently demonstrates the ethical value of the mitzvot by way of symbolic explanations: the unblemished bodies of the sacrifices indicate the unblemished hearts of those offering them (I, 259), in the same fashion as the rabbis derived lessons about people from the sacrifices or the ark of testimony. The circumcision of the flesh teaches about the circumcision of the heart (I, 8); the indicators of ritual purity in animals — the split hooves and chewing of cud — teach every student that he is obligated to explore and meditate on what he learns and to repeat it (IV, 107). Already in the Letter of Aristeas we find similar reasons for the details of the dietary laws.

Utilitarian Reasons

To a certain extent, the Hellenists also believed in utilitarian reasons. The rabbis knew that the performance of mitzvot differentiates Jews from the nations of the world and even enacted certain decrees "to discourage intermarriage," but only the Hellenists taught that the purpose of the dietary laws (Letter of Aristeas 142) and circumcision (Josephus *Antiquities* I, 192) was to protect Jews from the threat of assimilation. Philo distanced himself considerably from the method of the rabbis when he said that circumcision has hygienic reasons (*On the Special Commandments*, 1, 4ff.): it protects one from a certain disease, and facilitates procreation.*

Motivations of the Hellenists and the Rabbis

The Hellenistic Jews of whom we are speaking loved the Torah (in utter contrast to the earlier Hellenizing Jews in the days of Antiochus Epiphanes**) no less than the rabbis and they also observed the great majority of the

* The fact that some gentiles practiced circumcision for medical reasons was also familiar to the rabbis (see BT *Avodah Zarah* 26b). (IH)

** The 2nd Book of Maccabees was written in Greek on the basis of the longer account of Jason of Kyreine — a Hellenistic Jew, as his name attests. Both, of course, condemned the extreme Hellenizers and their cohorts. (IH)

written mitzvot. But the factors that motivated them to explain the mitzvot are completely different from those of the rabbis. The factors that had only a very limited effect on the rabbis — the scientific, the apologetic, and above all the religious-theoretical — are precisely the ones that laid the greatest impress on the Hellenistic explanations. Faith in revealed Torah, even though they affirmed it, did not serve for most of them as a foundation for their religious lives. Therefore, they strove to find *sufficient* reasons for the fulfillment of mitzvot — reasons that would be sufficient for Jews and non-Jews alike for whom the faith in the Torah of God in its traditional understanding no longer existed or at the very least was quite shaky. Many of the reasons that we indicated, the authoritarian and the rational, can also be found in modern Jewish literature. Undoubtedly they carved out a new path that could be walked both by believers and by those of less-than-perfect faith.

Pros and Cons of the Hellenistic explanation

This difference has its basis in their evaluation of the sources from which our obligations emanate. The Hellenistic Jews, influenced by the outlook of their non-Jewish surroundings, had great reverence for the natural, as opposed to the rabbis, who especially emphasized that the word of God had gone out to the people of Israel. This difference was heightened by the fact that the educational culture of the Hellenistic Jews was very different from that of the rabbis. The Hellenistic Jews used the Greek language — not only the spoken but also the literary language — which was much better adapted for expressing analytical matters than the Hebrew and Aramaic that the rabbis used. We should acknowledge the odd fact that Greek rhetoric also helped them with their work: it made it possible for them to organize, to clarify, and to articulate models of abstract matters just as they were done, for example, in the story of Philo about the four good virtues.

And yet the profit of these cultural accomplishments came at a cost. Rhetoric was the cursed affliction of Greek culture. It attracted one's attention more to the elegant style of a book than to its content and encouraged a lack of intellectual scruple and even a lack of honesty in classical literature. This applies also to the Jewish-Hellenistic literature,[28] whereas the philosophers of the Middle Ages were men of science who intended only to bring out truth for its own sake. Greek displaced Hebrew. Philo read the Torah in Greek translation. For this reason he almost never talks about the ideal of holiness,[29] and does not cite even once the verse "and you shall love your neighbor as yourself" (not even in his book *On Philanthropy*), because the Greek language lacked the proper terms for the concepts of holiness and religious love.[30]

Did Greek Culture Impoverish their Jewish culture?

We should add: Greek culture also displaced Jewish culture to some extent. At times Philo cites the books of Prophets and Hagiographa, but he is no expert in their religious-traditional content. For example: in his proclaiming that God does not desire the sacrifices of evil-doers, he relies exclusively on Greek thinkers without even mentioning the words of the prophets![31] It is a shameful, even tragic, fact that grieves the soul that these Jews, who sought to enrich the culture of the world from their own national archives, did not know how rich they were. This tended, certainly, to diminish the value of their work for the following generations. Without a doubt, they strove to implement their program using insufficient means. However, what of the program itself? Their attempt to explain the commandments of the Torah on a human-ethical foundation and the social idea to which the Greeks gave a scientific formulation — did this experiment derive from the absence of knowledge in the Hebrew sources? And is it therefore worthless for the Jew who "reigns in his house and speaks the language of his people"? Not at all! On the contrary, we can say: If Philo had been more familiar with the ethical treasures of the Bible, this would only have reinforced and strengthened his faith in the common denominator of Greek idealism and his ancestors' wisdom, and would thus have confirmed the major premise for his explanation of the commandments. From a certain perspective one could say about him "he prophesied and did not know what he prophesied," as when he struggles to prove this common aspect by way of symbolic explanations and allegories and passes over in silence the verses that would prove the ethical strength of our religion.

The memory of the Hellenistic Jews was almost lost from the hearts of our nation for hundreds of years. Their explanation of the commandments was not suited to make a strong impression on people brought up on the Bible. But the correctness of their basic intentions would be substantiated in the Middle Ages. In that later time Jewry would be blessed with thinkers who filled their vessels both with the wisdom of Israel (the Talmudic literature included) and the treasuries of other nations, and they would try yet again to explain the Torah's commandments by relying on world knowledge.

Chapter 5
Views of the Medieval Philosophers

General Introduction

The two streams in Judaism that we have discussed, the Talmudic and the Hellenistic, were not able to influence one another significantly in advancing the solution to our question. Indeed, Philo knew the heteronomic explanation, which was also accepted among the more traditional Jews in Alexandria; on the other hand, it is likely that Hillel, in his explaining the mitzvot to the pagan as a "commentary" of general interpersonal ethical obligation, was alluding to and basing himself on the Hellenistic method, that all the particular commandments only seek to explain and elaborate on natural law. But just as the Hellenistic Jewish thinkers could not rest content with a theoretical stress on obedience, neither could Philo's outlook, which did not recognize the fundamental difference between divine Torah and human invention, satisfy the rabbis.

Three Medieval "Schools" and Their Interaction

This situation was different in the Middle Ages. In this era the river of Jewish thought had three principal branches: the Talmudic, the philosophical, and the mystical, but the common ground of the principal Jewish spokesmen was more extensive than in the older era. None of them were Hebraically illiterate. Even those books written in foreign languages (especially in Arabic) were translated into Hebrew. The philosophers and kabbalists also read the books of the halakhists, and the latter knew the compositions of the philosophers and kabbalists (e.g., the *Mishneh Torah* and the *Shulḥan Arukh*). Poems imbued with philosophy (e.g., *Shir HaYiḥud, Adon 'Olam*, and *Yigdal*) or kabbalah (e.g., the majority of Sabbath *zemirot*) also had an echo throughout the Jewish Diaspora. But philosophical books like the *Kuzari* and *Duties of the Heart* were used as well — and are used by many to this day — by those who in all their lives did not have direct experience of general philosophy.

However, even though they knew each other and there were even mediators among the three approaches, this does not mean that these *influenced* each other to a noticeable extent, specifically in the matter of explaining the commandments. Maimonides, for example, had a complete mastery of Talmudic and Geonic literature, and was convinced that some of the rabbis would have endorsed his philosophical method. But there were anti-philosophic views among the rabbis, too; either he appropriated them for his approach by giving them his own explanation or he belittled them as solitary views not "in accord with halakha." Thus, these views could not shake his faith in Aristotelianism. Most of the members of the "Talmudic" faction read the books of the philosophers and the kabbalists, not in order to absorb their outlook, but only to reinforce their faith and love of the commandments. Therefore they adopted the philosophers' conclusions, but their basic method — to find rational or mystical reasons by relying upon one's thoughts and feelings without relying on Torah and tradition — did not influence them. If, among the conclusions of the philosophers, they found opinions that appeared to contradict the tradition, they tried to "explain" them, and when they did not succeed, they opposed them explicitly (e.g., Maimonides' explanation of the sacrifices).

Disagreements among the Schools

We should therefore not be surprised to find among these three schools of thought important disagreements in their explanations of the commandments.

Members of the Talmudic school were even more inclined to heteronomy than the rabbis were.* They saw almost no reason to engage in explanation of the reasons for the commandments and to add to those reasons that were already found in the talmudic literature. For example, it is not Rashi's way to give reasons for the commandments. In his explanation of the forbidden foods (Leviticus 12:2), he briefly quotes the well-known midrash "since the Israelites cleave to God and it is proper that they be alive, therefore God separated them from impurity," and so forth. His grandson Rashbam indeed refers to commandments "that are recognized [by reason], for example stealing, sexual offenses, coveting, civil justice, and

---

* Characteristic of this view is what R. Obadiah of Bertinuro wrote in his Commentary to Mishnah *Avot* 1:1, after the philosophical and mystical books were already widespread: "Inasmuch as this tractate is not based on written commandments of the Torah as other Mishnaic tractates are, but consists entirely of ethical injunctions; and inasmuch as the gentile sages also wrote ethical treatises on proper interpersonal conduct, but did so out of their own private invention; therefore the Tannaitic author of this treatise begins, 'Moses received Torah from Sinai,' to inform us that the ethical injunctions in this treatise were not the private invention of the sages of the Mishnah, but these too were uttered at Sinai." See above, Chapter 1, on the view of the author of the *Tur*.

hospitality"[1] and on occasion proposes additional reasons. Rashbam gives a humanitarian explanation not only for the prohibition of sacrificing parent and child animals on the same day, and the commandment to send the mother bird away from the nest [before gathering the eggs], but also for the prohibition of milk and meat (Exodus 23:19).[2] He also mentions the hygienic benefit of the [laws concerning] forbidden foods (Leviticus 11:3), and finds a reason for the commandment of Sukkah (Exodus 23:16; Leviticus 23:43), for precisely in a time when our houses are filled with plenty, it is incumbent on us to recall our previous poverty, and to thank the One who satisfies our needs. However, one should give great weight to his words: "He who wants to give a reason for the commandments according to *derekh eretz* [i.e., universal standards of common propriety] and in order to reply to heretics" (Leviticus 11:34). He testifies about himself (Leviticus 19:19) that he succeeded in persuading "heretics" [i.e., Christians] with his reasons for forbidden mixtures. His inquiries, therefore, are motivated not so much by a scientific need, but rather by the necessity to reply to Christians or "to deflect them with a reed"! Indeed, it is no accident that it was specifically Rashbam who considered this need and struggled to find new reasons.* This enthusiast of the "plain sense" was much closer to the students of philosophy than to his colleagues in Christian lands. However, his explanation for the commandments is not methodical. And his exceptional case does not negate the general rule that halakhic scholars did not take an interest in finding reasons for the commandments.

The approach of the philosophers was altogether different. Even Baḥya, who was far removed from cold rationalism, sharply opposed those who said that "the received tradition takes the place of speculation."[3] It is our obligation to use reason, which is "a gift from God on high," in order to establish a world-view appropriate to Torah. This obligation was regarded by the Jewish philosophers as not only theoretical, but also religious. Nearly all of them (Halevi was nearly the sole exception) explained the verse "Know your father" (I Chronicles 28:9) thus: Know God through philosophy. Therefore Rabbi Saadia Gaon, in his introduction to "*The Book of Doctrines and Beliefs*," denounced those who slough off the task of science

---

* His disciple, R. Joseph Bekhor Shor, cites logical reasons for the dietary prohibitions and is of the opinion that it is "cruel" to boil a kid in its mother's milk (see Porges, *Joseph Bekhor Schor* 19). R. Mordecai Jaffe, author of the *Levush*, went further (as my relative Dr. A. Wiener showed me) when he said that the ancients gave him room for flexibility . . . they set their table with all kinds of delicacies; but it is like eating bland foods without salt . . . it is impossible to judge them without *ta'am* [a double entendre on "reason" and "taste"], just as it is impossible to eat without salt, and furthermore . . . by means of the reason it is possible to understand each and every law more clearly" (H. Tchernowitz, *Toledot Ha-Posekim* (1948) III:103).

as "wicked." Solomon ibn Gabirol calls the neglect of wisdom "rebellion," or in other words, a religious offense.[4] It is understood, consequently, that all of them strove to explain the commandments of the Torah not only from an apologetic need, which they felt much more than Rashbam, but rather primarily from scientific or "theoretical-religious" motivations. It is the way of science to investigate the reasons for things. Of all possible reasons, medieval thinkers (following Aristotle) preferred the "teleological" reason — for example, in order to understand a tool, we need to know for what goal and use it is made, and according to this general understanding we can then explain its individual parts. Similarly one may also ask regarding the commandments of the Torah: (1) What is the utility that fulfilling the commandments brings to the person performing them? (2) Why did the "Cause of Causes" see fit to issue commands to all the people of this world, and why specifically these commands? These thinkers made an effort to find, as much as possible, rational reasons for the commandments, both from the perspective of man and the perspective of the Creator.

The members of the third school, the mystics, also delved deeply into the reasons for the commandments, perhaps even more than the philosophers. Just as the stories of the Torah are like a garment, the "commands" (that is to say the moral content of the stories) are similar to the body, and the secret meaning, to the soul (Zohar III, 152a), so too is the matter concerning the mitzvot. They were not satisfied with explaining things according to their literal meaning (as Rashi did) and not by revealing their moral and scientific value (as the philosophers) but rather by ascribing mystical reasons to them. In particular, they demonstrated that the commandments were instituted in correspondence to the supernal world, and thus they are apt to influence it.

Chapter 6
Saadia Gaon

All philosophers, including Jewish philosophers, are in some sense "rationalists," that is to say: devotees of reason.[1] But they understand "reason" in different ways. Only by taking account of these differences is it possible to understand their explanations for the mitzvot.

The Different Tasks of Human Reason

In his discussion of the "Four Roots of Knowledge," Saadia ascribes two functions to reason: (1) Reason intuits axiomatic ideas that do not require proof, "such as that justice is good and lying is bad." (2) It is reason's task to deduce conclusions from its own axioms, from facts to which our healthy senses attest, and from reliable tradition. But this is not to say that it is adequate to establish a scientific theory of morality. Saadia discusses ethical matters in the appendix that he added to his *Book of Doctrines and Beliefs* (The Tenth Article), but his account is not systematic. He does not derive his opinions from one source, and he does not recognize at all the concept of "ethical science."[2]

In addition to these, our intellect has other important functions: (1) It is up to intellect to examine every tradition with regard to its veracity. It is up to it to decide if the content of the tradition is suitable to our experience and our logic. The judge before whom witnesses testified that Reuben owes Simeon the Tigris River need not even examine the trustworthiness of this testimony, as it contradicts experience.[3] Such is the matter regarding the religious tradition. If some would-be prophet says something that contradicts our knowledge, we are not required to examine the miracles he relies on for his legitimation. But if it is found that the content of his prophecies is in the realm of possibility and is confirmed by our experience and our intellect, and we see in addition that his purported miracles are creditable, then reason not only permits but even demands that we rely on them, and that we accept the knowledge offered through such prophecies as a complement to our knowledge from natural sources (the senses and reason). (2) Reason is determinative not only in matters of truth and justice, but also in matters of our physical and material well-being. Saadia does not cite this matter explicitly because it seems obvious to him.

This concept of "rational" differs considerably from that of the usual "rationalists."[4] Saadia neglects the scientific ethics that existed at the center of the rationalist outlook, but he values utility, experience, and tradition, and he does not see any fundamental difference among these different activities of the intellect. He knows and emphasizes that it is more difficult to know things that are "subtle" (such as the metaphysical) than things that are "crude" (such as the objects of sense perception). But he has no doubt that the same intellect that illuminates our everyday lives and lays the foundations for the secular sciences is an appropriate instrument to clarify and to illuminate matters of religion — as this intellect demands from us that we rely more on reliable tradition and on the Bible than on the natural ways of knowledge.[5] And both these ways, the natural and the traditional, are opened for us by the Creator.

Intellect can help explain the mitzvot

On the basis of these assumptions, we can now interpret Saadia Gaon's way of explaining the mitzvot. He definitely rejects the two extreme views: that of traditionalist Arabic thinkers who say that even were the prophets to have given us false commands, we ought to have obeyed them because we have no source for the understanding of our obligation other than the commandment of God,[6] and the view attributed to the philosophers of India[7] that there is no need to heed the mitzvot in the Torah forbidding us what was permitted to natural mankind, but only to heed the voice of our conscience. In his opinion, it is possible and also necessary to interpret the mitzvot of the Torah with the aid of our intellect and to complete the Torah of natural obligation by means of the Torah of traditional obligation. First of all he stipulates that the Holy and Blessed One gave the mitzvot "in order that we may attain complete, goodly, and perfect salvation,"[8] and in his view the prophet alludes to this when he says, "See, his reward is with him, his recompense before him" [Isaiah 40:10]. Of course, God could have presented us with "perpetual felicity" (in the World to Come) even without this precondition, but "reason teaches" that receiving good as a reward for toil is superior to receiving the same good without effort.

*The Rational and "Hortative" (**Shim'iyot**) Mitzvot*

Why did the Creator command us precisely these mitzvot? We must distinguish between "rational" [*sikhliyot* < *sekhel*] mitzvot and "hortative" [or "arbitrary" — *shim'iyot* < *shama'*, having the sense of "hear" and "obey"] mitzvot. The "rational" are those mitzvot that the intellect also requires us to observe, for which the Torah comes to clarify and explain the particulars. For example, reason requires us to express our thanks to the One who benefits us, whether in deed — in the instance in which He is in need of it — or whether in thanks — in the instance in which He does not need the recompense. For this reason, it was necessary for the Creator to command us concerning His service and how to thank Him. This is the case in the matter of prohibition against cursing God and impugning His honor, particularly through idolatry. Reason teaches that it is forbidden for human beings to harm each other, and thus it is fitting for the Creator to restrain them from doing so; therefore it was incumbent on Him to command them regarding truth and justice and to forbid murder, adultery, stealing, and so forth. We need to hear not only all of these general rules but also their particulars from the mouths of the prophets. Reason teaches, for example, the abhorrence of adultery and stealing, but not the proper ways of marriage and property acquisition (L118).*

Saadia called the second category of mitzvot *shim'iyot* ("hortative"**) because we received them through the sense of hearing (see his commentary on *Sefer Yetzirah* 1:1), but according to the opinion of the Arabic thinkers who preceded him[9] this term also signifies the "discipline" (*mishma'at*) that obligates us in regard to these mitzvot. This category includes mitzvot such as sanctifying the Sabbath, sanctifying the priests, the prohibitions of work,

* L = Landauer edition (standard Arabic edition of Saadia's *Book of Beliefs and Opinions*). The Rosenblatt (Yale) English edition refers to the corresponding Landauer pagination by angled brackets in the middle of the text; thus the reader will find the notation <118> in the middle of page 144 of the Rosenblatt edition, indicating the passage to which Heinemann is referring here. (LL)

** With trepidation (and over the objections of my students) I resort here to coining "hortative mitzvot" as an English equivalent to Saadia's term *mitzvot shim'iyot*. The Hebrew *shim'i* has the dual connotation of "what is heard" and "what should be obeyed." It is always used as a mutual complement to *mitzvot sikhliyot* ("rational commandments") but to call them "non-rational" would be subtly inaccurate, for though the *mitzvot sikhliyot* are known through reason and the *mitzvot shim'iyot* are known only through having heard them from the divine command, it does not follow that the latter are non-rational, only that they are not known to humans through reason, but they may very well be rational in their own right as well. Previous translations of *mitzvot shim'iyot* as "religious commandments" or "traditional commandments" do not get at the proper sense of the word, and lead to confusion in certain contexts, as the rational commandments also include some commandments of religious significance (such as avoiding blasphemy and worshipping the true God), whereas all the mitzvot — *sikhliyot* and *shim'iyot* alike — are included within the body of tradition.

"Hortative" suggests "hearing" (e.g., in relation to the German *hören*). I know this is a false etymology, as "hortatory" really comes from the same root as "exhort," but I will let it stand. (Anyway, "exhort" is significative of the same sense as *l'hashmi'a*, the causative verb related to *shim'iyot*.) With this explanation and apology, I beg the reader to just accept "hortative" as my coinage to fill the gap in English for a good translation of *shim'iyot*, and to let the meaning and significance of this term accrue from the various contexts in which it is used. (LL)

the prohibitions against marrying relatives, and the laws of impurity. And it is easy to justify their obedience from the human perspective, for through them one achieves the life of the World to Come.

Many Hortative Commandments Have Plausible Reasons

However, it is difficult to explain for what reason the Creator commands them, "for He does not create anything that does not have a meaning (that is to say, a purpose)." And yet when we look into the matter, we find some benefit for some of them: the festivals enable us to rest from our exertions, to meet with our friends and to discuss with them matters of wisdom and religion; the priests' holiness facilitates their task of guiding the community. Distinguishing between permitted and forbidden animals discourages us from the cult of animals, because we do not worship either what we eat or what we regard as impure. As for the laws of incest, had the women who live with us (for example mother, sister, daughter) been permitted to us in marriage, this could have led to problems, for in that case, the beautiful women would have married their relatives, and the rest would have had trouble finding mates, once their relatives rejected them. Forbidding unclean objects from coming into contact with the Temple increases people's reverence for the Temple and the religious cult. In Saadia's view, it is possible to find explanations such as these for the majority of the "hortative" commandments, even though it is impossible for us to plumb the depths of God's wisdom that surpasses our wisdom "as the sky surpasses the land." The critics of Scripture who said that some of the commandments run counter to wisdom are totally in error (L141). The sacrifices, for example, were only instituted because "the soul of all living beings is in their blood"; therefore sacrificing animals reminds us that our blood will also be spilled if we continue to sin. God commanded us concerning the building of the Temple and all of the sacred service in it, not because He, God forbid, is in need of this, but rather as a means for us to express our gratitude to Him. One should not be astonished that the ashes of the red heifer purify the impure and defile the pure; there is an analogy in the case of healing drugs that cure the sick but harm the healthy.

The method of Saadia that we have briefly summarized here has its virtues and drawbacks.

The Virtues of Saadia's Method

One may see Saadia as pioneering a new way. He is in fact similar to Philo (of whom he had no knowledge), for in his view, too, the special commandments provide a commentary on general natural law, but he diverges from the Hellenists in that he defends the Torah as God's commandments, and bases obedience on the relationship of the "servant"[10] to the master. Therefore he acknowledges explicitly that we mortals do not know the reasons for all of the commandments. He follows the rabbis in distinguishing between the commandments that "had they not been written, logic would dictate that they ought to be written" and those that are only known from the Torah's commanding them. But he did not rely on their statement and did not even quote them explicitly. This is not accidental. The distinction in wording indicates a difference of view: the rabbis do not call the first kind of commandment "rational" or say that our intellect dictates them, whereas Saadia reiterates this idea, in his desire to point out that there is also an autonomous source to our obligations.[11] Saadia tried and succeeded in maintaining an equilibrium between the heteronomous and autonomous reasons.

The Drawbacks of Saadia's Method

Saadia explains the value of our obedience from the human perspective and from the divine perspective.[12] He acknowledges the heteronomic character of the fulfillment of the commandments, at the very least regarding the "hortative" commandments, but he adds that this obedience is in our interest (specifically in terms of the reward in the World to Come) and therefore can even be regarded as "rational." One should not conclude from this that Saadia was, God forbid, one who "served his master in order to receive a reward." Love of God was rooted in the depths of his heart.[13] But it is something else if a Jew's warm emotions overwhelm his philosophical methodology! His emphasis on the utility of fulfilling the commandments brings Saadia's rationale for the mitzvot very close to the rationale of our everyday decisions. This tends to blur the all-important distinction between the actions we perform for our own enjoyment and the religious actions that we do "for their own sake" — a distinction that was already made in the explanation according to the rabbis.[14]

Saadia favors utilitarian reasons

This blurring is especially felt in his attempt to explain the commandments from the perspective of the Creator. The Torah gives the commandments ethical reasons, religious reasons (like "you shall be holy"), and historical reasons, but not utilitarian reasons. The utilitarian reasons are precisely what stand out in Saadia's explanation and are much more numerous with him than those advanced by the rabbis, the Hellenists, and Rashbam. These sober reasons give Saadia's methodology its unique characteristic.

According to Saadia, the religious commandments (such as the sanctity of certain days and certain human individuals) do not stand out as a special category with a distinctive "religious" reason. Rather, most of them are justified as "useful" to us. Social reasons, which Philo emphasizes, are not found at all in Saadia's work. He also does not assign the dietary prohibitions any educational purpose nor does he employ historical reasons. For Saadia, the narratives of the Bible are merely an anthology of examples of the doctrine of reward and punishment. How remote from him are the allegorical explanations* found in so much of Midrash and Hellenistic literature!

Saadia's explanation is indeed apt to counter the stumbling blocks that were the bane of the Arab skeptics and their Jewish students, but it also flattens the value hierarchy that is integral to the classic Jewish rationale: cool considerations and level-headedness rule our decision making and also, as it were, the decrees of the Creator-Legislator. Saadia's methodology leaves almost no shred of the wonder and mystery that are the life-blood of religious practice.

However, reservations like these do not apply to Saadia's basic methodological conception, but only to how he carried it out. His historical achievement is secure. He pioneered a way of understanding the commandments that would hold great possibility, and what he was lacking, his students came and completed.

---

* Ibn Ezra, in his "short" commentary to Exodus (Prague edition, p. 80), writes that in Saadia's view there are three cosmoi: the macrocosm (the universe), the "middle" cosmos (the Temple), and the human being, who is the microcosm. In order to illustrate this view, Saadia cited analogies (such as the analogy of the bird in heaven, the fowl-sacrifice in the Temple, and the wing-shaped configuration of the pair of lungs in the human body) that bear similarity to the analogies in the Midrash (such as Exodus Rabbah 33:4) and even more so to those in *Sefer Yetzirah,* but this is not the same as the Hellenistic view that the Temple was a symbol of the cosmos.

Chapter 7
Baḥya ben Joseph Ibn Pakudah

The purpose of ***Duties of the Heart***

The first thinker to follow up on Saadia's work was Rabbi Baḥya ibn Pakudah. The objective of his work *Duties of the Heart*[1] is altogether different from that of Saadia's *Book of Doctrines and Beliefs*, but only through the framework of the earlier work is it possible to understand Baḥya's remarks about the reasons for the commandments. Baḥya comes not to reconcile science and Judaism, but rather to help the Jewish reader arrive at his life's task. "The Creator created the soul and wants to raise and elevate it to the level of His special treasure, His pure chosen ones, close to the light of His glory."[2] But the soul's being situated in this world poses great dangers for it: it must decide between what in Arabic is called *din* and *dunya* (i.e., between the requirements of religion and the demands of the lower world*). Because not all of the demands of this world are unjustified, it is not easy for the soul to choose the right path. Therefore God gave the soul a trusted advisor, namely the intellect. However, the intellect does not speak to everyone in a way that addresses the heart. Therefore, R. Baḥya took it upon himself to serve as a spokesman of this wisdom, to warn the souls about its duties, and to point out the value of the duties of the heart in order to live a pure life in this world and thus merit eternal rest in the World to Come.

But if all our salvation depends on the activity of our intellect, then why did God send prophets to the people of Israel to tell them the duties of the heart that the intellect itself requires of us? Why did God give them "commandments of the limbs," some of which apparently bear no relation to the duties of the heart? This is an important and pressing question, especially as Baḥya knew the stance of those Moslem philosophers who

---

* It is a great pity that the medieval Hebrew translator Ibn Tibbon did not translate this pair of words — which in a certain sense is the focus of Baḥya's thought — correctly. He translated the first as "Torah" and the second as "*olam* (world)." Not only did he eliminate the assonance that heightens their opposition, but *dunya* has a sharper connotation than "world," whereas *din* has the broader connotation of all religion (not only Judaism). When Baḥya wants to refer to the Torah he uses the term *shar'iya* or adds the possessive pronoun. (IH)

rejected all historical religions in the name of "true religiosity,"[3] just as some modern "enlightened" thinkers have done. In any case, Baḥya did not prove the value of the mitzvot directly. Rather, he approached it in a roundabout way, in keeping with the purpose of his book, by explaining the connection between the fulfillment of commandments and the *religiosity of the heart* to which it leads. This connection is in two parts. The Torah already assumes that the obedience of the forefathers is a sign of their piety. We also see that according to the Torah the commandments were designed to elevate the Israelites to the level of "a holy people." This dual connection was not unknown to the thinkers who preceded R. Baḥya, but only he succeeded in articulating it adequately, which was testimony to his ability to investigate the depths of the heart and analyze human motivation. From his psychological proofs we can learn much about the ethical-religious question of the value of the commandments.

The Heart — Source for Performing the Mitzvot

Baḥya has no doubt that the proper performance of mitzvot stems from purity of the heart and is evidence of that purity. The patriarch Abraham proved his love for the Creator precisely by performing the mitzvah of circumcision and being ready to offer Isaac as a sacrifice.

The Levels of Mitzvah Performers

On the other hand, it is the way of the evil impulse to incite us to cast doubts on the Prophets, on the tradition of the Sages, and even on the value of our worship by saying that God does not need the worship of God's creatures. (DH 5:5) Unlike Saadia, Baḥya knows of no serious arguments against our obligations to perform the mitzvot aside from the rationalizations of our evil impulse. Obviously, we are obligated to keep them with all due care; however, this is not enough. We cannot perform the obligations of our limbs in full unless our hearts are willing (DH, Introduction). There are ten levels of mitzvah performers (DH 3:4). The lowest level is that of those who "loathe the Torah." They deny the miracles of the Torah and its value, and so they cast off the yoke of the mitzvot, but they "are not drawn by the reins of reason" either. The reason for their heresy and insubordination is that "passion overwhelms their intellect." Members of the second and third levels hold that the Torah exists only to improve worldly matters — that is to say, they do not attribute any religious value to the Torah.[4] Members of the fourth and fifth levels, even though they believe in the World to Come, "their heart is in this world." We should not view these people as religious. Members of the sixth level "do not understand the reward in the World to

Come or its delights."* Members of the seventh and eighth levels are "like servants who serve the Master in order to receive a reward," meaning that they hope for the reward from the Creator or fear God's punishments. But members of the ninth and tenth levels, even though they believe in reward and punishment, "are intent on serving God alone." The former, indeed, do not take proper care to avoid pride, but among the latter are counted "the prophets and the saints who are devoted to God and who made a covenant with God . . . and who gave God their souls, their children, and their possessions." These words, of course, allude particularly to the patriarch Abraham. Clearly Rabbenu Baḥya ascribes great value to the performance of mitzvot in this way. However, we cannot arrive at a level without also paying attention to the duties of the heart not detailed in the Torah. Just as the Torah study of "those who ignore the duties of the heart" is defective,[5] so too is their performance of mitzvot, for "even though it leads to a path of salvation in the World of Rest,"** it is valueless for seven reasons, especially because they perform only out of fear and hope (that is to say, they do not surpass the members of the seventh and eighth levels of mitzvah performers, and it is difficult for them to stay away from hypocrisy and the obstacles posed by desire).[6]

The Propadeutic Value of the Written Torah

And yet, just as "tradition is no substitute for speculation,"[7] so too it is not the proper place of speculation to usurp the place of the tradition. In order to prove the need for both approaches, Baḥya (DH 3:3 — see examples) cites seven reasons for the value of the written Torah.

He has already emphasized that "the awakening of Torah leads to the other [i.e., the awakening of the intellect] and is a step by which we ascend to it"; thus it has a propadeutic value. The Torah's authority is based on signs and demonstrations that "address all persons equally through their senses" (beginning of reason 7); therefore it is apt to attract the heart of the whole nation (reason 3), at least until they arrive to the highest level through the awakening of the intellect (reason 5). Particularly at the time of the giving of the Torah, "the Israelites were overcome by their bestial desires" and thus "they were too weak-minded and muddle-headed to

* All this goes to show how much Baḥya values the relation between religiosity and the prospect of immortality.

** See the start of the Third Gate. There he distinguishes between "the awakening of the Torah" (the first awakening for those wholly asleep) and "the awakening of reason," but in his explanation of the 3rd and 7th reasons for the minimal value of this first reason, he says explicitly, "the fact that it is only from the Torah." Compare Vajda, REJ (1937) 101 on this "awakening." (IH)

apprehend many of the rational precepts." Because of this, God also gave them hortative commandments in the Torah "whose validity reason cannot explain. The strong-minded and clear-headed individual will accept (the rational commands) as binding in both respects (the authoritative and the rational), whereas one whose intellect is too weak to perceive their rational ground will accept them on the basis of the Torah alone, and will treat them as hortative precepts" (reason 6).*

The Value of the Torah for the Educated Also

But besides the propadeutic value, there is a great value in fulfilling the commandments for those whose faculties allow them to listen to the voice of reason and science. Saadia Gaon has already remarked that reason is insufficient to define our religious obligations (reason 2). When the Torah established these commandments, it took into consideration that we are composed of soul and body, and further that speculation brought a number of people "to have contempt for the world and withdraw from civil society." This view is very important. Perhaps Baḥya believed that if he, too, were to rely only on "reason," that is to say on what the Arab philosophers deduced from intellectual considerations, he would stray from the right path and forget that God "put in our hearts (also) the world," that is to say this terrestrial world (9:1). With regard to his position on "the boundary of abstinence and the need of the men of the Torah for it [9:2]" Baḥya mentioned the definitions that the "(Arab!) sages" established,[8] some of which were very extravagant, and of one ("deprivation from all physical rest and enjoyment, and subsistence on those bare necessities without which one cannot survive") he says that it "is more (appropriate) to resort to the abstinence that is described in our Torah, rather than the other definitions which we have mentioned." This example is enough to demonstrate to what extent even the philosopher who relies on his own opinion is in need of "the awakening of the Torah!"

The Commandments of the Limbs Attest to the Commandments of the Heart

Thus are explained the value of several "rational commandments" of the Torah, and we are also led to consider some of the "hortative" commandments from a completely new perspective. Obviously, "services

---

* On the relation of the hortative mitzvot and Israel's weak-mindedness at the time of giving the Torah, about which Baḥya speaks only allusively, we will deal later when we speak of thinkers who raised the issue explicitly. (IH)

of God [i.e., religious rituals] — human beings are obligated to perform them, in accordance with the benefits they enjoy" (reason 4); and as The Holy and Blessed One "chose us by bringing us out of the land of Egypt and parting the Sea of Reeds, and through acts of grace that came after this" we are obligated to render additional service, "and there is no way to know this from reason alone." Baḥya repeats this argument at the end of the chapter.[9] There he adds that the Aaronid priests were given twenty-four special commandments corresponding to the twenty-four good benefits that the Creator had conferred on them: these are the twenty-four priestly gifts [owed by the lay Israelites to the priests]. Baḥya was satisfied with this general kind of explanation of the commandments. As for the reasons for specific commandments, he addressed them only tangentially. In his view, in agreement with the principles that we have expressed, their objective is to remind us of God's existence and to guide us to His service. The commandments of tefillin, mezuzah, and others (DH Intro:1, 7:5) remind us to remember the Creator and to love Him; the commandment of the Sabbath testifies to the creation of the world (5:5). "The Torah cautions us against many foods, kinds of clothing, sexual relations, possessions and deeds" in order to prevent the overflowing of passion that causes the intellect to weaken (3:2).* And the mitzvot affect us not only through removing stumbling blocks. The purpose of most, if not all of the commandments of the body, is to awaken us to the commandments of the heart and the conscience, as they are the pillars of ritual and the roots of the Torah, as it is written: "You shall fear God your God . . ." and it says, "For this thing is very close to you, in your mouth and in your heart, to observe it," and "What does the Lord your God ask of you . . ." Because this demand exceeds normal human ability and cannot be fulfilled without withdrawing from animal passions, God gave us the mitzvot of the body and the limbs. "And when one who believes in his heart and his conscience strives to do them, God opens for him the gate of spiritual virtues** so that he can reach that which is beyond his normal ability, and he can serve the blessed Creator with his body and his soul, in the visible and invisible modes . . . and a parable has already been told of the man who planted a tree and trimmed its roots, and fertilized them, and afterwards he looked forward to the fruits from the hand of God; but if he had ignored their tending and looked expectantly toward them, it would not be fitting that God give him their fruit" (3:8.21). In this way he elucidates the saying of the rabbis, "Torah leads to deeds and deeds lead

* That is also the reason Aaron was commanded to raise the ashes, so that he should not be haughty in his heart (6:6, end).

** The Hebrew *ma'alot* has the double sense of "ascensions" and "virtues." (LL)

to scrupulousness . . . purity leads to saintliness." According to this idea, to which Baḥya alludes in other places,[10] observance of the commandments does not serve as a necessary and sufficient cause for piety of the heart, just as agricultural work does not ensure the fertility of the tree,* but each of them invites God's help — and we should mention that Baḥya did not believe in absolute free choice as Saadia did, but rather he too believed that in a certain sense the fear of Heaven comes from God.

Religiosity of the Heart and Fulfillment of the Commandments

From all that has been said it emerges that there is no contradiction between the religiosity of the heart and the correct fulfillment of the mitzvot, but rather complete compatibility. Our obedience to the Creator's mitzvot follows from our religiosity and brings about our religious-ethical education, in addition to which it complements the rational commandments and also fills in for reason for the weak-minded. Even though Baḥya particularly emphasizes the value of general human ethics, he does not differ from his predecessors on whom he relies, namely the Talmudic rabbis and Saadia, in his appreciation of the commandments that God gave just to the people of Israel. But he differs from them noticeably in the mode of his explanation. Through these differences it is possible to grasp the unique character of his thought more clearly.

Baḥya is apparently very different from the rabbis, both in the methodical form of his proofs as well as in their substance. Surely the rabbis did not disparage those for whom "the tradition stands in place of inquiry"![11] They did not require examination and inquiry into religious theory.[12] They did not prefer "the awakening of reason" to "the awakening of Torah." They repeatedly emphasized the heteronomous character of religious discipline,[13] whereas according to Baḥya we ought to choose the practice of the mitzvot voluntarily. It is incumbent upon us to mold our souls, so that we shall abhor what the Torah forbids us, just as it is in our nature to abhor eating mice (9:5); one who acts correctly because of his reason is superior to one who does it only because he is commanded (3:3).

How does Baḥya's outlook differ from Saadia's?

And yet he is surely not less remote from Saadia, not only in detail, but in the thrust of his vision. According to Saadia, every advance in wisdom and science is to the good. Baḥya greatly limits the authority of the intellect and its ability to judge on religious matters. He knows that to the extent

* We shall see that Judah Halevi also makes use of this metaphor. (IH)

that we imagine we know God through common sense, we in fact recede from Him,[14] for "man is not able to see Him and live." The "reason" that excites Baḥya's admiration is not the same as Saadia's, which also arranges economic affairs — thus Baḥya excludes all utilitarian considerations from his explanation of the Torah's mitzvot.* Nor is it the scientific reason of the Aristotelians, but rather first and foremost the "practical reason" in Kant's sense, or more precisely the voice of conscience, in which love of morality and devotion to God are rooted. The means that this reason employs are indeed logical and to some extent scientific, but its intention in addressing us is only religious-ethical. The factor that especially motivated Baḥya to explain the commandments is precisely the "religious-practical": he seeks to educate his reader in order that he will fulfill the commandments in full devotion and correct intention. This is the same factor that we find in the explanation of the rabbis.[15] It is necessary background for understanding the fact that Baḥya, the advocate of reason, found fertile ground for his book precisely among the devotees of the "kabbalah" (that is to say the "tradition") and that they accepted his book to some extent as "tradition." Thus the book *Duties of the Heart* has not only a scientific value, but first of all an educational value; R. Baḥya is counted among the great educators among the Jewish people. He saved its religious life from petrifaction and protected the "divine fire" from being extinguished by mechanical actions.

Yet there is a recognizable difference between the educational program of the rabbis and that of Baḥya. The rabbis did not minimize the value of the "duties of the heart,"[16] but they did not limit their care to the soul's happiness, for they were not individualists. Aristotle's rule that "the whole takes precedence over its parts" fits their outlook on the value of religious life. The social commandments bind us to each other and they also strive "to repair the world." The festivals and fasts serve as a remembrance of God's beneficences and afflictions, but at the same time they shape the historical awareness of this "perennial nation." Of Baḥya, by contrast, one may say that his aspirations are centered on the World to Come. The difference between this world and the World to Come, and also the connection of religion to our true, eternal happiness, jumps out from the original Arabic text more than from its Hebrew translation.** Therefore, everything depends on the soul's purity. With its help we shall acquire our world, together with the pure, elect individuals from all the nations of the world. Thus there are absent from Baḥya's work all the social explanations that both the rabbis and the Hellenists taught. His explanation, therefore,

---

* However, our virtues yield benefit for us in the World to Come (DH 4 Introduction, end; 6:10). (IH)

** See the footnote to page 57 on the Hebrew rendering of *din* and *dunya*. (IH)

is one-sided. But we cannot blame the author for this. He did not write his work in order to exhaust all the depths of the question; he wanted to make a contribution toward a solution to the extent that his work demands it. And we should acknowledge that his gift was considerable because the "one side" to which he gave his eyes is an important side, perhaps the most important side in the reasons for the commandments. R. Baḥya was qualified to consider this side not only because of the purity of his heart and his comprehensive expertise in the ethical literature of the nations of the world, but principally because of his knowledge of life and of humankind. He was a psychologist no less than a moralist, and he was well equipped to shed clear light on the reasons — both imaginary and real — that people employ in their life-decisions. Thanks to these virtues, Baḥya succeeded in elucidating the influence of Torah on our inner lives. Even though its primary thrust was educational and practical, his book also has considerable theoretical and scientific value. The reader can derive not only enjoyment but also great benefit from its many details, precisely with respect to explaining the commandments.

Chapter 8
Rabbi Judah Halevi

Purpose of the Kuzari

Rabbi Judah Halevi's well-known book, the *Kuzari*, bears the original title *A Book of Proof and Argument in Defense of a Despised Religion*.* The book lives up to its name. It comes not to verify human ideals and to prove that we Jews share them, but to clarify the special, unique quality of our history and religion. Therefore, it justifies the mitzvot not by their human value, but first and foremost — if one may say so — by their Jewish value, that is to say, as a means to the fulfillment of the special Jewish task.

Halevi's outlook concerning the Jewish people's role is based on the standard understanding of nature in his time (1:31 etc.). All beings were divided into four ranks: inanimate, vegetable, animal, and human. Each rank has a special quality in addition to the characteristics of the ranks below it. However, members of the top three groups will not achieve perfection unless they have proper seed (race), environment, and care. The Ethiopian,** for example, was regarded as "only sufficiently fit to receive human shape and speech in the most deficient form" (1:1), because of the defects in the climate as well as lack of education.

The Mitzvot Seek to Train Us for Coming Closer to God

Halevi adds a fifth rank to the four existing ones, which he calls (4:3) "people of God."[1] Its members show their superior worth over other creatures through their closeness to the Divine, which is manifested in two ways: (1) through miracles that are performed by or for them, or (2) they know the Creator not only by the philosophers' way, as the generic

* I cite the Hirschfeld edition of the book, which includes the Judeo-Arabic original and the Ibn Tibbon Hebrew translation. See also my article in the collection *Rabbi Judah Halevi*, Jerusalem 1941, Mossad Ha-Rav Kook. Halevi deals with our central question especially in Book III of the *Kuzari*. (IH) Note: The English version in this chapter, where possible, is taken from Heinemann's abridged translation in *Three Jewish Philosophers*. (LL)

** The racially pejorative outlook Halevi expressed here was unfortunately all too common in medieval and early modern times. (LL)

"God" — that is to say, the Prime Mover — but also through the personal name YHWH, the Father who watches over His creatures and who desires their worship (4:15). The perfection of this rank also depends on the three conditions mentioned above: the proper race, environment, and care. "People of God" in the fullest sense are found only among the *seed* of Israel (the patriarchs, and before them, Adam and Noah), when living on the *land* of Israel and practicing the *cult* of Israel. This is not the place to discuss the first two conditions, but in this context we should emphasize that the role of the mitzvot is to guide us — not to human completeness, but to a higher form of completeness, that is: closeness to God, which is the special mark of the "chosen people."*

Mitzvot Necessary to Arrive at the Top Rank

Is it possible for intellect, which members of the fourth rank also achieve, to understand the special conditions of life in the fifth level? Halevi answers this question in the negative, and supports his answer especially** with two reasons: (1) intellect does not understand the conditions of life, even on the lowest levels; for example, based on its simplistic assumptions, it cannot prove why a hatching egg requires a certain temperature or why reproduction is impossible without the copulation of a male and female (3:13). Intellect must learn these facts by experience! (2) Science can penetrate the secrets of religious life even less. Socrates himself admitted (5:13, 14): "I do not deny your wisdom of God. But I am wise only in humanity." Therefore, one should not be amazed by the philosophers, and we must not blame them for saying of our mitzvot that they are not fit to attain the knowledge of God, which (they claim) only philosophers can achieve.

To reach God, perform the divine commands!

From here, we come to the cardinal principle in Halevi's approach: "One can only arrive at divine order through divine ordinance, that is to say, through actions ordained by God" (1:98).*** In Halevi's view, it is impossible:

---

* This term (Hebrew *segullah*, commonly translated in English as "treasure" or "chosen people") is but a translation of the Arabic *safwa*, which indicates an elite. Ahad Ha-Am rendered it more precisely as *tamtzit* (essence, e.g., the essence of perfume squeezed out of a plant — see *Al Parashat Derakhim* II, 67). [In Heinemann's translation of *Kuzari* in *Three Jewish Philosophers* he renders it as "the pick." — LL] See also my article, "R. Judah Halevi's Historical Outlook," *Tziyon* 9:155.

** In addition to his general strictures against the pretensions of reason.

*** The play on words ("order, ordinance"), taken from Heinemann's abridged English translation of *Kuzari* in *Three Jewish Philosophers*, imitates a play in the reconstructed Arabic

(1) to *create* the necessary conditions to approach godliness, without relying on any religion, as the philosophers and hermits did (2:49, 3:1); (2) to *imitate* the conditions that God passed down to us, according to the ways of the other religions (namely Christianity and Islam), which accepted circumcision or a weekly day of rest, because their enactments only superficially resemble ours "as much as statues resemble live human beings"; (3) to *explain* the details of the commandments according to our intellect without relying on the correct tradition, as the Karaites do (3:22); (4) to institute *enactments* "with the appearance of coming from the Torah," unless such enactments are done under divine inspiration. This condition is fulfilled by the rabbis (3:39,41); therefore the Karaites err and sin in opposing these enactments.

Halevi's Approach is Not Magical

To the extent that Halevi distances himself from the rational position, he draws closer apparently to a magical position, which found its supporters from within the Neo-Platonic school and had noticeable impact on many philosophical-religious systems (as in the Hermetic tradition).[2] But Halevi differs from the magical approach inasmuch as he does not recognize the intrinsic efficacious power of religious actions unless they are performed with the proper intention. "There are two essential axioms of the Torah: the first is that the Torah should be viewed as coming from God and the second that the Torah should be accepted with a sincere heart by the congregation" (3:23). But once these conditions are met, "there necessarily (!)[3] follows the outcome which is the descent of the Divine Presence (Shekhinah)." An additional difference between Halevi and the magical approach is that the main purpose of the latter is to give us the power to control our fate and the external course of our lives, whereas in Halevi's view the fulfillment of the mitzvot, prayer, and the Temple service influence first of all our inner experience and our religious abilities. Even the destruction of the Temple caused only the strength of Israel to be weakened, due to suspension of the commandments that depend on the Temple (2:32), and not the strength of the entire world, as would be the case according to the magical approach.*

---

version (*al-'amr al-ilahi / amr ilahi*). The word "*davar*" in Hebrew has the same double sense (essence/matter, word) as *'amr*. On the central Halevi term *'amr ilahi* (in Hebrew: *'inyan elohi* — in English, "divine word/power/essence"), see Heinemann's article in *Tziyon* 9:168. (IH/LL)

* According to the view of Rav Ḥisda, which influenced some of the kabbalists. (See Becher, *Aggadot ha-Bavliyim* 70; Max Grunwald, *Gesammelte Aufsätze,* 17.)

Our Reason Cannot Understand All the Mitzvot

We should note that Halevi (in common with the philosophical enthusiasts of magic) does not deny the value of the rational, even though he restricts its authority. We saw that it is possible to know "God" (though not YHWH) through scientific proofs. Reason, in the broad sense of the concept (as, for instance, Baḥya conceived it), also plays ethical and religious roles: it governs our senses and our volition (3:11, 2:26). The rabbis were right to place the prayer "for reason and knowledge" before the rest of the petitions of the Amidah because "through them, a person will approach closer to God," and they also placed it next to the blessing of "who desires repentance," in order that "this wisdom, knowledge and understanding will be in the way of Torah" (3:19). But up to what point can reason explain the commandments? Halevi also acknowledges that there are rational or generally known commandments (3:7, 2:48), some of which are "spiritual,"* such as the commandment of faith in God, and others "behavioral," such as the ethical mitzvot (3:11). These are open to rational understanding "with some addition" (from the revealed side), because in fact reason is unable to demonstrate particular providence (*ibid.*) and cannot determine the quantitative measure of the ethical obligations (3:7). Moreover, one cannot explain by pure reason why a woman becomes forbidden to ordinary men by means of betrothal and available to them by means of a writ of divorce (3:57). But all the rational commandments are nothing but "premises and preambles" to the "divine" commandments such as the Sabbath, circumcision, and the like (2:48). And happy is he who accepts the God-given Torah "with all his heart, without scrutiny or scruple; he is superior to the man who scrutinizes and investigates. He, however, who descends from this highest grade to scrutinizing, does well to seek a wise reason for these commandments, instead of casting misconstructions and doubts upon them, leading to corruption" (2:26, end). Few are endowed with a sturdy soul that is not enticed by the stray opinions it encounters (5:2). Halevi tries to find an explanation for the divine commandments as well. It may be possible — not on the basis of the simplistic assumptions of the intellect, but rather to some extent on the basis of historical, physiological, and psychological *experience*.

* These are called "philosophical" in the Hebrew translation but not in the Arabic original.

History Testifies to their Value

Historical experience testifies to the value of the commandments only indirectly, but this testimony is very important. The Christians and the Muslims also acknowledged that the Divine Presence rested on the nation of Israel and its elect during the time that the Temple stood. This fact becomes clear according to the scientific premise that the "godly" life requires proper "care." Once the building of the Tent of Meeting was completed, the descent of the Divine Presence necessarily followed (3:23). And once the Temple worship was suspended, our religious — and even our essential — strength became weary, and we were practically regarded as dead (2:32). The consequences of the service of the Tabernacle are connected to its organization and particulars, and it is not in reason's power to invent them (3:53); "were it so, the philosophers would have been able, through their great wisdom and intellect, to duplicate that which the Children of Israel arrived at" (1:99).

Life of Body and Life of Soul Parallel

Natural science sheds more light on the problem. For indeed nature is uniform and one God rules over all the ranks of its creatures. Therefore the conditions of life on the highest level are substantially similar to those of the bottommost and not just in a negative sense (that is to say, that one cannot prove them on the basis of simplistic assumptions), but also in their positive qualities. The philosophic view, that the perfection of humankind (that is to say, of those on the fourth level) depends on "the quality of air, land, food, and water"* (1:1), is close to the Jewish perspective, which says that the Land of Israel (2:10) and the dietary prohibitions (3:49) facilitate the achievement of the level of the "people of God." Halevi describes this parallel of ordinary human life to godly life more precisely in other places; prayer is sustenance for the soul, just as foods are the sustenance of the body; "the beneficial effect of one prayer continues until the set time of another prayer, just as the energy one derives from the daytime meal lasts until one feasts again in the night time" (3:5). Also on the Sabbath, "the body will crave (or make up) that which it was lacking during the six days of the week, and it will prepare itself for the future; and similarly the soul will remember what it was lacking because of the troubles of the body,

* Halevi alludes here to the titles of two books that were ascribed to the Greek physician Hippocrates: *On Air, Water, and Places*, and *On Foods* (as factors contributing to our health). The Khazar king emphasizes that there are acceptable ideas in the speeches of the Philosopher, the Christian, and the Moslem.

and it is as if on that day it was healing itself from the sicknesses of before and preparing itself to ward off the sickness of the future" (*ibid.*). And just as our bodies are fitting for the mind to reside in them only according to a certain God-given natural order, so the Holy and Blessed One established the Temple in a manner similar to our bodies: "the fire rested on the fatty parts of the sacrifices — like a natural heat that rests in the minute fat-globules of the blood"; the purpose of the sacrificial altar, "that the revealed fire will cling to it, and the golden altar was sanctified to a lighter and thinner fire; but to the lampstand was attached the light of wisdom and knowledge . . . the ark and the cherubim were suited to heart and to vision"* (2:26). The parallel is continued. This explanation is not symbolic, like the Hellenistic explanations that equated the Temple to the cosmos, nor is it similar to the analogical interpretation of Saadia;** rather, the goal is to explain the relationship between this order and the activity of the higher life. Halevi even explains the laws of ritual impurity (4:68) by way of analogies, teaching about material and spiritual damage that comes from ritually impure things.[4]

Psychological Explanations

The pious Jew fulfills all of the commandments of the Torah, without differentiating between their types (3:11), and his whole life bears their impress. Certainly the prophets admonished Israel that they did not fulfill those commandments without which even gangs of thieves are not able to maintain themselves. But it did not occur to them to disparage those commandments unique to the people of Israel. For "is it conceivable that an Israelite will be satisfied in performing the law of love and mercy, but neglect circumcision, the Sabbath,*** and the rest of the laws, and be happy

* Just as the neurochemistry of the brain is somehow mysteriously associated with the phenomenon of ordinary mental activity, so in Halevi's view the correct functioning of the sacrificial ritual in the Temple was necessary to provide the physical basis of prophetic inspiration. (LL)

** On the analogy that Saadia draws between world, Temple, and man, see footnote to page 56. (IH)

*** The Hebrew translation adds: "and the laws of the Pesaḥ," based on a misreading of the Arabic. Halevi alludes to an additional reason in *Kuzari* 3:11. This should be translated: "A person remembers his good to his God if he suffers pain in His service," and interpreted: "A person finds satisfaction in his being able to render good, as it were, to his Father in Heaven by fulfilling His will, and also in the pain that he suffers for that purpose." Indeed the book of Job rejects this view ("If you are righteous, what can you give Him?" [35:7 — compare 3:20, 22:3] and the traditional Ne'ilah prayer echoes this view: "If [a person] be righteous, what can he give to You?" But on the question of whether God "yearns for the prayers of the righteous" and is in need of their service, the views in the Aggadah are

with the result?" (2:48). The commandments' influence on our lives and our vitality is not simply religious, but in a certain sense also utilitarian: the blessings provide us with a "pleasant life" insofar as they highlight our enjoyment (3,13); the Sabbath affords us rest of body and soul such as kings are not able to attain, because their souls are not settled on their day of rest" (note that the *King* of the Khazars said this! — 3:10). But this utility is related to the character of a unique nation; the "sweetness" that is generated by the blessings is composed (of course) of emotions of thanks and affection to God, the creator of good (3:17); Sabbath rest is a "secret" means that God uses "in order to preserve us"; had it not been for our "keeping" the Sabbath, "not one of us would be wearing clean clothes, and there would not be a meeting-occasion for us to remember our Torah in the persistent exile that is upon us" (3:10).

Explanations like these are superior to Saadia's utilitarian speculations. They are based on the recognition that the Torah seeks to elevate our spirit, and that our pure happiness is desired by God no less than our submission (2:50, 56) — in contrast to several Jewish philosophers who were influenced by ascetic tendencies and mistrustful of the value of joy in living.

Halevi also emphasizes — also in complete agreement with the Torah — that many commandments were given in order to remind us of God's deeds and our obligations toward Him: the Sabbath and festivals are a reminder of the Creation, the Exodus from Egypt, and the giving of the Torah (3:10); by means of the tefillin we sanctify "the place of thought" and "the springs of energy" for the work of the Creator; the garment-fringes protect us "so that we will not be ensnared by our feelings (3:11); the commandment of circumcision distances us from licentious living (1:115). Halevi explains the prayer-liturgy thoroughly in a manner reminiscent of the method of Rabbi Samson Raphael Hirsch, who says that its purpose is to direct our thoughts aright; in Halevi's view, too, prayer comes in order to instill in our hearts the faith in the Creator's wisdom, providence, etc. (3:17, 19).* Nevertheless there are "divine actions" (i.e., divinely ordained commandments) that "our intellect does not comprehend," and one of these commandments is circumcision, which was given to Abraham as a sign "to connect him and his seed to the divine principle" (3:7). It appears that Halevi senses also the composite character of the notion of "holy" that we discussed above. "'Holy' is a term for God

divided (see *The Ways of the Aggadah* 183ff.). The view at which Halevi hints is approached by Buber: "God needs you" (*I and Thou*, 1923, 97) and Heschel: "God is in need of man" (*Man Is Not Alone*, 1951, 248).

* In Saadia's view, "the main purpose of prayer is petition" (*Siddur Rav Saadia Gaon* 90).

indicating that He is high above any attribute of created beings; and if he is called by them, this is by way of metaphor; and thus Isaiah heard 'holy, holy, holy' without end; and the reason is that He is so sanctified and elevated that He is not at all affected by the impurities of the nation among whom his honor dwelled . . . and when Israel is called holy, it is an epithet indicating that the Divine Principle is attached to them" (4:3). Because the "divine principle" is different in kind from the "rational, the animal, and the natural" (1:49), it is perhaps possible to say that God is called holy because His attributes surpass those that can be known by reason. In any event, the idea of holiness is the absolute opposite of the idea of impurity. Therefore the "rabbi-scholar" in the *Kuzari* said in his explanation of the laws of purity: "Impurity and sanctity are opposites; you will only find one in the context of the other . . . since the notion of impurity is nothing but a quality such that whatever possesses it is forbidden to come into contact . . . with whatever is sanctified to God" (3:49, beginning). Indeed we must admit that Halevi did not clarify the matter (in the same place he speaks of the Karaites!); nevertheless his approach is very different from the rational, sober explanations of impurity and sanctity that we find in Philo and Saadia.

God of Religion vs. the Metaphysical God

Ideas like these serve as a transition to the emotional explanation for the commandments that Halevi did not articulate explicitly, but whose traces are found in the *Kuzari* and in his poetry. In contrast to the majority of people in his era, he saw with clarity the difference between the philosophical and the religious knowledge of God: "The heart yearns for YHWH . . . but logic leads to *Elohim*" (4:16). Therefore, to some extent the religious person is similar to a poet who is unable to give a quantitative analysis of a poem's metrical qualities, but who "intuitively tastes the song's meter." He may fall short of the erudite who can cite you chapter and verse of the laws of prosody, but he — the poet — "can teach a natural (who is naturally gifted like himself) with a slight hint. So, too, the nation that is naturally gifted with respect to Torah and closeness to God (!) will catch fire in their souls from the sparks in the words of the pious, and light will surge into their hearts" (5:16).* Thus Halevi believes that the Jews'

* We need not dwell here on the relation between Halevi and Ghazali, who compared the religious person to one intoxicated, in order to emphasize the difference between knowing something and possessing it (Obermann, *Subjektivismus Ghazalis*; Benet *Kneset* 1942 311ff.), nor on his relation to the thinkers of our own period such as Schleiermacher and Rudolph Otto (see especially Chapter 3 of *The Idea of the Holy* on religious emotion).

approach to God (which finds concrete expression especially through their doing His will) causes the "divine principle" to draw near to them.

The Emotional Experience

This is the meaning of Halevi's poetic declaration: "When I went out to greet you, I found You greeting me."[5] Halevi succeeded in expressing the experience of fulfilling the mitzvot in his poetry. The rabbis wrote in the prayer-book, "The Sabbath day utters praise and says: 'A psalm for the day of Sabbath.'" It seems that Halevi was the first[6] who paid attention to this song and made himself a lyre for the song of the Sabbath day. Longingly he awaits its arrival because "this is my day of rest, this is my beloved and friend."[7] And this experience is not only personal, but is also national (in agreement with the doctrine of the "chosen people" that we explained); God promoted the importance of the Sabbath day in order to "separate Israel from among the nations," because one who equates "their days to my holy day" would as easily confuse "*iddim* (sanitary napkins) with *addayim* (ornaments) and the dead with the living. We should not say that Halevi based the performance of mitzvot solely on the experiential aspect. In his method, feeling stands alongside historical faith and not in its place. Just as the aesthetic conception of religion was very remote from him, so too secular-national reasons did not cross his mind. However, whereas the majority of his colleagues only saw the rational side of Jewish religious life, Halevi recognized its many-sidedness and thus anticipated to some extent the "Romantic" streams that came about during the modern era and influenced Judaism as well.

The "Practical-Religious" Value in Halevi

By our reading, we may say that even though Halevi's intention was only apologetic — and therefore he did not see any need for well-adjusted naïve believers to consider the explanations of the commandments — nevertheless, his ideas have a very important "practical-religious" value. He prevents his audience from resting satisfied with mechanical performance of the commandments. He awakens within our hearts feelings of mourning and repentance, feelings of joy and security in response to the divine

---

Of course, it never occurred to Halevi to minimize the value of historical tradition as these thinkers have done, but we cannot emphasize too much that the common denominator between them still stands. Thus Halevi was a forerunner of the Romantic school, which also influenced the German-Jewish poet Heinrich Heine, especially in his *Romanzero*, which includes the two famous poems "Princess Sabbath" and "Judah ben Halevi." (IH)

mitzvot, and all human and Jewish aspirations find an echo in our hearts. The practical-religious energizing effect of his work adds to the logical value of his ideas; one who fulfills the commandments in agreement with his guidance will understand and will feel the truth of this great principle, that with the help of "God's word" one can come closer to God.

Halevi's Personality

Halevi's ability to bring out the many-hued character of Judaism is rooted in his own varied personality. He remains both poet (the man of feeling) and doctor (the man of experience and vision) in his theoretical work. One can say that to a certain extent Halevi was able to base his faith upon his art and upon his profession,* explicitly in his explanation of the commandments. Three strengths that were bubbling up within him came together in a friendly conglomeration. These strengths did not get in each other's way; rather each complemented the others. In one respect Halevi set limits to reason, but in another way he expanded the territory of its work inasmuch as he was all-inclusive, uniting each of the aspects of Judaism within his scientific conception.[8] Saadia and Baḥya were lovers both of the people of Israel and the land of Israel, but because their thought was mainly humanistic and ecumenical they passed in almost complete silence over these emotions.** Halevi, on the other hand, raised a monument for these emotions within the walls of his spiritual building. Therefore the reasons he went to the land of Israel were different than those of many others during his period. He hoped that one of the conditions on which the renewal of prophecy depended would be realized through settling the land.[9] The same applied to the performance of the commandments, and in particular those whose reasons are hidden from us. For example, we know about the necessary connection that exists between worship in the Temple and the revelation of God's presence. Reason is not able to contradict this fact, just as it is not possible to contradict any fact in the world. Rather, it explains this by comparing it to the conditions of higher beings in general. Therefore, the mysteriousness surrounding the hortative commandments is not a difficulty or something suspicious for Halevi as it was for Saadia. Even that which is above reason is compatible to a certain extent with our way of thinking. If it is possible to call "rational" a person who seizes on the fitting method to bring him closer to his objective (e.g., one who listens

* It is impossible in translation to reproduce Heinemann's wordplay of *emunato* (his faith), *ommanuto* (his art), and *ummanuto* (his craft or medical profession). (LL)

** Saadia tends to understand the unity of Jewry as purely religious: "Our nation is not a nation except through its religious laws" (ED 3, L 128). (IH)

to the voice of an expert physician even though he does not understand his orders because of his experience or knowledge), surely it is possible to call "enlightened" one who fulfills the commandments that religious life requires for its existence. This observance is "rational for the one who observes" because it is the only path leading to the objective of our lives, which itself transcends reason.

Halevi was an innovative thinker throughout his thought-system, and in particular in his explanation of the commandments. He dwelt apart and was not numbered among "the philosophers," either in his own estimate or in his colleagues', mainly because Aristotelianism was the reigning philosophy of the day. However, his achievement confirms the judgment that the outsiders to the academy sometimes outperform the "experts." Only at the end of the Middle Ages, and even more so in the modern age, did Halevi come to enjoy the appreciation that he deserved.

Chapter 9

Abraham Ibn Ezra

Rabbi Abraham Ibn Ezra devoted sections 5–9 of his book *Yesod Mora* (*The Foundation of Faith*) and many entries of his two commentaries to the Torah to the explanation of the mitzvot. He knew the views of the thinkers who preceded him; he knew that of Halevi both from his writings and from oral communication — and he learned from them all.[1]

The Value of Knowing the Reasons

In Ibn Ezra's view we are obligated to receive the yoke of the mitzvot even if we do not understand their reasons,* like a child who eats bread though she does not understand how it is baked (YM 8). But we should not deduce from this that whoever does not investigate the reasons of the lawgiver is therefore to be praised (as Halevi would have said). "Our lord Moses said of all the mitzvot, 'Surely it must be a wise and understanding nation' to have received it! And if they have no reasons by which we are to know their nature, how are the nations to say that they are perfect laws, and that we who observe them are wise?" (*ibid.*). Ibn Ezra rightly points out that the Torah itself added reasons to several of its laws** (YM 8). But it was content with hints and did not explain its reasons completely, for just as our limbs serve many functions, so do mitzvot have more than one reason.[2] We should find them with the aid of our intellect, which is "the messenger between mankind and God."[3] This intellect only achieves its full perfection by many-sided enlightenment: "One who is wise in the tradition but has learned no other wisdom is like a camel carrying silk: the camel does not benefit the silk, nor does the silk benefit the camel" (YM 1). It is thus understandable why Ibn Ezra interprets the mitzvot of the Torah particularly in the light of "other wisdoms," especially mathematics and astronomy, in which he was proficient.

---

* But of course he emphasizes the intention of the heart, in similar terms as Baḥya (YM 7).

** "Sometimes the Torah gives an explanation of the law's rationale, which is not the case in the Amoraic law-collections" (Cassuto, *Commentary on Exodus* (1952), 183.

Utilitarian and Ethical Reasons

With respect to their method, his interpretations recall in part the three thinkers who preceded him. Utilitarian explanations are rare in his commentaries. He notes that the plague of leprosy, even though caused by sin (see his commentary on Leviticus 13:45), "is among the contagious diseases," and therefore the Torah distanced the leper from his fellows (verse 2). "The mitzvot and enactments [of the rabbis] all come to correct the heart" (YM 7). In explaining this principle (*ibid.* 5), he does not distinguish between mitzvot that have an effect on our virtues and those that recall the kindnesses and power of the Creator: "Essential mitzvot, that are not dependent on place, time, or other circumstance, are planted in the heart . . . and these were known by rational consideration before the Torah was given through Moses . . . Some mitzvot come to remind us of these essential mitzvot. Thus the Sabbath is a reminder of the creation, and the slave's rest is a reminder of the Exodus from Egypt; similarly Pesaḥ, matzah and maror, the sukkah, mezuzah, and the tefillin of the hand and the head." In connection with asceticism he is even more stringent than Baḥya and praises those people "who left the world and served the Lord alone" (YM 10 end); this applies particularly to sexual relations, "for the Lord loves the one who isolates himself in order to serve Him and heed His word, and [the abstinence in preparation for] Mount Sinai proves this" (Exodus 19:15), also the "first," and this is the secret of "the man" (referring to the sin of Adam, the first man); and because man's urge is like an animal's, it would not be proper to forbid all females, so here he forbids those who are habitually found with him" (Ibn Ezra on Leviticus 18:6). The command of circumcision also comes to restrain our urges (YM 7).

Ibn Ezra followed Halevi when he said that the Sabbath "renews the strength of our intellect" (on Genesis 2:3) and "it is the time for souls to receive an extra measure of wisdom greater than all the other days" (on Exodus 20:8). Ibn Ezra employed the various methodologies known to him, but in an original manner, and he was also inclined towards paths upon which the philosophers of the Middle Ages had not trod before him.

Symbolic Reasons

(1) Even though he objects to the Christian allegorists who abrogated the contextual meaning of Scripture, he agrees that "there are places in which both (the contextual and the hidden meaning) are actually connected — and the two of them are faithful and clear, on the bodily level and the intellectual level, for example the circumcision of the flesh and the foreskin of the heart."[4] His intention in this is not the verse: "and you shall circumcise the

foreskin of your heart," as there the plain, contextual meaning (the peshat) is rejected, of course[5]; rather the circumcision itself, even though it can be supported according to its plain, contextual meaning, has an additional secret meaning. "And know that the word *orlah* means weightiness, and thus 'uncircumcised' (*arel*) of the heart is synonymous with 'heavy is the heart of Pharaoh' . . . and here the commandment includes that you should be responsive to the Lord . . . and you should not make your hearts heavy as Pharaoh or Ahaz did."[6]

Ibn Ezra explains symbolically the purification of the leper as well (Leviticus 14:14): "The big toe symbolizes all deeds, and the right hand for the sake of the strength of the right side, and the earlobe is a remembrance to heed that which He commanded."

Secret Relations Between Mitzvot and the Forces of Nature

(2) **Mitzvot that correlate with nature and the forces acting in it.** On this, Ibn Ezra speaks more allusively than explicitly (YM 9). He opens with the verse, "Open my eyes, that I may perceive the wonders of Your Torah" (Psalm 119:18), thus announcing that he has in mind to reveal secret relationships that only people educated in the sciences will be able to understand completely. He begins:

> "This month (i.e., new-moon[7]) shall be for you the beginning of months" (Exodus 12:1) — the day of the *molad* (the conjunction of the sun with the moon just prior to the sun's entering the sign of Aries) is truly the "head" (beginning), and on it the Tabernacle was set up (because on it the sun and moon were conjoined and the sun entered the constellation that is considered its place of honor). And on the tenth (on which the Israelites were commanded to select the lamb for the Paschal offering) is the "triple cord" (Eccles. 4:12) — one in honor (the moon enters the sign of Cancer,[8] in which its power rises to its climax), the other in disgrace (Mars, the moon's rival, sits humiliated because in this astral configuration all the signs are in opposition to Mars). And thus on the tenth of the [opposite] month [of Tishri] (i.e., on Yom Kippur when we fast because the astral configuration is in Mars' favor) . . . The matter of the "seventh" is also known; the seventh year, and the cycle of seven sabbatical years culminating in the Jubilee to proclaim liberty corresponding to the rule that [the Levites] "at the age of fifty shall retire from the work force" (Num. 8:25). And the "Second Passover" [observed in Iyyar 15 for those unable to observe the regularly scheduled Passover] corresponds to [the extra month added] in leap year. And "do not seethe a kid in its mother's milk" corresponds to "[A mother and her young] do not slaughter on the same day," "do not take a mother [bird] together with its young," "do not plow (with an ox and an ass together)," "do not breed [cattle of different species together]," "do not practice in your

land (castration)," "[a woman] shall not wear a man's clothing, nor shall a man [wear a woman's clothing]" — all of these overturn the work of the Lord. Similarly the passage "You shall observe my *hukkot*" [the word that the rabbis and Saadia understood as hortative laws without stated reason, which Ibn Ezra seems to reinterpret as the ways of God as expressed in the workings of nature = natural law].

The end of the section that we quoted proves that according to Ibn Ezra, the Torah forbids whatever "overturns the work of the Lord" (i.e., whatever is contrary to the workings of nature). That is his approach for explaining the mitzvot in this section; thus he does not base the prohibition of meat and milk and similar laws on humanitarian notions, and thus in this list he did not include "do not muzzle" [which would point to a humanitarian motive], but rather he thinks that whoever takes the milk that is designed to give life to the kid (young goat) and uses it in order to cook opposes the natural order. His explanation of Leviticus 19:27 also fits this method: "Since the hair of the head and the beard were created to beautify, it is not appropriate to destroy it."

Mystical Arithmetic

The aside in the quoted section, "The matter of the 'seventh' is also known" hints at the mysterious force in the number 7, according to the Pythagoreans' theory that 7 is the "perfect number" (Ibn Ezra on Leviticus 26:18). Also in his explanation of the seven altars of Balaam (Numbers 23:1) he writes: "There are secrets that will not be understood except by a handful of people, as in [the role of the number] seven in the days,[9] and in the months and in the years and seven sacrificial sheep and seven sprinklings of blood . . . and in rendering the perfect to the perfect (seven sacrifices on seven altars [see Numbers 23:1]), so that then there will be renewed the spirit of understanding (Balaam hoped that the spirit of prophecy would be induced in him), and "the intelligent will understand" [i.e., this is a riddle — figure it out!]."[10]

Astrological Explanations and Their Limitation

Both Ibn Ezra's numerology and the ideas expressed in the beginning of the above-quoted section are rooted in astrology. As it is known, most medieval thinkers accepted astrology or at least did not completely reject it. The radical astrological opinion that viewed people's characters and the events of their lives as totally dependent on the astral powers could not, of course, be accepted by mainstream Jewish religious thinkers. Some of them maintained that Jews were completely exempt from the influence of the constellations (as the Talmudic rabbis said, "Israel has no mazal"*[11]). Some thought that it is possible to influence the astral powers either directly through magical practices or indirectly through religious actions that call forth the will of the Creator "for the astral powers govern mankind, and God governs the astral powers"; "The astral powers hearken to God's voice, and God hearkens to the voice of His pious worshippers."[12]

To what extent Ibn Ezra distanced himself from the radical astrology (of the fatalistic kind), becomes clear from his remarks in the *Yesod Mora* (YM 7, middle): "'The Host of Heaven is apportioned by God to all of the nations' [Deuteronomy 4:19: see Commentary *ad loc.*]: this is the meaning of 'God will punish the Host of the high Heaven' (Isaiah 24:21), and this is also opposed to the teaching of astrology. God adopted Israel as His special possession and removed them from the authority of the astral powers, for as long as they place themselves under His authority by doing what He commanded in his Torah. That is what the ancients meant by: 'Israel has no *mazal*,' and what [Moses] meant by: 'that we — I and Your people — may be distinguished' (Exodus 33:16). And you ought not to object: how can God change the constitutional laws of heaven and earth? Here the case of Noah will prove." Ibn Ezra acknowledges, therefore, that God changes natural law for the benefit of His followers, and also, of course, that He hearkens to prayer.[13] But we should not conclude from this that the astral powers do not have any influence at all on our life-events or that it is enough to lead an upright life in order to cancel their influence. In Ibn Ezra's view, powerful dangers lie in wait for us in connection with specific stars or astral configurations, and the Torah advises us how to avert this danger through certain actions. This first becomes clear in the law of the festivals that Ibn Ezra hints about in the most obscure language (in his commentary on Leviticus 23:24, and in parallel places).[14] The gist of his words is: the commandment of the Sabbath and its designated sacrifices was instituted in order to counteract the negative influence of the Sabbath Star (i.e., the planet Saturn), which is called the "evil spirit" by the astrologers.**[15] Also on Rosh Hashana and in the middle of the months of Nisan and Tishri the conjunction of the stars is very inauspicious, and worship on these days, including blowing the shofar, have the function of negating the resulting danger.

* I.e., Israel's fortunes are not ruled by the stars, but by God directly — compare Deuteronomy 4:19–20, 32:8–9 (and JPS Commentary *ad loc.*), and Psalm 82. (LL)

** See also in Solomon Ibn Gabirol's poem "The Royal Crown" Saturn "stirs up wars, spoliation, captivity and famine . . . his service is foreign." As for the connection between the planet Saturn and our Sabbath (Saturday), this was believed by the Greek and Roman astrologers, and their view was familiar to Philo (*Education of Philo* 155). He determines that there was an integral connection between the Sabbath and the legends of Chronos/ Saturn, in whose days people lived in bliss according to the laws of nature.

The Arrangement of the Temple and Its Affairs

Ibn Ezra also gives an astrological explanation for the structure of the Temple, which symbolizes the microcosm (i.e., the human being),[16] as well as the macrocosm. The latter correspondence is given in three parts: the Holy of Holies symbolizes "the First (highest) World" (i.e., the dwelling place of the Divine Presence [Shekhinah]); the Shrine, site of the golden altar and its vessels, was instituted corresponding to the "middle" world, the world of constellations and spirits; the courtyard, in which the copper altar is found, symbolizes the sublunar world of "perishing and becoming." However, Ibn Ezra also saw the Temple as a means "to bring down the divine strength to earth, to elevate the nation in whose midst the Temple resides to the rank of prophets, and to defend it in an extraordinary way from its enemies' attacks."[17] This became clear especially in his shorter commentary on Exodus 25:4: "And all the time that they observed the Temple worship, the sword did not pass through their land." This viewpoint also embraces his explanation of the clothes of the High Priest[18] and some of the reasons that he offers for the sacrifices. On Leviticus 1:1 he writes: "We find a single covenant for two things[19]; it is also possible for there to be one commandment for the sake of many things like the commandment of the burnt-offering and the ordinary sacrifice; for through giving each portion in its time, there is saved the portion [i.e., the soul] that has a portion in the World to Come*; thus the root-meaning of the word *le-khaper* [to atone] is: 'to give a ransom,' as is attested in the passage of the head-tax ransom (Exodus 30:11–16)**; and therefore [Moses says to Pharaoh the people must sacrifice to God] 'lest he strike us with the plague' (Ex. 5:3). Burnt-offerings also have secret powers regarding the futures [these cancel the evil futures that are to come upon us according to the astral configuration]. Also from each sacrifice is to be understood the secret of the generations.*** And the sin offerings and the unleavened bread (eaten by the priests) are to keep alive the teachers of Torah." Not only to the sacrifices does Ibn Ezra attribute a secret power, part of whose basis is in astrology, but also concerning the incident of the Golden Calf he says (in his shorter commentary on Exodus, page 99 in the Prague edition): "Whoever understands the workings of the heavens will

---

* "When the portions of the animal are given in ransom for your own limbs in this world, you are saved for the World to Come" (Rosin MGWJ 42:127). Rosin, who discusses at length the atoning power of the sacrifices, believes that Ibn Ezra is referring to the entire people of Israel, who collectively have a portion in the World to Come. (IH)

** There the word *kofer* is used for "ransom," and it says that the payment of money (a half-shekel) is for the purpose: "There will be no plague when they are counted."

*** The animals and fowl that are eligible to be brought as sacrifices are pure and non-aggressive (Neter in his commentary to Ibn Ezra), and thus they serve as an example to their owners. (Compare Philo above, p. 44)

understand [why they chose] the form of the calf," that is to say, they aimed to bring down the energy of the constellation of Taurus" (Rosin 42:358).

Toward an Understanding of the Esoteric Explanations

These astrological reasons that are characteristic of Ibn Ezra are doubtless strange to us because the time of astrology has passed. For this reason, some may see Ibn Ezra as offering alien fire on God's altar and might feel like saying to him: "You of all people, champion of the plain-sense reading, the first and almost the only one in your era who searched out the reasons that the Torah itself gave for its ordinances — did you not sense that it would have never dawned on the Torah to give these kinds of reasons for the mitzvot?"* But Ibn Ezra could have answered that he did not explicate these reasons but only alluded to them, with the special intention of giving satisfaction to those Jews who innocently believed in astrology, and thus to prevent them from the graver error of adopting the more extreme astrology that surely contradicted Judaism. And if such an explanation amazes us, it doubtless would have found approval from his contemporaries — and not just Jews. It should be mentioned that Melanchthon, a friend of Luther and the great linguist and "plain-sense" biblical commentator, explained the periodic restriction of marital relations on the grounds that it was the way of menstruation to occur during the conjunction of the sun and the moon, and that this occasion caused weak babies to be born.[20] This was the opinion of a Christian thinker who was not interested in the justification of our commandments. It did not occur to him to doubt that the Torah also knew and appreciated astrology. Ibn Ezra's explanations were also occasioned by his scientific faith; he had grounds for hoping that he would be able to explain the esoteric secrets of Torah and thus be able to add to the Torah's honor in the eyes of his people, as well as in the eyes of Christians who rejected the commandments in their plain sense.[21]

Mitzvot that seek to preserve racial purity

(3) The third idea that Ibn Ezra added to the accepted wisdom of his age was that the commandments guard the purity of our race. A propos of the prohibition of the sciatic nerve, Ibn Ezra writes [YM 5]: "it recalls the kindness that God showed Jacob — that he alone is our father (others were not descended from him), and nobody else shared it with us as was

* We must qualify this objection by noting that Gunkel (in *Schöpfung und Chaos* 126) agrees with the astrological interpretation of the candelabra, whereas Cassuto, especially in his Commentary on Exodus (1952), emphasizes the mystical significance of the numbers in the Torah. (IH)

the case with Abraham and Isaac. Therefore, we do not defile ourselves with their food or drink their wine as is mentioned in the Torah: 'Cursed be Canaan,' for they shall not mix with the Israelites." In his explanation of the prohibition of ordinary wine of gentiles, he suggests that it was instituted "because of their daughters" [i.e., against intermarriage], and he attributes the same reason to the dietary prohibitions, the first of which is the prohibition of the sciatic nerve. Also regarding the prohibition of "rounding the corners of the hair" (Leviticus 19:27), Ibn Ezra writes, "as the other nations do, to be distinguished from them."

Ibn Ezra's Common Cause with the Jewish Hellenists

All of these explanations prove that Ibn Ezra did not consider unimportant these commandments that Saadia (but not Ibn Ezra!) called "hortative," even though those commandments "that are planted in the heart, known by rational consideration before the Torah was given" were in his eyes "essential" (YM 5). Precisely in the explanation of these, Ibn Ezra's distinctive character stands out. Nevertheless if we compare his methodological innovations to the ways of his unknown predecessors, namely the Hellenists, we shall find surprising similarities. To be sure, Ibn Ezra differs from them regarding the astrologic explanation, even though Philo did not categorically reject belief in the astral influence on our lives. Nevertheless, there are several similarities between them: (1) the Hellenists also used allegorical methods, generally without annulling the plain meaning, whereas the rabbis only resorted to metaphorical or allegorical interpretations by way of casual supports[22]; (2) the Hellenists also taught that the mitzvot were given in correspondence to nature and the forces at work in it — such as numbers[23] and the movements of the stars — whereas the rabbis and medieval philosophers were satisfied with noting the *parallels* between the mitzvot and natural events*; only in the eyes of the Hellenists and Ibn Ezra does the Temple symbolize the cosmos and its segments; (3) the Hellenists — for example, Aristaeas (142) and Josephus (*Antiquities* I, 192) — noted that certain mitzvot were given in order to prevent assimilation and absorption.

Ibn Ezra — Mystic of Science

It is a common method of scholars to explain such similarity of views by literary influence. Indeed, Ibn Ezra knew the allegorical method from the Christian commentators, not all of whom rejected the contextual meaning.

---

* Ibn Ezra himself (on Numbers 19:2) cites Saadia's explanation of the red heifer's power to purify the impure and defile the pure, by reference to known herbal remedies.

It is also possible that he found Philo's explanation of the Tent of Meeting in their books (without knowing that its origin was Jewish![24]). Ibn Ezra certainly derived the method of numerology and the knowledge of nature from those same Greek sources on which Philo and Josephus drew. These connections are certainly valid; however, they do not resolve the main question: Why did Ibn Ezra see fit to follow just these views, whereas his contemporaries, such as Halevi and Ibn Daud, opposed them and rejected them outright? There is only one way to answer this question: There was a spiritual-intellectual kinship between Ibn Ezra and certain thinkers, Jews and non-Jews that led him to seek methods such as theirs; the "cultural experience" did not create the "primary experience," but rather his character and tendencies brought him close to his colleagues-in-thought in order to create, with their help, a scientific formula for the appropriate concept. This applies especially to the Pythagoreans, who overwhelmingly influenced most of the schools of the Hellenistic period — including Philo! Love of the revealed and that of the hidden met in their souls as they did in Ibn Ezra's. They were experts in mathematics and physics, but they also discovered secret relationships between the world of numbers and constellations and our world below, and they founded a religion that included ethical and "hortative" mitzvot (which is what they called, for example, their prohibitions of certain foods), which they explained in a symbolic and allegorical way.[25] The similar aspects between them and their Greek and Jewish students and Ibn Ezra, such as the tendency towards allegorizing and explaining the lower world through the influence of the astral world, are rooted in their similarity of character; both were "scientific mystics." The science that discovered the relationships between numbers and what is done on earth came to confirm their faith that the revealed requires clarification by way of the hidden, "and there is the secret and the foundation." We understand that Ibn Ezra did not make a great impression on the students of Aristotle, the soberest of the Greek scholars, but his methods lived on and influenced people who were "scientific mystics" like himself, within the scientific branch of the kabbalists.

Chapter 10
Abraham Ibn Daud

Rabbi Abraham Ibn Daud was the first Aristotelian among Jewish philosophers. In his and his successors' eyes, the views and method of "The Philosopher" were identified with those of science in general. They took his words as true until disproved. From these assumptions they also arrived at a new method of explaining the mitzvot.

Both the "rational" and "hortative" mitzvot are eternal

Already in his discussion of the question of "abolishing the mitzvot" (*Emunah Ramah,* ed. Weil, pp. 75 ff.), Ibn Daud expresses certain views and assumptions that are important for our question. He distinguishes, as Saadia did, between the rational mitzvot (which he calls *mefursamot* — "commonly held") and the hortative ones. There is no thought of abolishing the former, of which even a band of robbers has need. Nor should one abolish the hortative mitzvot, inasmuch as the Torah has called them perpetually binding. The prophets who said, "My soul hates your new moons and festivals," or "What point to Me are your many sacrifices?" and so forth, had no intention of abolishing the mitzvot (did not Isaiah himself exhort concerning observance of the Sabbath in other places?) but only of condemning the "combination of ritual observance with social injustice." Similarly Ibn Daud rejects the "worthless arguments" against certain mitzvot, such as applying the original (Egyptian) Paschal blood to the doorposts and lintel, which seemed to skeptics to deny God's omniscience. Rather, the purpose of this mitzvah was that "on account of their faith and obedience to the divine command, He deflected the damage from them" (79). For us, the last article of his book (98 ff.) is the most important, but unfortunately it is not well organized.

"Practical philosophy" has the purpose of achieving happiness. We shall arrive at this objective through (1) correction of personal virtues, (2) household management,* and (3) political practices.** We are led — in vain — to expect this classification to serve as a basis for the entire article.

* That is to say, mitzvot that pertain between a person and other members of his household. (IH)

** That is, mitzvot that pertain between one person and another (not of his household).

The mitzvot as acknowledgment of our gratitude

He devotes the whole first half to explaining the concept of "equity," whose explanation applies to theoretical philosophy as well as to the second and third parts of practical philosophy. This equity, "on which heaven and earth depend," also determines our religious obligations,[1] for it commands us to treat well whoever has treated us well. "And if it is impossible" for us to thank Him "with all our power, then inasmuch as God's kindness surpasses every kindness in the world, it is incumbent on us to render service and express our thanks to the greatest extent" (*Emunah Ramah* 99).

Interpreting the Ten Commandments

He interprets the Ten Commandments in accord with these assumptions: The point of origin is the emphatic assertion that the Exodus from Egypt was the act of God, not simply the effect of astral influences. This principle (which is not pragmatic but theoretical) requires us to serve Adonai alone and to revere His name. The Sabbath also recalls the Creator's power, whereas honoring one's father and mother directs us to honor our Father in heaven. The remainder of the mitzvot determine our political conduct. The command "do not covet" surpasses everything that the great philosophers taught in their ethical treatises. The principles that were articulated at the Sinai revelation, and specified in detail through the 613 mitzvot, govern the relations "between the servant and his Master, and between the servant and his peers." The command "love your neighbor as yourself" comprises also love of God, for we cannot love what we do not know, and we should know not only God's "attributes and actions," but also the fact that all our fellow-persons come to us not from God directly "but through natural causes." From this knowledge there follow: (1) the proper "fear" of God (which is wholly dissimilar to the fear that we have of wild animals and the like); (2) "service" of God, which is not restricted to the observance of prayer, but embraces our entire life insofar as possible; and (3) "attachment" to God. So that we should persevere "in the remembrance and fear of God," the Torah has established "aids" such as tefillin, fringes, mezuzah, and the festivals* that recall the kindness that He exhibited to us.

The first half of this article thus demonstrates that science and reason require of every person not only ethical but also religious behavior. In giving a scientific account of our obligations, Ibn Daud was undoubtedly

* Ibn Daud includes among the festivals Purim and Hanukkah, although these are not mentioned in the Torah. (IH)

influenced by Saadia, who had taken note of our obligation to express thanks to God for His beneficence. But the plan of his article is also similar to the approach of the Hellenists (of whom he was certainly unaware), who regarded the Ten Commandments as the specification of natural law and the 613 mitzvot as the specification of the Ten Commandments. The role of the mitzvot in reminding one of the kindnesses that God wrought on behalf of the people of Israel had already been taught by Baḥya and Abraham Ibn Ezra.

The continuation of the article is based on the announced topical division; however Ibn Daud is not speaking only of our obligations. He demonstrates, in accord with his book's purpose, that the Torah contains, in the most fully developed way, all the requirements of philosophical ethics, whether in the realm of personal virtue (such as generosity and humility), household management,* or political governance** (101, end).

Ranking the "hortative" mitzvot

Especially important is the portion dealing with those mitzvot whose utility we cannot discern, such as those pertaining to the sacrifices and their details. He mentions that they have been called "hortative mitzvot" but he prefers to label them "subtle matters instituted in wisdom." These mitzvot would seem to constitute a category in themselves, but in fact the Torah includes only four categories: (1) faith, (2) ethical mitzvot, (3) "household management" (i.e., those mitzvot that improve private life), and (4) "political governance" (i.e., those mitzvot that improve public life). The "hortative mitzvot" are simply a sub-category of the ethical. The value of these categories is not equal: faith is on a higher level than the mitzvot. Those mitzvot whose reason is hidden from us "are on a very weak level"; this is attested by the words of the prophets (I Samuel 15:22, Jeremiah 7:21, Isaiah 1:11 and 66:3, Psalms 50:8). However, they do have reasons, though the reasons are "weak." For example: whoever brings a sin-offering will certainly reveal his sin to the priest, and by doing so he takes precaution against relapsing or despairing of God's forgiveness. The institution of the sacrifices also has symbolic reasons: the rabbis have said that the suspected adulteress brings barley, which is animal fodder, because her action was of a bestial sort. They also gave a reason for the sacrifice of birds that was brought by one being purified of leprosy, because the sinner was a babbler like birds (leprosy was associated with the sin of slander). The slaughter of

* Here Ibn Daud mentions rabbinic commands, such as the enactments of Usha.

** Here, and not in the domain of personal virtue, he cites the verse "you shall love your neighbor as yourself" and other social injunctions. (IH)

animals is a kind of "scolding" of our animal nature. Ibn Daud also alludes to magical and astrological reasons given for the sacrifices, as well as to the episode of Zipporah (warding off the danger through circumcising her son), but he does not accept such reasons as plausible.

In praise of Abraham for not second-guessing God

Ibn Daud attributes special value to those mitzvot whose reasons we do not understand, "for obedience is good" (i.e., in performing them a person shows that he is heeding the word of his God, without questioning His ways). Indeed, a person is entitled to pursue all kinds of wisdom, "especially" those that lead him to know God. But because a prophet with proven credentials has been sent, and he commanded us laws that reason does not contradict and that we can live with, whoever accepts these mitzvot "in the way of faith and right" is to be counted a believer, and whoever wishes to second-guess and ask what is the use of abstaining from the flesh of animals that lack cloven hooves or do not chew their cud, or from fish that lack fins and scales, is not following in the ways of those ancients who risked their lives in order to fulfill their Creator's command. When the patriarch Abraham was commanded by God to sacrifice his son, he did not second-guess and argue, asking what had happened to all the promises and hopes that God had implanted in him. To be sure, God knew that Abraham would devote himself to fulfilling the mitzvah. He tested him only so that his devotion would stand as a shining example. This, then, is the utility of those "matters ordained in the way of wisdom" through which it is possible to distinguish "between denial and faith." With this sentence, Ibn Daud concludes his book *Emunah Ramah*.

"Weakness" of the hortative mitzvot: Ibn Daud's relation to Saadia and the modern rationalists

These arguments are the words of a man who is both enlightened and believing. To a noticeable degree, his rationalism is similar to that of Saadia. Saadia also taught that we believe in prophets because reason forces us to rely on miracles that attest to their credentials. He also emphasized that the mitzvot of the Torah — including the hortative ones — are not contradicted by reason. However, Ibn Daud deviates from Saadia inasmuch as for him, the mitzvot whose purpose eludes us do not constitute a separate class. Maybe for this reason he refuses to call them "hortative," for this term seems to indicate that such mitzvot have no rational reason at all. But in point of fact, he, too, distinguishes between two kinds of mitzvot, even with respect to their value. The less-understood mitzvot are of a "weaker level." This expression can have two meanings. When we say, for example, that the juvenile works of some poets are of lesser value than their mature works, we mean that the earlier exhibit deficiencies, or at any rate their artistic value is slight. By contrast, when we say that the tutor must soothe the child, drill him, and educate him, and we add that among the enumerated tasks "the last is most important," there is no doubt that faithful fulfillment of the earlier-mentioned tasks — the lesser, as it were — will be considered no defect but to his credit. Clearly, only one who disbelieves in revealed Torah will regard certain commands of the Torah as of negligible value in the first sense. As is known, in the modern period critical scholars of the Bible arose who drew a distinction between "prophetic Judaism" and "legalistic Judaism"; they based themselves on the verses that Ibn Daud quoted and saw in them opposition to the religious value of the sacrifices (whose laws were not written down, according to these critics, until Second Temple times!). They hailed Ibn Daud, who in their view had opposed "the prejudice that all parts of the Torah were of equal value,"[2] thus demonstrating his courage and honesty.

Did these scholars deceive themselves and not sense the great difference between their approach and that of Ibn Daud — a man who had devoted his energy as a historian and philosopher to defend the Jewish tradition? Just as Ibn Daud had never heard of the method of Wellhausen, who thought that the prophets predated the Priestly Code, so it never occurred to him that the prophets disparaged the sacrificial offerings or Sabbath observance, or that many (or even the majority) of the mitzvot of the Torah exhibited a "deficient" religious outlook. In Ibn Daud's eyes, the hortative mitzvot were also "ordained in wisdom," (i.e., in God's wisdom that inspired the prophets, and whoever believes in them and performs them eagerly is worthy of praise).

There is thus no doubt that Ibn Daud understood the "weakness" of the hortative mitzvot in the second sense that we indicated in the last paragraph. No criticism is intended thereby. Ibn Daud follows the example of the rabbis, who also distinguished between "light" and "heavy" mitzvot,* and between those whose reason is known and those whose reason is hidden.

* The material was collected by Wohlgemuth, *Das jüdische Religionsgesetz in jüdischer Beleuchtung* II, 19 ff. However, the expressions are ambiguous (*ḥamur* can mean either "difficult" or "important"; see Albo *Principles ('Ikkarim)* I, VI, 20 on this difference). Therefore not all the passages that Wohlgemuth cites indicate difference of value, but the rabbis' words concerning the three mitzvot for which we should be prepared to sacrifice our lives, and the value of Shabbat, circumcision, and prohibition of idolatry, demonstrate that they too recognized a ranking of the mitzvot in the sense that we have pointed out. (IH)

But in the rabbis' view, the first distinction and the second distinction are not equivalent. The identifiably "Jewish" mitzvot of unknown reason include some that are "heavy" and important, such as circumcision and the Sabbath.* Why, then, did Ibn Daud see fit to give preference to the "rational" mitzvot over the others? Indeed, he emphasizes (at the end of the same chapter) that even a band of robbers needs them, but this fact, which Halevi also acknowledges (*Kuzari* 2:48), is not calculated to raise the estimation of these and to reduce the value of those mitzvot in which only the chosen believers participate!

Why Ibn Daud Preferred the Rational to the Hortative Mitzvot

In order to find Ibn Daud's answer to our question, we should recall that the rational portions of the Torah do not stand on the same level, either: "The essential pillar of the Torah is faith." Afterwards come the moral laws and social enactments. Such a hierarchy is not unusual in his method. He similarly orders natural phenomena in their rank of value (p. 44), from matter "which does not exist for its own sake" to the human being "who is the purpose of this whole natural realm of existence." Similarly he ranks our various faculties — from the vital and the animal up to the rational,** "above which no further power exists, hence it is the purpose of it all."

It follows from this that "the many sciences are in a hierarchical ranking, and the supreme purpose of all of them is the knowledge of God, may He be blessed and exalted." The science of medicine, for example, "is quite honorable, because through it the human being will perpetuate his life in this world, by whose aid he can arrive at perfection and the supernal existence." But whoever thinks that this is the supreme goal of human existence, "and spends all his time in pursuing it, does violence to his soul . . . all the more so,[3] one who spends all his time in lesser matters than this," such as the details of mathematics. He compares such people to a servant of whom it was told[4] that they promised him his freedom and would even make him king on condition that he go on pilgrimage (to Mecca), and he wasted his time in embroidering the threads of his bag, to the point that his preparation spoiled the opportunity to go on the journey.

* Of course the words of the prophets, on which Ibn Daud relies, found an echo among the rabbis, despite their generally positive evaluation of the sacrifices, which shines clearly through the majority of their utterances. See for instance JT *Rosh Hashanah* 56b: "Your practice of justice and righteousness (David) is dearer to me than all the sacrifices, as it is said, 'Doing righteousness and justice is preferable in God's eyes to sacrifice.'"

** The Hebrew *medabber* (Arabic: *nakt*), translations of the Greek *logikos*, all of which have the dual sense of "speaking" and "intellectual." (IH)

Why, if all mitzvot are valid, do they differ in rank?

Go and infer: in Ibn Daud's view, everything follows the final goal. To the extent that something is closer to the final goal of existence, and to the extent that any of our actions is closer to the purpose of our life, they have greater value. As for those deeds that are remote from the final goal, their value is generally positive, but on the occasion that the diligent application that we invest in a deed (and especially in the fine details of that deed) distracts us from the ultimate purpose, we should regard the value of that deed as negative. Our overall purpose on this earth is to perfect our intellect generally and to acquire true knowledge of divine matters in particular.[5] Therefore the most important part of the Torah is that which enables us to acquire correct knowledge of the blessed God. But the ethical mitzvot are also important because they assist the intellect to establish control over the lower forces in the soul and the body. Of lesser value are those mitzvot (including "love your neighbor as yourself"!) that are only directed at the proper ordering of our bodily existence. Among the mitzvot between the person and God are many that are of great value, such as the Sabbath (which Saadia counts among the hortative mitzvot), tefillin, and the like. By contrast, the value of the commands of the sacrifices, which only indirectly aid our moral perfection (which itself is not the prime purpose of our life), and their details (which have no effect on us because we do not know their reasons) are very remote from the ultimate purpose, nor can we attribute to them any important educational value. We already saw, in discussing Baḥya's method, that one should see the performance of the mitzvot both as the seed of our piety and its fruit. Just as Baḥya taught of the patriarch Abraham that he showed his love by accepting his Creator's command as incumbent on himself (see also *Kuzari* 3:7), so Ibn Daud praises precisely the "faith" that he thus showed,* in order to draw a connection between the lowest-ranking mitzvot to the highest rank that a mortal human can achieve.

* In the rabbis' view also, Abraham demonstrated a love without limits. Perhaps Ibn Daud intended to counter the familiar Christian view that Abraham was the original paragon of faith, for whom faith, rather than deed, was "reckoned as justification" (based on Genesis 15:6, as interpreted by Paul in Epistle to Romans, Chapter 4). Ibn Daud suggests here that faith and deeds are not mutually exclusive, but rather faith is the foundation for deeds, including those that Christianity rejects. In all his exchanges with Christianity Ibn Daud exercised great caution, and his tragic end (for he died a martyr's death) demonstrates how necessary this was!

Similarities and differences in Baḥya's and Ibn Daud's rankings

Gradations such as these had already been established by Baḥya Ibn Pakudah. He opens his book with a classification of the sciences. Even though he does not emphasize the difference in their value, it is obvious that in his view natural science and the "auxiliary" disciplines such as mathematics are of inferior rank to "the divine science," which consists in "knowledge of the blessed God, of His Torah,[6] and the other intellectual truths." The same applies to the mitzvot. Was not his entire book written in order to attest to the value of the "duties of the heart," (i.e., the obligations of knowledge and ethics, which Ibn Daud also raises to the highest rank)? Already in the introduction to his book, Baḥya tells of a sage "who would sit with other people until the middle of the day, and while together with his friends he would say, 'Give me the hidden light'" (i.e., the wisdom of the heart). To one sage, who asked him an unusual question concerning the laws of divorce, he responded, "You are the man who asks concerning what will not harm us if we do not know it. Do you know all that you are obligated to know of the mitzvot . . . that you have turned aside to consider foreign questions whose knowledge leads to no great improvement in your learning and faith, but you do not seek to improve what is wrong in the virtues of your soul?" Only this appreciation of the mitzvot of faith and ethics explains the superiority of "intellectual awakening" over "awakening of the Torah," which we have discussed. And it is also clear that both of them, in according preference to the duties of the heart, are close to the Arab thinkers.[7] But the difference between them is also instructive. Baḥya speaks explicitly only about the superiority of the intellectual mitzvot, but not of the "weakness" of the hortative mitzvot. He deflects with his left hand the excessive application that was devoted to some of the hortative mitzvot in order that he can draw near with his right hand the obligations of the heart. In contrast, Ibn Daud emphasizes the meager value of the sacrifices (and even the value of deeds in comparison to that of the principles of faith), in order to draw traditional Judaism closer to the scientific-philosophical conception. For scientific knowledge is very precious in his eyes, not only because intellect is our crowning glory, but also because reason — and only reason — can defend Judaism against the attacks of its opponents. Just as his *Sefer ha-Kabbalah* (Book of Tradition) proves the reliability of the tradition, in order to refute the views of the Christians and the Karaites, so the purpose of his philosophical book (a purpose that he deliberately obscures in his introduction) is to prove that only Judaism is worthy of being called an "exalted faith" (*Emunah Ramah* — the book's title), because all its principles are in agreement with the doctrines of *the* Philosophy, namely the Aristotelian. This objective is easy to achieve in the theoretical realm, but difficult in the practical realm. Did not Christianity, in denigrating most of the hortative mitzvot — including those of the Temple service — seem vindicated by philosophy, which depreciates the value of all ritual forms, as Halevi (speaking through the Philosopher at the beginning of the *Kuzari*) points out? Therefore Ibn Daud demonstrates that there are rational reasons even for those mitzvot that Saadia called "hortative," but their practice is not as effective in achieving the ultimate purpose to the same degree as ethical living and especially correct knowledge.

Therefore their value was originally depreciated — not by the Christians, but by the prophets of Israel; appreciating them, however, is entirely in accord with philosophical assumptions.

Ibn Daud, Halevi and Ibn Ezra

The oft-repeated formulation in which Ibn Daud speaks of the "weakness" of the hortative mitzvot attests to a certain sensitivity, which we should try to understand. He undoubtedly was familiar with the appreciation of these mitzvot by other thinkers. Ibn Ezra thought the sacrifices were useful for negating the dire influence of the astral bodies; Halevi[8] sees the rational mitzvot as "preparatory foundations for the divine commandments" (*Kuzari* 2:48), the latter of which raise us to the supreme human level. However, in Ibn Daud's view (p. 45) "there is no other power higher than reason" that performance of the mitzvot can impart to us. The astrological method, which Ibn Daud knew not only from Ibn Ezra's books,[9] may have sparked his fierce opposition, for the students of Aristotle knew that "true philosophers" did not deem such a method even worth mentioning.[10] In his view, these two attempts to assign a special and superior significance to the hortative mitzvot only obscured the splendor of our "exalted" and scientifically correct faith and weakened our power to defend it against Christian attacks.

These comparisons illuminate the innovation in Ibn Daud's method. The kind of reason on which he relies in order to justify the mitzvot is *scientific* [i.e., philosophical] reason. Indeed, the science of that period (especially in the view of thinkers who were partial to religion) was not a science whose job was just to address theoretical questions; such a "science" (in the philosophical tradition of Plato and Aristotle) opened the gates both to ethical life in this world and to eternal felicity in the next world. Ibn Daud believes that the activity of reason has no more important objective than searching out the truth. Therefore he does not attribute any utilitarian motives to the religious mitzvot that are given for all time,[11] not in the materialistic sense of Saadia (for whom forbidding incestuous unions to close relatives had the purpose of facilitating marriage to others), nor in the more "refined" sense of Halevi (for whom the rest of the Sabbath enables us to bolster our morale through the trials of exile). He does not believe in the influence of the mitzvot on supernatural phenomena. Prophecy does not depend on the Temple service (73, etc.) and it goes without saying that the sacrifices do not negate the dire influences of the astral bodies (103). The purpose of the hortative mitzvot is to remind us of the principles of our faith and the beneficences that God has wrought for us in general and to purify our hearts — in complete accord with the purpose of our life, as philosophy would have it.

The debate between Ibn Daud and Halevi — who were contemporaries and compatriots — is apt to shed light on the development of the approach to our question over the generations. Both of them acknowledge the value of the mitzvot, the value of philosophical science, and, furthermore, that it is extremely difficult to explain the importance of the religious mitzvot on the basis of Greek rationalism. Halevi emphasizes this (4:15) perhaps even more than Ibn Daud. Both of them therefore had to decide whether to broaden the domain of scientific investigation in order to make room within its rubric for those values characteristic of religion, or to reduce (but not annul!) the value of specific mitzvot in order to bring Judaism closer to the rationalist outlook. This debate was not born in the period of these two thinkers; it did not end there, and it will never end as long as the common basis that we have mentioned remains standing.

Chapter 11
Maimonides

The Different Points of View in His Various Books

Maimonides dealt with the reasons for the commandments in several places, especially in the *Mishneh Torah* and in the *Guide of the Perplexed*,[1] but for different purposes. In books that were intended also for readers with no philosophical background, he discussed our question only tangentially, and his intention was not "theoretical-religious" but rather "practical-religious": he wished to guide his readers in the direction of a correct and knowledgeable fulfillment of the commandments, and to wean them away from any religious understanding based on nonsense and superstition. This objective applied both to the Biblical and the rabbinic commandments. In the *Guide*, by contrast, his intention was purely theoretical. There he speaks on divine providence and the governance of the world. Just as he discusses the question of injustice ("why does the righteous experience evil, and the wicked experience good?") only from the standpoint of the Creator (i.e., why does God bring suffering to His pious followers?) and not of heads of state (i.e., why do they not punish the wicked?), so too he generally restricts the question of the reasons for the mitzvot to the domain of the God-given commandments.[2] These explanations are addressed to philosophically educated readers, to whom he can present ideas that are not intended for the masses.

1. Is it possible and permitted to explain the mitzvot?

In our discussion of the Biblical treatment of this topic, we saw that the mitzvot can be viewed as irrational from the perspective of the performer but rational from the perspective of the Lawmaker. Maimonides also emphasized this duality of nuance, in stark contrast to the views of some his "enlightened" modern interpreters, who have neglected the "irrational" aspect in his thought and tried to bring it closer to their own outlook.*

* Translator's note: I must say that I tend to agree more with the "modern enlightened" commentators (such as Hermann Cohen) than with Heinemann at this point, at least as

Permitted to explain the mitzvot, but not to reject them

We read in the *Mishneh Torah* (at the end of the Laws of Sacrilege):

> One ought to consider the laws of the holy Torah and to penetrate into their ultimate significance as much as he can. If, however, he cannot discover the reason and is ignorant of the basic cause of a law, he should not regard it with contempt. "Let him not break through to ascend to the Lord, lest He break out against him" (Exodus 19:24). His thinking about it must not be like his thinking concerning secular matters. Consider, for example, how strict the Torah is with regard to sacrilege. If wood and stones, earth and ashes, became consecrated as soon as the name of the eternal Lord was called upon them [and anyone who put them to secular use committed sacrilege and required atonement even if he acted unwittingly], how much more should man take care not to rebel against the laws which God wrote down for us, simply because he happens to be ignorant of their basic reason. One must not impute to God things that are not right, nor regard the precepts as he would secular things. It is indeed written in the Torah: "You shall faithfully observe all My statutes and laws and perform them" (Leviticus 19:37). The Sages interpreted this verse to mean that we must observe and perform the statutes [*ḥukkim*] the same as the laws [*mishpatim*]. What *performance* denotes is known, namely one must do the statutes; *observance*, on the other hand, means that one should be careful about them and not imagine that they are less important than the laws. The laws (*mishpatim*) are duties the reason of which is obvious, and the benefit derived in this world from doing them is known; for example, the prohibition against robbery and bloodshed, or the precept of honoring father and mother. The statutes (*ḥukkim*) are precepts the reason of which is not known, and of which the Sages said, 'These are statutes that I [God] have set down for you and you have no right to question them, even though a person's evil urge nags at him concerning them and the nations of the world raise arguments against them — such as the prohibition against pork and that against meat-milk mixture, the laws concerning the heifer with the broken neck, the red cow, or the scapegoat that is sent away to the wilderness.[3] How King David was troubled by the Epicureans and the pagans who raised arguments against the *ḥukkim*! But the whole time that they harried him with these false arguments that are devised in accordance with man's fallible intelligence, he would increase his devotion to the Torah, as it says, 'Though the arrogant have accused me falsely, I observe Your precepts wholeheartedly' (Psalm 119:69) . . . And all the sacrifices are included in the *ḥukkim*. The Sages said that the world endures by virtue of the sacrificial worship, for through performing the *ḥukkim* and the *mishpatim* the upright

---

pertaining to Maimonides' view in the *Guide*! To be sure, in the *Mishneh Torah* he takes a different standpoint — more reflecting the rabbinic tradition than his own private view. But this is an opening to a much larger discussion, connected with the issues raised in my Preface. (LL)

> merit the life of the World to Come. The Torah places the commandment concerning the statutes (*ḥukkim*) first, as it is written: "You shall observe my statutes and my laws, by the performance of which man shall live" (Leviticus 18:5).

Perhaps these things are worded this way here in accord with the objective of the *Mishneh Torah*, which comes to describe the mitzvot and to endear them to mankind. It did not occur to Maimonides to give the *ḥukkim* preference over mitzvot whose reasons were recognized. Therefore, there is no doubt that he formulated these last words in a one-sided manner. But in the rest of his books, too, he emphasized his obligation to affirm the mitzvot whose reasons are unknown to us, and supported this view with rabbinic sayings that express the heteronomic character of the mitzvot. The rabbinic dictum, "a person ought not say, 'I don't like pork,' etc." he explains in the "Eight Chapters"* (Chapter 6) as applying to the *ḥukkim* alone, in accord with the examples that were cited by the rabbis. He also cites their statement "greater is one who is commanded and acts than one who is not commanded and acts" in *The Guide of the Perplexed* (3:17), without elaborating on it [thus implying that he simply agreed with it]; he emphasizes that even in the case of one who is not commanded but performs the mitzvot, God rewards him, as per the view of the rabbis.[4] In the *Guide* (3:24) he praises Abraham as he stood in the trial of the binding of Isaac and was prepared to fulfill the commandment of his God, the reason for which he, of course, did not know. He who knows the criticism that Abraham Geiger directed at Abraham's "blind obedience" can imagine the difference between Maimonides and the free-thinking theologians of the 19th century, even though they tried to base their views on his method.

The performance of the mitzvot is heteronomic from the human side. But there is no doubt for Maimonides that the Creator gave them to us for certain reasons. And it is only because of the insufficiency of our intellect that the reasons for some of them are unknown to us, and our investigating them is truly praiseworthy.

Those who forbid us to consider the reasons for the mitzvot have erred

Indeed, according to Maimonides there are two rabbinic statements forbidding such inquiry: the dictum disparaging the prayer formula "Your mercy extends to a bird's nest" (*Guide* 3:48), and possibly also the statement

* "Eight Chapters": Maimonides' ethical treatise that he inserted as his introduction to Treatise Avot in his Commentary to the Mishnah. (LL)

"What does God care if one slaughters from the neck or from the nape? Rather, the mitzvot were only given to purify humankind through them,"* though the latter could also be interpreted in accord with Maimonides' method (3:26). In the latter place he emphasizes that he agrees with the majority of the rabbis who said that King Solomon "knew reasons for all of the mitzvot except for the red heifer" — hence, there are reasons for all of them, and what was taught concerning the whole Torah, "it is not an empty thing for you," means the giving of these mitzvot (i.e., the whole Torah) is not an empty thing without a useful purpose, and if it appears of any of the mitzvot that such is the case, the deficiency is *from you,* in your lack of comprehension. Now, the verse that the people of Israel have *ḥukkim u-mishpatim tzaddikim* — righteous (or just, perfect) statutes and laws — is also pregnant with meaning. Maimonides gives it a straightforward interpretation, taking *ḥukkim* in the rabbinic sense of laws whose reason is hidden from us. This agrees with Ibn Ezra's interpretation, whereas Ibn Daud understood it in the sense of theoretical principles of religion.[5] Reason requires us to acknowledge that God's mitzvot have reasons; otherwise "man would be more perfect than his Maker" (3:31), for no action is considered good unless the actor intended it for a particular objective (3:25).

And yet this rule, that there are reasons for all the mitzvot and it is incumbent on us to inquire about them, is in need of a double qualification.

Caution is required in investigating the reasons for the mitzvot

(1) Maimonides cites (3:26) the rabbinic dictum that the Torah did not reveal the reasons for the mitzvot because King Solomon came to grief precisely in connection with those mitzvot whose reasons had been stated. One should not infer from this that it is forbidden to reveal the reasons for the mitzvot to the laity at all. Maimonides knows that reasons for the mitzvot are not so rare in the Torah (*Sefer Ha-Mitzvot* "The 14 Principles," Principle 5), but he understands that the enlightened person must exercise great *caution* in revealing the reasons for the mitzvot to a public of simple readers. Therefore he only added the reasons for the mitzvot in the *Mishneh Torah* in order to *endear* them, to discourage *superstition,* or to justify the *order* of the mitzvot in his book (such as including the prohibition against

* Maimonides must have understood "to purify humankind" in this saying as meaning "to prepare us for the World to Come through obedience to the Creator's command." Had it meant "to improve us," then the author of the saying would be in agreement that the mitzvot have intrinsic worth [which could be investigated by reason]. (IH)

shaving the corners of the beard among the laws concerning idolatry: see *Hilkhot Avodah Zarah* 12:1). However, he emphasizes in the *Mishneh Torah*, too, that it is proper to investigate the reasons for the mitzvot as much as possible.[6]

Impossible to Explain All the Details

(2) The second limitation touches on the details of the reasons. In the *Guide* (3:26) he writes, "the mitzvah of sacrifice has obvious great benefit, as I plan to explain. But the fact that the one sacrifice is of a sheep and another of a ram, and that they number a specific number, for this it is altogether impossible to explain the cause. And anyone who bothers himself to give a reason for each part of the ritual, in my eyes goes crazy in a prolonged insanity . . . and whoever imagines that the details have such-and-such a reason, is as distant from the truth as the one who imagines that the commandment taken as a whole has no real benefit. And know that wisdom requires this — and if you prefer to say, necessity demands — that there will be parts that do not have an explanation . . . so that if you say: why was there a sheep and not a ram — the same question would have been necessitated if you said ram in place of a sheep, for it would be impossible to have a sacrifice without some species or other; and similarly, if you ask why were there seven sheep and not eight — one would ask the same question if there were eight or ten or twenty, for it would be impossible to specify the command without some number or other." The commentators were justly amazed at this harsh attack,[7] especially after Maimonides himself wrote at the end of his explanation of the commandment (3:49, end): "I have now dealt one by one with all the commandments included in these classes and we have drawn attention to the reasons for them. There are only a few and some slight details for which I have not given reasons, even though in truth we have virtually given reasons also for these, which it will be easy for the comprehending person to derive from our words." We shall see that Maimonides gives a reason for the veneration of the number seven in the Torah, and also explains why the Torah specifically chose a ram for the sin offering. This is not an outright contradiction, as there obviously remained some details whose reasons he did not explain. Still, there are opposing emphases here. It appears that Maimonides wanted to take a stand against the preachers who attempted to show the wisdom of the Torah precisely on the basis of those details that were caused by necessity. It also appears that he forcibly rejected the explanations of those who defended the Torah with blatantly unscientific arguments. In his passion for these issues, he expressed himself in a one-sided manner.

2. The Foundations of Maimonides' Explanation

There is a *purpose* to the mitzvot of the Torah, but what is it? It is obvious that God is not at all in need of His creatures' worship of Him (*Guide* 3:13). The mitzvot, therefore, are intended only for the benefit of humankind. But what is the nature of that benefit?

The Torah's Intention: Perfection of Soul and Perfection of Body

Maimonides responded to this question in Chapter 27 of Part III of the *Guide,* which introduces the whole larger section (Chapters 28–49 of Part III) explaining the mitzvot. "The intention of the whole Torah (its narratives and its precepts) is directed at two things: perfection of the soul and perfection of the body. It is for the soul's perfection that the masses should be taught true opinions, in accordance with their power of understanding, whereas the perfection of the body consists in arrangement of the conditions of their livelihood with each other." These are arranged in two ways: by "prevention of violence among members of society[8]" and by "their instruction in beneficial moral qualities, to the point that affairs of state are well-ordered." We should know that the perfection of the soul has precedence in rank of value, whereas perfection of the body has precedence in nature and in time, "for it is impossible to arrive at the higher goal until the lower goal has been achieved . . . and the human being's ultimate perfection is to achieve enlightenment and self-actualization* to the extent that he knows whatever is in human capacity to know of all existing things . . . clearly this ultimate perfection has nothing to do with deeds and ethical virtues, but is purely contemplative**. . . It is doubtless the most honorable state, and only it is the reason for perpetual life (in the world to come). The true Torah, then, which we have already made clear is unique, namely the Torah of Moses our Master, has come to bring us both perfections together . . . It informs us that the end of this Torah in its entirety is the achievement of these two perfections. For He, may He be exalted, says: 'And the Lord commanded us to do all these statutes [*ḥukkim*], to fear the Lord our God, for our good always, that He might preserve us alive, as it is at this day.' Here he puts the ultimate perfection first because of its superiority; therefore it says, 'for our good always' — i.e., to arrive at the world which is perfectly good. On the other hand, the

* According to Maimonides, every person has the potential to actualize his/her reason but does not achieve full perfection (or "self-actualization" in more modern terms) unless this intellectual potential is properly developed. (IH/LL)

** It is by contemplation that we develop our knowledge and achieve intellectual actualization. (IH)

formula 'that He might preserve us alive' alludes to our corporeal state (which is the lower perfection)."

Three Assumptions for Explaining the Narratives and Precepts of the Torah (With Consideration for Non-Intellectuals Also)

Chapter 27 serves as the basis for explaining the entire Torah, including all its precepts and narratives, and it is based on three assumptions:

(1) The Torah is a divine book. Just as the laws of nature are for the benefit of the majority of creatures but do not take cognizance of exceptional cases, so the Torah has consideration for the majority of humankind (3:34). Therefore Maimonides emphasizes at the start of the chapter (3:27) that its purpose is to impart true views "to the masses." It is taken for granted that ordinary people are more in need of ethical improvement than philosophers, but this does not mean that only the laity have need of the mitzvot. Maimonides himself, who was not shy about showing off his scientific knowledge, acknowledges (3:51) that in terms of his religious personality he does not stand on the same level as the patriarchs. To some extent we may say that precisely the enlightened, who understand the secrets of the Torah and its esoteric meaning, can properly appreciate the wisdom that is revealed both in its narratives and in its precepts.

(2) The Torah is a divine book. Therefore there is a difference between it and man-made laws "as the difference between an idol and a human being."* Its objectives aim higher than the "political governance" that is the objective of the legislation of the Greeks, the devisings of the (pagan) Sabians, and the like, for just as its narratives have not merely a historical value (3:50), so its precepts have not merely a pragmatic value. In each case it is its purpose to guide human beings toward their supreme perfection, either directly or indirectly.

(3) The Torah is a religious book. "Our Torah's entire root and pivot around which it turns is to wipe out these opinions (pertaining to idolatry) from people's hearts" (3:29 end). Therefore Maimonides does not hesitate to agree with the Greek sages, who said that mankind's ultimate perfection is *perfection of intellectual knowledge,* and ethical perfection is only a means to achieving the ultimate perfection.

* This citation from *Maimonides' Letter to Yemen* is altogether reminiscent of Halevi's views. Neuburger cites other similar passages (25).

Maimonides is thus sure that he is interpreting the Torah's intention in this chapter in accordance with its own views and values. In his eyes there is no opposition between our tradition and the ways of "scientific" (i.e., Aristotelian) philosophy; the teleological method, which reveals the purposes of both the narratives and the mitzvot, will demonstrate the meaning and value of the Torah in all its clarity, and whoever denies these purposes appears to Maimonides as impugning the honor of the Torah and its Giver.

According to this outlook, Maimonides establishes in this chapter the criteria that one should employ in order to prove the purpose and value of the mitzvot. However, one may well ask if the results that follow from his assumptions (and especially the third assumption) do not endanger somewhat the value of the mitzvot, and whether Maimonides himself would have agreed with all these conclusions.

From Maimonides' proofs it follows that not everything that is written in the Torah is equally close to its ultimate goal. For that goal is intellectual perfection, and actions of whatever kind are only means to arrive at that goal. Closest to the goal are the narratives that expound God's actions (creation of the world and His providence) and the mitzvot that exhort us concerning the knowledge and love of God (for there is no love without knowledge). Somewhat more distant from these are the mitzvot that recall God's deeds (such as Sabbath, tefillin, Pesaḥ, etc.), as well as the ethical mitzvot (such as "love your neighbor as yourself"), and the political and social mitzvot. Still more remote are those that act on our moral qualities only indirectly, such as the prohibitions on food and sexual intercourse. The same applies to the narratives (3:50).

Thus there is a *gradation* of the mitzvot. But this does not mean that mitzvot that are more remote from the goal should be treated lightly. Maimonides always emphasizes (also in 3:27 in sentences that we have omitted) that the lower objectives are prior conditions for achieving the supreme objective; therefore the value of the mitzvot that lead us to it still stands. The Torah is our guide; what shall we say of the guide who is insistent only on the academic learning of his student and neglects his moral education and his health? Therefore Maimonides explicitly condemns those who belittle the value of the historical narratives (3:50).

And yet, even if there is a rational value to all the mitzvot, we may nevertheless make distinctions, according to Maimonides' assumptions, as to the relative value of the different categories of mitzvot. Can we detect such a distinction in Maimonides' works?

Examples for the Above Principle

We find very little gradational ranking of the commandments in Maimonides. In the *Guide* (3:47)[9] he emphasizes that the Torah does not put a heavy burden upon us, but rather "seeks to lighten the load of religious service; and if you think that some of the mitzvot incur pain or great inconvenience, it is because you are not familiar with the common customs and outlooks of ancient times. Recognize the difference between the idolatrous custom of immolating one's child to the worship of his god and our commandment of sacrificing a dove to the worship of our God!" After citing verses that support his outlook, he proves at length that the Torah restricted access to the Temple through the rules of purity and impurity, and he also remarks that the laws of family purity in the Torah are much less onerous than those of other nations. This is characteristic of Maimonides' position on these matters, and it stands in contrast to the well-known sayings of the rabbis, that the Holy and Blessed One "gave us an abundance of Torah and commandments"* until we are "filled with mitzvot like a pomegranate." His preference for spiritual-intellectual matters over the practical is also prominent in his "Laws of the Fundamental Principles of Torah" (4:13), where he quotes the rabbinic saying (BT *Sukkah* 28a): "A great thing — the work of the divine Chariot,** and a small thing — the disputes of Abaye and Rava." This preference is also manifested in his outlook on sacrifices (*Guide* 3:32): "If the Torah were to have abolished sacrifices, then it would have been asking the people to accept what was inconceivable for them to accept, since human nature has always tended to the customary. It would be similar as if a prophet were to come in our days calling for worship of God and saying: God commanded that you should not pray to Him, or fast, or ask for His salvation in a time of trouble, but rather let your worship be inward thoughts without any action." These last words remind us of his opinion (3:27) that ultimate perfection "consists not of actions but virtues," and they seem to contradict the value of the practical commandments. If we recall that the commandment of Sabbath was given because "correct opinions, if they have no actions to reinforce them, publicize them, and perpetuate their memory among the masses, will never

* Maimonides cites this dictum of R. Hananiah ben Akashya (from the end of Mishnah *Makkot*) and interprets it in the sense that only through the love out of which we perform the mitzvot do we merit the World to Come, and "insofar as they are numerous, it is impossible that a person should not in the course of his life perform at least one of them with its full intentionality, and in doing that mitzvah, his soul will achieve eternal life through that deed." (IH)

** "Work of the divine Chariot" — which for Maimonides meant metaphysical studies and especially Aristotelian philosophical theology. (LL)

survive" (*Guide* 2:31), one can perhaps see Maimonides as approaching the view of the philosophers, who credit the fulfillment of the commandments with only an educational value for the simple masses.*

Joy in the mitzvot that Maimonides showed in his life and works, vs. what he says in certain places

However, we receive an entirely different impression when we discuss the value of Maimonides' commandments not according to lone aphorisms, but according to his actions and literary output. He did not rest content, as is well known, with the keeping of commandments that were sworn upon on Mount Sinai, but rather took upon himself and upon the members of his household a fast to remember his being saved from the tempest of the sea.[10] Whoever is expert in the *Mishneh Torah* knows how much Maimonides appreciated that special "joy of mitzvah" that comes not merely to ordinary people but especially to those who know the deeper nature of the commandments. It is enough to cite his closing words concerning the Festivals of Joy ("Laws of the Lulav" 8:15): "The joy that a person feels in performing the commandment and in the love of who commanded it, this is great worship. And whoever keeps himself from this joy ought to be punished, as it is written: 'Inasmuch as you did not worship the Lord your God in joy and with a good heart.'" Only the appreciation of religious life and affection for the mitzvot can explain how Maimonides (in his introduction to his commentary on the Order *Kodashim* of the Mishnah) could bewail the humiliation of suspending the sacrificial commandments, or how he could invest in them perhaps in the majority of his work on Halakhic literature. From here one can understand the opinion of the scholars who posited a contrast in the evaluation of the commandments as between "Rambam" the legislator and "Maimoni" the philosopher, or "between his halakhic teaching and his religious consciousness."[11]

Tensions with regard to actions

This contrast exists between what he says in *Guide* 3:27 (discussed above) and what is revealed in his work and his way of life. But just as Maimonides has the habit of formulating his opinion in a one-sided way, so it may turn out that this chapter is not the whole of his thought, but rather needs to be complemented based on what he says elsewhere. According to this chapter, our actions have merely an instrumental value.

---

* We shall discuss later whether there are a few mitzvot that were instituted in keeping with the people's ignorance. (IH)

However, in the introduction to his *Commentary on the Mishnah*,[12] he cites the view of the rabbis who say that God has nothing else in His world but the "four cubits" of halakha, because the ideal person of the lower world is the scholar, and "study leads to action." Even more important is his commentary on Mishnah *Peah* 1:1 ("these are things whose fruits a person eats in this world, while the principal remains for the World to Come"). There he distinguishes between two kinds of commandments: the first kind, "that pertain to the person as a private individual in the relationship between himself and God, such as the garment-fringe, tefillin, the Sabbath, and the prohibition of idolatry," whereas the second kind "depend on the utility of human beings to each other, such as the prohibition of theft, exploitation, enmity, and grudge-bearing . . ." Hillel was referring to the second kind in his dictum: "what is hateful to you, do not do to your fellow," and the Mishnah teaches us that even though their performance yields benefit in this world ("if a person behaves thus, others will follow his example"), nevertheless it is also reckoned to his credit for the World to Come. "And if you probe this matter further, you will find that the study of Torah is considered equal in weight to everything else; because through the study of Torah a person comes to achieve all of this (the two types of commandments), as we explained earlier (in his Introduction), that study leads to action."*

Tensions with Regard to Feeling

Secondly: in Chapter 3:27, there is no place for emphasizing the religious sentiments, love and fear, for a person comes to "ultimate perfection . . . when his intellect is fully actualized and he knows everything that is within the human capacity to know." This perfection depends only on religious knowledge. However, in all of his works Maimonides attaches great importance to our religious emotions, in particular to the love of God, about which he talks in several places, sometimes at length and sometimes briefly.[13] And perhaps he agreed with Halevi (*Kuzari* 4:16), that it is through the emphasis on love that "Abraham's teaching surpasses Aristotle's."** We

* In keeping with his delimited conception of action, especially ethical action, he interprets the "woman" referred to in Proverbs as a symbol of matter, whether good or evil, and does not rest content with the moralistic sense of these texts (*Guide* III, 8). Of course, he does not abolish the plain sense either.

** In the marvelous chapter, *Laws of Repentance* 10:2, Maimonides writes on the person who serves out of love: "This quality is a great virtue, and not every wise person attains it; it is the quality of our patriarch Abraham." Hermann Cohen (in the collection *Maimonides* I, 123) believes that this is directed against Aristotle; however Maimonides is not speaking of love of God generally, but in the specific context of observance of the Torah. Still, it is a fact that Aristotle did not mention love in his *Metaphysics* (alluding to it

saw that according to Baḥya it is possible to justify the fulfillment of the mitzvot by the relationship between our actions and the love of God — in two ways: the fulfillment of the commandments *proves* our love (and in that sense is the fruit of love), while at the same time it *generates* love. This double relationship appears also in Maimonides' writings. In his view too (as in the views of Baḥya, Halevi, and Ibn Daud), the patriarch Abraham is God's lover *par excellence* because he acceded to all of God's commands, even to the harshest of all; he agrees with those who say that this trial was decreed on Abraham in order to make known to the world the strength of love (3:24), and he adds (to demonstrate the value of religious feeling) that the goal of the entire Torah is one thing — namely fear of God, and not only knowledge of God. He continues: "The purpose of the deeds prescribed by the Torah is to help people achieve perfection (so that they will achieve the emotion) . . . to fear God may He be blessed . . . the Torah says: 'If you do not faithfully observe all the words of this Torah . . . to fear this revered and awesome Name . . .' It thus makes clear that the intention of all the words in this Torah is one purpose, which is to fear the revered and awesome God" (3:52). Clearly this "fear" that Abraham manifested is different from the fear that constitutes the second step of piety ("Laws of Repentance" 10:1), and it is much closer to love.* It is in accordance with this that we should understand the most important passage (3:51 at the beginning of the "comment") that mediates to some degree between the intellectual goal (of 27) and the sentimental (of 52): "The intellect which flows toward us from God (may He be blessed) is the bond between us and Him. You have the choice: if you wish to strengthen this bond — you can do it, and if you wish to weaken it little by little until you sever it — you can also do that. This connection can only be strengthened by your employing it in loving God." He does not count the sages or the pious of the nations of the world among the people who fulfill this requirement (as Baḥya does), but only Moses and the three patriarchs. And because the correct fear of God and love of God are close to one another, as we have explained, there is no absolute contradiction between his commentary on the Mishnah, which says that the love we show through fulfilling the commandments entitles us to a share in the World to Come, and the end of the *Guide* (3:52), which remarks that "through the views that the Torah teaches us we come to love God" (see also 3:28), while our deeds inculcate fear of God. Generally the

---

only in his *Ethics* and *Rhetoric*), and that Maimonides, when speaking of love of God, based himself on Jewish sources, and learned from Halevi particularly with respect to the difference between the religious relationship connoted by the different divine names *Elohim* ("God") and *Adonai* ("Lord").

* See Ibn Daud, *Emunah Ramah* 100, on the two kinds of fear, and Albo's differentiation of two kinds of religious emotion below.

Guide ascribes to the mitzvot and their performance much value besides the "intellectual," which is stressed exclusively in Chapter 3:27. Their performance demonstrates and also reinforces our religious sentiments, in which the great personalities of Jewish tradition, including the patriarchs, excelled; it elevates us in this world and strengthens the connection between us and God, on account of which we will merit life in the World to Come.

The relation between theoretical and practical man

The value placed on action and religious feeling certainly qualifies the intellectualism that one senses in Chapter 3:27 and softens its pungency to some extent, but it does not cancel the distinction between "men of action" and Maimonides himself, a man of theory and knowledge. This distinction is made clear in the *Mishneh Torah* no less than in the *Guide*. Whereas Jacob ben Asher, author of the *Tur,* prefaces his description of the commandments with the dictum of Judah Ben Tema: "Be strong as a leopard, light as an eagle, quick as a gazelle and strong as a lion to do the will of your Father in Heaven," Maimonides begins: "The foundation of foundations and the pillar of wisdom is to know that there is a First Cause that gives being to all of existence," and in the second chapter he adds: "This honored and awesome God commands (us) to love and to fear him." Correct knowledge purified of every superstition constitutes the necessary basis of all our religious feelings and actions, according to Maimonides. Such a level-headed intellectualism does not, of course, contradict the appreciation for the mitzvot that Maimonides showed in his life and in his writings, especially in his description of the ideal of the pious sage who sanctifies God through the way in which he lives, "engaged in study of Torah while wrapped in tallit, crowned with tefillin, and scrupulous in all his actions beyond the requirement of the law" ("Foundations of the Torah," 5:11).

However, we should not forget that Maimonides expressed his intellectualism more forthrightly precisely in connection with the most important of topics — in establishing the basis for the explanation of the commandments (3:27). We must inquire to what extent the foundation shaped the larger structure, and then explain the reasons that motivated this one-sided formulation.

3. The explanation of the Commandments

Maimonides divides the commandments into fourteen groups in order to explain them (*Guide* 3:35) and gives a reason for each group. It is impossible, of course, to describe his explanation here in detail. We will only try to elucidate Maimonides' characteristic methodology. For this purpose, it is enough to point to a few examples of his explanations.

Explanations that Maimonides rejects

Maimonides' style of thought is distinctly discernible, not only in those explanations that he accepts and innovates, but also in those that he rejects. In this he is a complete rationalist, in that any explanation that is incompatible with a scientific outlook is null and void for him. Therefore, he passes silently over any explanation that smacks of superstition; "even though blowing the Shofar on Rosh Hashanah is an apodictic decree," it is given "in order to awaken the sleeping from their slumber" (Laws of Repentance 3:4), but he does not mention the reason "in order to confuse Satan,"* and he vents all his wrath upon "those who write inside (the mezuzah) angelic or mystical names . . . surely they forfeit their place in the World to Come; for these fools, it is not enough for them that they have violated the commandments, but they have turned the greatest commandment, namely declaration of the Unity of the Holy and Blessed God, along with the love and worship of Him, into an amulet for their private benefit."[14] And because astrology is only a superstition for Maimonides, he does not cite the astrological explanations of which Ibn Ezra was so fond.

*Casual supports (**asmakhta**)*

There are other explanations that a scientific approach rejects, not because of their assumptions but because of their methodology. With complete justice, Maimonides emphasizes [*Guide* 3:43] that the Rabbis, in discussing the reasons for the mitzvot, often did not aim to identify and explain the original reasons of the legislator, but rather to graft their own wise or moral insights onto the text. Maimonides did not question the educational value of such comments, but they are not useful, according to him, for the purpose of explaining the commandments. As an example of this procedure, he cites the explanation of the "four species" [of the lulav and etrog brought on Sukkot]. He similarly rejects the aggadic explanation for the prohibition against metal work on the altar (3:45). He would rather acknowledge that he does not have a sufficient answer

* This picturesque rabbinic explanation is found in the Babylonian Talmud, *Rosh Hashanah* 16b. But the 15th-century philosopher Isaac Abravanel interpreted "Satan" in this passage as referring to the evil urge.

for the use of the cedar tree and the scarlet [in the purification ritual of Numbers 19] than to accept the aggadic explanation (3:47, end). He dismisses the explanation of the gifts of the priesthood without even mentioning it (3:39). So too with the matter of the punishment of property theft and personal robbery (3:41 — see above, page 27). Not only does he explain the difference between them with a sober reason, but he disagrees with the assumption that the punishment is proportionate to the transgression. However, he agrees with the view that leprosy is a punishment for slander, perhaps because of the episode of Miriam. Mystical reasons are very rare for Maimonides, as are symbolic ones (see *Guide* 3:46 regarding the scapegoat) or purely emotional ones (3:46) such as his explanation that the purpose of the laws of impurity is to inculcate reverence for the Temple. It is possible to call almost all of the reasons that he cites "rational," but they are quite varied, even though it is not his way to add multiple explanations like Ibn Ezra.

Utilitarian Reasons

Because the Torah aims also at our benefit, it stands to reason that utilitarian explanations are not completely absent in his works. The incense purifies the air in the Temple so that the odor of the meat will not spoil our reverence; the pig is forbidden because of the dirtiness involved in raising it, as evidenced by the experience of Christian lands (3:48), for the Torah maintains cleanliness (3:33); the commandment of circumcision, the commandments of the Sabbath, and the prohibition of the licentious all have utilitarian purposes (3:49).

Of course, the moral explanations are more important in his eyes.

Some of the Moral Explanations are Social

The Torah is based on justice, especially in matters of penal law (3:41). Maimonides emphasized according to the plain meaning of the text — and in the *Guide* he seeks to explain only the plain meaning, not the traditional understanding* — all punishments are completely appropriate

* So he says explicitly near the start of *Guide* III, 41, using the term *fiqh* (which Ibn Tibbon renders "Talmud"). He also says that he will share his view on the Talmudic interpretation of *lex talionis* only "face to face." It would seem that he did not agree entirely with the accepted traditional interpretation, though he ruled according to it in the *Mishneh Torah*; he does not specify to what extent his personal interpretation differed from the tradition. We should not be surprised that he interpreted some verses contrary to the received law, albeit rarely. See Hanokh Albeck's remarks in *Jubilee Volume for B. M. Lewin*, 93, on the methods of the translators and certain plain-sense commentators of the Middle Ages.

for the action of the sinner, even though it is possible to soften the penalty in all cases except for the sin of murder. He notes (3:33) that the Torah is strict on setting limits to our desires, which distract us from pursuing our ultimate goal. In this manner he explains the sexual and dietary prohibitions (3:48), as well as the commandment of circumcision (3:49), even though he also cites other reasons for these types of commandments (such as the prohibition of pork, or the mixture of meat and milk). He emphasizes the social character of the Israelite religion in his commentary on the Mishnah (introduction to Tractate *Peah*) and in the *Mishneh Torah* (at the end of "Laws of Gifts to the Poor," as well as in his description of the proper celebration of Purim in "Laws of Megillah and Hanukkah 2:17: "There is no greater or more splendid rejoicing than gladdening the hearts of the poor," etc.). In the *Guide* he deals only briefly with sociological reasons (see his discussion of *tzedakah* and tithing in 3:39 and the end of 3:26). However he does consider the prohibition of cruelty to animals to explain ritual slaughter and the prohibition of slaughtering an animal and its offspring at the same time (3:48); in connection with this commandment he learns from the exegetical principle of "minor to major" that from the compassion we are required to show animals, all the more so are we forbidden to bring trouble to our human neighbor. (See also 3:42, end, concerning the love of humankind.) It is impossible, therefore, to say that Maimonides expresses an asocial outlook here.*

However, Maimonides tried above all to find an *intellectual* value for the commandments in four ways:

(1) Commemorating historical facts

The mitzvot remind us of historical facts that are laden with religious value: not only is the Sabbath a commemoration of creation, and not only are the three major festivals a commemoration of the Exodus from Egypt (3:43), but Maimonides (*ibid.*) adopts the view that on the Day of Atonement Moses went down to the people in order to announce the good news that God had pardoned them for making the golden calf (3:46). He also agrees with those who say that the sacrificial bull of the high priest "atoned for the sin of the golden calf." He does not even condemn as

* Such an argument is advanced by Neuburger (13 and 40). He rests his case on *Guide* III, 54 (speaking of the fourth and highest perfection, the "rational"): "Therefore you ought to desire to achieve this thing, which will remain permanently with you, and not weary and trouble yourself for the sake of others" (Pines English translation 635). But these words should be interpreted in the context of Maimonides' previous remarks. Our obligation to achieve intellectual perfection ranks higher than the practical mitzvot, but does not abolish them! See the summary of the present chapter.

"weak" the midrashic explanation according to which the sin offering of the male goat alludes to the goat of the Joseph story,* despite the criticisms he directed against similar explanations in the aggadic literature. In line with the positive valuation of emotion that we mentioned, he points out that the remembrance of our torments in Egypt and in the wilderness is likely to implant in our hearts feelings of thanksgiving to the Creator, that God brought us out from a life of suffering to a pleasant life, whereas the memory of sin awakens our hearts and brings us to repentance.

(2) Cosmological explanations

In contrast to Ibn Ezra, cosmological explanations are uncommon for Maimonides. However, Maimonides emphasized that the same wisdom that is revealed in the work of nature is also visible in the Torah (3:32, 34), but the idea that the Torah "is always similar to nature" (3:43) is only exemplified by pointing to the number seven, whose value is known in the Torah and in the works of nature.

(3) Inculcating the Fear of Heaven

There are many mitzvot whose purpose is to implant within our hearts "the perpetual remembrance of God, fear and love of Him, observance of all of the commandments, and belief in God (may He be blessed), for it is necessary to all religious people to believe in him. These are the commandments of prayer, recitation of the Shema, the blessing after meals, and whatever pertains to them; as well as the Priestly Blessing, tefillin, mezuzah, the garment-fringe, acquiring a Torah scroll, and the obligation to read from it frequently" (3:44). He only devotes a few lines and alludes to what he has written about all of these commandments in his "Book of Adoration" [*Mishneh Torah* Book 3], not because these commandments are regarded as minor (for indeed they leave their imprint on all our daily lives, and there is no commandment that he values more than the study of Torah), but rather because "it is all so obvious and well-known."

(4) Distancing Us from Idol Worship

Typical of Maimonides' explanations is his striving to prove that the Torah wanted to distance us from idol worship and from the disgusting practices connected to it. He believed that to this end, the Torah utilized two means: first, it forbade several practices that were associated with idol

* Slaughtered by the brothers to use its blood to stain Joseph's cloak. (LL)

worship, and second, it preserved the sacrifices out of a worry that the people would totally break faith and sacrifice to pagan gods if the offering of sacrifices were to be completely forbidden. The germ of the first reason (see *Guide* 3:29), and, according to Maimonides, also of the second (see below), is hinted at in the Torah itself. However, in order to amplify the first and realize its value to the fullest, he invested considerable effort to investigate the practices of idolatry, and the more he delved into them, the more he became convinced of the unsightliness of their ritual and in the right-mindedness of the Torah in outlawing their ways. The relationships between the mitzvot of the Torah and the practices of idol worshipers that he exposed were very important in his eyes: they enable him to discover the unseen reason for several of the mitzvot (3:28), to attribute to these mitzvot a theoretical value, and to prove accordingly his assumption (3:27) that "our entire Torah has its root and the pivot on which it revolves to wipe out these opinions from our hearts" (29 at the end).

Already in the *Mishneh Torah* he listed the prohibitions of tonsure (cutting the hair) and cutting the beard among the laws against idol worship (12:1) "because he found them surrounded in front and back with mitzvot that are forbidden because they are practices by idol worshipers" (these are the words of Joseph Caro's *Beit Yosef* on the *Tur Yoreh Deah* 181). In the *Guide of the Perplexed* he writes at length especially about these issues (3:37). There, he clarifies the relationship between sorcery and the worship of pagan gods (and particularly the worship of the astral bodies) and notes that it was specifically women who performed these acts of sorcery, and thus the punishment for "sorceresses" is clarified. In addition to the prohibitions against cutting the hair and beard, he also mentions the prohibition of *sha'atnez* (mixed fabrics), as idol worshipers used to wear wool and linen together, and would also, as part of their ritual, dress men in women's clothing and vice versa. He adds that this practice was forbidden because it leads to prostitution. Of utmost importance to Maimonides is the fact that the agricultural worship of the nations of the world was connected to unsightly and filthy acts; therefore, the Torah forbade eating the fruit of trees during the first three years (*'orlah*), grafting, and cross-breeding in the vineyard. According to Maimonides, the statement of R. Josiah, which forbade cross-breeding in the vineyard "only if wheat and barley and grape-seeds were planted together with one hand-throw" proves that already "he saw the essence of this matter in the ways of the Amorites." Maimonides also sees the Torah's intent in this matter that the beasts that the nations of the world idolize were allocated for our sacrifices (3:46), and there he notes that only the goat for the new month was called "a sin-offering for God" because the Egyptians used to sacrifice to their gods specifically on new moons.

The Sacrifices: Weaning Us from Idolatry

However, despite the fact that the Torah forbade anything having to do with idol worship, there is one major exception, namely the sacrifices. Maimonides explains these mitzvot on the basis of the fact that all nations of the world brought their sacrifices to their gods. Therefore, Israel was also used to this type of worship, and if God were to forbid them from all acts of sacrifice, they would be driven back to idolatry (3:32). For God did not lead the people to the land of Israel directly "lest they have a change of heart and return to Egypt." God certainly had the ability to strengthen their hearts so that they would be prepared immediately to fight the Anakites, but it is not God's way to manipulate our character. Similarly, God did not do away entirely with the familiar ritual, but gave it a place in the monotheistic cult. Together with this, there are, indeed, special reasons for details of the cultic practices*; but the basic rubric of the Temple worship was established or, more precisely, was permitted in order to distance the people from sin.

His Proofs

Maimonides indeed knows that this idea will be a stumbling block for many readers (3:32),** but he is certain that it has a basis in the Bible, in philosophy, and in educational theory:

(1) The Torah itself hinted at its intention when it commanded to bring every animal about to be slaughtered to the Tent of Meeting so that the nation should not sacrifice to the goat-satyrs (see Leviticus 17). However, its opinion about the value of the sacrifices stands out because it placed no restrictions on prayer or on the mitzvot of tefillin, mezuzah, and the like, but only on access to the Temple, both by prohibiting worship in other high places (3:32) and by the laws of impurity (3:35, 47). The prophets revealed what the Torah demonstrated through its commands when they said that God does not desire "burnt-offerings and sacrifices, so much as hearkening to the voice of God," and in other speeches similar to this statement (3:32).

* See above concerning the scapegoat and the High Priest's bullock-offering. (IH)

** My student and friend Dr. Ephraim Urbach has made me aware of the words of R. Joseph ben Todros Abulafia (in Koback's *Jeshurun* 28:36): "It was told to us some years ago that our Teacher the author of this work sought to suppress Part III which speaks of the reasons for the mitzvot, but he was not able to do so because it had already been published among the farthest isles. He thought it had crossed the line in suspending mountains from a thread." How far one should trust such hearsay evidence is doubtful, but it is credible that Maimonides himself recognized even more keenly, from the debate occasioned by this portion, the difficulties to which his speculations gave rise. (IH)

(2) Regarding the question of why the Torah and the prophets saw fit to diminish the value of the sacrifices, philosophy answers: "Since this way of worship . . . is in keeping with the 'second intention' [i.e., a means to an end], whereas spontaneous outcry, prayer and similar types of worship are closer to the [primary] intention and are necessary to arrive at God (that is to say, to arrive at the primary intention)" (*ibid.*). The Torah did not attribute independent value to the sacrifices; their value is only indirect, as a means for countering idolatry, whereas prayer plants directly in our heart the proper knowledge of and cleaving to the Divine.

(3) By not requiring from the Israelite nation only the "service of the heart," but by also maintaining, ordering, and in some sense authorizing the ritual mode that was customary for the people of that time, the Torah demonstrated unparalleled wisdom. In its stories it imparted to the masses "true doctrines to the extent of their capacity of understanding" (3:27), and because of this it spoke more than once "in human language," that is to say by way of parables, whose true sense is revealed only to people of science. Similarly, in its injunctions it showed consideration for the level of ordinary human beings, and it commanded and forbade only what they could tolerate; those with deeper understanding should explain its intentions.

Maimonides, Ibn Daud and Modern Rationalists

Maimonides utilized this explanation — that the Torah acceded to certain mitzvot in order not to place a stumbling block before those inclined towards idol worship — only for the explanation of the sacrifices. He knows, of course, that the nations of the world also have celebrations that are similar to ours (3:43) and laws of purity and impurity (47), but it never occurred to him to say that the Torah enacted what it enacted because the people were used to these practices,* and needless to say, he never gave a similar explanation for the other "hortative" mitzvot, such as prohibitions of specific foods, which it certainly had not been Israel's habit to eat in Egypt. On this matter there is also a difference between the mitzvot of the sacrifices and the other "hortative" mitzvot, for the Torah restricted the Temple worship to a great extent. Maimonides' view on the sacrifices is based, however, not only on the speeches of the Prophets and the philosophical viewpoint, but also on the Torah; in this he deviates from Ibn

* Only in the case of levirate marriage did Maimonides emphasize (III, 49) that the practice existed prior to the Torah and the Torah allowed it to stand. (IH)

Daud, who attributed a certain "weakness" to all of the "mitzvot enacted in wisdom." However, both of them measured the Torah's mitzvot with the same rational criteria; this commonality stands out in Maimonides' more comprehensive explanation than the short chapter that Ibn Daud dedicated to the mitzvot. Because of this, Maimonides has received in our days a strange "honor": some saw him as a pioneer for the supporters of the fictitious "Prophetic Judaism," who say that the Prophets, in opposition to the Torah, were fed up with all of the ceremonial mitzvot, especially everything having to do with the Temple worship. Those who say this err concerning the essence of Maimonides' conception. Indeed, he deviates from their idea that the Temple worship was "the worship" *par excellence*, and he differs with Halevi and Ibn Daud, who say (each in his own way) that it is impossible to attain the results of the sacrifices through a different ritual such as prayer. According to Maimonides, the value of the sacrifices is not equivalent the value of "service of the heart." But this does not say that the enacting of this ritual testifies to a "religious concept of inferior value," like the opinion of Geiger and Cohen and their colleagues. The Prophets did not oppose the sacrifices (according to Maimonides) but would "rebuke the people for their excessive zeal in bringing sacrifices, and explained to them that they are not the object of a purpose sought for its own sake, and that God can dispense with them" (3:32). They opposed the excessive esteem of this mitzvah and the superstition into which most people of their time certainly fell: that it is possible to influence God with "gifts." Indeed, Maimonides emphasizes that the Torah had consideration for "those of weak opinion," just as Baḥya did before him, but as for the "developmental hypothesis," which says that throughout the generations human beings will develop from religious naïveté to a more sophisticated conception — only minuscule beginnings of this method* are found in Maimonides, and they are less daring than the opinions of some of the Talmudic rabbis who say that the mitzvot will be nullified when the Messiah comes.[15] According to Maimonides, did not the patriarch Abraham reach the pinnacle of religious perfection (*Guide* 3:51 etc.)? In several places in all of his books Maimonides emphasizes that God will never nullify even one of the statutes of the Torah.[16] Therefore, he dedicated great effort to the mitzvot of the sacrifices. We have already noted that in his introduction to the explanation of the "Book of Sanctities" he criticizes those many Talmudical scholars who neglect these mitzvot,

* Maimonides believed in the progress of knowledge (*Guide* III, 14, end). But the Greeks already made the distinction between scientific knowledge which advances, and religion whose most perfect exemplars were found in antiquity. (See my *Poseidonions metaphysische Schriften* I, 88ff.) From *Guide* III, 33 we can deduce at most that it is possible to raise the popular masses slowly to the level where the greatest of the ancients stood. (IH)

and in his halakhic masterpiece he deals with them no less than the rest of the mitzvot in the Torah — even though the halakhic decisors who came after him dealt only with those mitzvot that apply in our day.

Summary

More Than Just Intellectualism

The explanation of the commandments in the *Guide* is one-sided and does not express the outlook of Maimonides in its entirety: first, because its fundamental approach, as expressed in Part III, Chapter 27, emphasizes the value of intellectual beliefs in comparison with actions and emotions. Second, because it was Maimonides' purpose in this book only to resolve the difficulties that were encountered by his colleagues who had a prior positive view of both Torah and science, he did not deem it necessary to delve at length into social and emotional rationales whose value the philosophers already conceded.[17] Our lengthy treatment of the *Guide*, therefore, needs supplementation. In order to do so, we cannot be satisfied with the reasons that he offered in the rest of his books. Is it not the case that in "the Book of Love" of the *Mishneh Torah* he spoke not at all about love, but rather assumed that the reader would justify the name of the book from his religious experience? — Precisely that which is self-evident and needs no explanation reveals the roots of the author's thoughts and his intentions. It is up to us to complement the intellectualism contained in the proofs of the *Guide* on the basis of his life, which testifies to his devotion to the commandments, as well as those sparks of religious enthusiasm that flash forth from a number of different places in his works, as we explained above in "Foundations of the Explanation."

But a review of the details of the explanation confirms what we have already emphasized: his appreciation of emotion comes only to soften, and not to annul, the intellectual character of his approach. We can summarize his basic view as follows: The correct understanding of faith, bringing us to good deeds, and connected to the emotions of love and fear, constitutes our ultimate perfection; the mitzvot were given in order to implant it in the hearts of all the Jewish people, to secure it and protect it.

A Comprehensive, Many-Sided Approach

This, of course, is a kind of rationalism. But the rationalism of Maimonides and its foundation are clarified further when we methodically compare his explanation to those of the philosophers who came before him. It surpasses all of them in its wide scope, its many-faceted character, and its overall unity. It encompasses all the commandments that are difficult to explicate (such as the commandment of levirate marriage). Maimonides' explanation "brings its food from afar" (cf. Proverbs 31:14), even more so than the explanation of Ibn Ezra, which indeed used the pseudo-science of astrology, but not the perspective of history. His explanation is even more precise than that of Ibn Daud in proving that there is one purpose and one reason for every mitzvah in the Torah. Maimonides' explanation is hence more "scientific" than the explanations of the philosophers who came before him. Maimonides recognized that he alone absolutely rejected all unscientific explications, as we observed previously.*

The astounding fact is that Maimonides (and again it should be added: and only he) recognized and emphasized explicitly that there are those who oppose all explanations of the commandments, not from among the lay Jews of his era alone, but even from within the rabbinical circle. They constitute only a minority, and every lawmaker, as is known, has the right to follow the majority. But in any event, he acknowledges that the central question is also debatable among men invested with religious authority, which they received from the prophets (*Guide* 3:14, end).

Three Kinds of "Believers," Two in Error

These two facts (the emphasis on scientific method and the controversial aspect) are related, and can be understood on the basis of the general assumptions of his thought-system, which are especially prominent in the exposition of his theology.[18] He considers three types of "believers": (1) Those who ascribe physical attributes to God; they are complete heretics in his view, and it is a great mitzvah to enlighten them. (2) Those who believe in spiritual attributes, like our psychological attributes; we ought not debate with them, even though they err, so that they will not become confused. (3) Only those of the third group — "so few, that they can scarcely be called a group"[19] — are able to hold onto both Torah and philosophy until "there is a unity of the two"; this group will not succeed until after they have struggled prodigiously with the matter. To such struggles, the *Guide* itself is testimony! And what is their reward for all their labor? Not only do they present the truth in its full clarity, but they also penetrate into the genuine intention of the Torah and bring to light all of its right and truth, which have been hidden from the eyes of the people. For it is the true understanding of God's unity, which contradicts all the positive attributes (except for the attributes of action, which are not to be called "attributes"

* See above, page 108.

in the proper sense) that one cannot know except by relying on scientific reasons. The Torah is in need, therefore, of scientific elucidation, just as a diamond does not reveal its luminosity unless it is properly polished.

Advantage of all the mitzvot

All this applies not only to the theoretical content of the Torah, but also to its commandments. On this point Maimonides diverges from Ibn Daud, to whom he is otherwise closest. With regard to the verse "this will be proof of your wisdom and discernment to other peoples, who on hearing of these laws will say 'Surely, that great nation is a wise and discerning people,'" Ibn Daud explains (*Emunah Ramah* p. 4): "This is not said regarding the hortative commandments; for there is nothing wondrous about them in the eyes of those who are not of our nation. Nor is this said regarding the political laws and ethical virtues; for every thinking person is able to posit them as a rule for himself . . . but rather this was said regarding the amazement of the nations when they inquired of the roots of the Jewish faith." By contrast, Maimonides explains the verse according to its plain meaning (*Guide* 3:33) and takes it upon himself to bring to light the value of *all* the commandments — indeed not to the eyes of the general populace, but to the scientific-minded of the other nations. According to his view, this objective could not have been achieved by the methods of Philo (whom Maimonides did not know), Saadia, or Baḥya. Emphasis on the ethical and social content of the mitzvot could succeed only in shutting the mouths of the adversaries who completely deny the utility of the Torah, and could serve at most to prove that our commandments are superior *in degree* to the laws of the other nations, but not to give evidence to the *qualitative* and essential superiority of the Torah, which is "alone called a divine law, whereas the rest of the political regimens were instituted by politicians, not prophets" (*Guide* 2:39).[20]

Why is only the Torah called a divine law?

This distinction between the divine Torah and all human devisings was not emphasized in such a sharp manner by the previous philosophers, except for Halevi, and Halevi's way of doing this was not possible for Maimonides, who did not believe in "the religious superman" who constitutes a separate species in his own right. Thus there remained before him only one path: to connect the commandments with the religious intention (and together with this — the scientific) of the Torah — the intention that distinguishes between the Torah and secular regimens in order to guide us to acknowledge the absolute unity of God. In carrying out this idea, it became clear to him that specifically these commandments that were a stumbling block to the philosophers, such as the commandment of the sacrifices, the prohibitions of cross-breeding, fabric mixtures, and the like, were directed to this theoretical goal, inasmuch as they remove from our hearts the erroneous ideas and repulsive practices whose foundations lie in these ideas. Perhaps there will be critics who will say to Maimonides: Indeed, you have set out to emphasize also action and emotion, which are characteristic features of the Jewish way, but you remained stuck in mid-course[21] and were not able to free yourself from the chains of Greek rationalism. But to this criticism Maimonides would reply: On the contrary! The ones who are stuck in mid-course are those, who look only at the ethical and utilitarian value of the commandments — a value that is found also in the laws of the nations of the world (how many nice adages of the pious of the nations of the world did R. Baḥya cite!), or who rejected the reasons for the commandments and regarded them as without purpose — as if one of the gods ruling over humankind in the manner of despots had given us the Torah! My own explanation has its foundation in the faith of the nation of Israel: The God who is perfect in His ways wants to reward us by means of that which will teach us the path to ultimate perfection, and specifically those commandments that lead to this goal only by indirect means. For example, the sacrifices demonstrate to us the wisdom that we admire in the arrangement of nature (*Guide* 3:33), and they give evidence of the godly source of the Torah.

We have not come either to defend Maimonides or to judge him, but rather to explain his views and his reasons and thereby to elucidate his explanation of the commandments, in which all his finer qualities are displayed: his sharpness, his perseverance, his command of the sea of Talmud, and the breadth of his knowledge that encompasses the literature of non-Jews, both philosophical and cultural. All those who took an interest in him after his time would ask this question: To what extent was he correct in his explanation of the reasons for the commandments? In the following chapters we shall expound the views of the thinkers who enlarged on or retreated from the method of Maimonides.

Chapter 12
Gersonides

Comprehensive Explanation for All Narratives and Mitzvot

Rabbi Levi ben Gershon (in Latin, Gersonides) was also one the students of Aristotle, and even the most radical among them: his views on the creation of the world and on divine providence are much closer to those of Aristotle and his commentators than the views of Maimonides are. We might have assumed on that basis that regarding the value of the hortative commandments (especially the sacrificial service) and their details he might have strayed far from the traditional position and confessed their "weakness," even more than Ibn Daud and Maimonides. However, if we read his commentary on the Torah from this assumption, we will be completely surprised. We shall not find a single one of the sages of Israel who invests more diligence than he in the explanations of *all of the details* of the commandments. And these efforts of his have their foundation in an approach no less scientific than those of his predecessors; his introduction to his commentary on the Torah[1] declares that all parts of the Torah, including the commandments, were given "to guide us to the true perfection that is the 'fruit' of every human being," and his explanation of the "fruit" is "that we shall ponder the truths of existent beings" (137c), in agreement with the views of Maimonides (*Guide* 3:27). He also rejects decisively all rabbinic interpretations that appear unscientific (2c). On the contrary, we can say that his efforts to pile up the innumerable "benefits" of all of the commandments of the Torah and all of its stories (for the Book of Esther he attributes fifty benefits!) derives overall from his sober character, in which he is similar to Aristotle, and from his preference for the "final" (purposive) cause,[2] requiring a teleological explanation, which he took from Aristotle's teaching. To be sure, he diverges from the method of Aristotle and his school in a direction that he believes is no less scientific than the philosophical method. Gersonides — the famous mathematician and astronomer — agrees with Ibn Ezra* in affirming that

* Gersonides regards Maimonides and Ibn Ezra as his mentors. (See the start of his commentary to Genesis 2, beginning "the middle world.")

the "middle" (celestial) world, especially the constellations, has an effect on our lower (terrestrial) world, and that it is possible for us to annul its evil influences by means of specified deeds, among which are those deeds concerning which the Torah commands us. Finding his scientific ideas in the words of the Bible, especially those ideas that are remote from the spirit of the text, enabled Gersonides, with his marvelous ingenuity, to delve deeply into the mitzvot (and similarly into the narratives) in order to confirm his views and to raise the prestige of the Torah at the same time.

We shall identify the various viewpoints that he takes in explanation of the mitzvot, and we shall show the manysidedness that he displays in his interpretation of certain mitzvot that he believes are especially important.

Hygienic Reasons

If the principal intention of the Torah is to bring us to spiritual perfection, nevertheless "what follows from observing the commandments of the Torah and its laws and statutes are wondrous physical benefits, and not just spiritual benefits only, and from their neglect ensue great physical evils, not only spiritual evils" (*Commentary on the Torah,* Portion *Ekev,* Application 26). This is not just a matter of providential supervision. The dietary prohibitions also have hygienic reasons; the animal that possesses the two well-known signs "is more suited for a human's physiological temperament to be nourished from it" (Leviticus 11), "and the doctors have already said of a woman who becomes pregnant in the days of her menstrual impurity, that her child will be a leper" (*Commentary, Shemini* end, 138b).

Many mitzvot act on our moral qualities

Many commandments have an effect on our moral qualities, especially to moderate our appetites. Circumcision was commanded, "as Maimonides mentioned," to temper our sexual potency (Leviticus 15, Application 3); the regulations of ritual impurity also limit the same act, which should not be done "unless there is a need, and not for pleasure-seeking" (*Shemini,* end); and the Torah's injunctions concerning the impurity of seminal emissions caution one against evil thoughts (Deuteronomy 22:13, Application 10).

Relatively uncommon are social reasons. Of course he emphasizes the social reasons for the laws governing slavery (Exodus 21:1, Application 1) and the sabbatical year (*Behar,* end and Application 10), and he also explains the rule of sending away the mother bird and the prohibition of milk-meat mixtures by the principle of cruelty toward animals (Deuteronomy 26:6), but he dedicates no more than eight lines to the commandment of "you shall love your neighbor as yourself" (161a).

More important in Gersonides' eyes, and also more common, are *spiritual-intellectual* reasons, based on the assumption that the Torah seeks to teach us true opinions. He thinks that only through knowledge of nature is it possible to arrive at knowledge of God, from which flows also religious love (as mandated by the verse "You shall love the Lord your God [Deut. 6:4]). Therefore, to Gersonides, the Torah is somewhat of a study-book of natural science, and its mitzvot serve likewise as the means to this study. The Torah commanded us to recite the Shema morning and evening, so that we should have occasion to observe the motions of the stars (which are testimony to God's providence: Deut. 6–7 Application 5). The utility of the fringes is not only ethical (on this, Gersonides cites the rabbis) but also "so that a person be guided to acknowledge God's existence . . . for the four corners symbolize the four elements . . . and the woven fringe symbolizes the many things that arise from their combination, whereas the blue thread binding the fringe together symbolizes the heavenly powers which are similar to them in their blue appearance" (he elaborates on all these points in his commentary to the portion of the fringes, Numbers 15). He explains the command of the red heifer with the aid of his views on the immortality of the intellect (not the whole soul), which survives into the world to come but cannot acquire any more additional knowledge because it has become separated from the senses. For this reason one must select a heifer that has not borne the yoke and thus cannot do any additional work, like this intellect that can no longer continue in its activity (*Parah,* and see also what he writes about the broken-necked heifer, Deuteronomy 21). These examples are sufficient for us to understand Gersonides' method without having to disclose all the details of his philosophy.

These matters will be clarified still further when we add the explanation of the two mitzvot for which Gersonides offers many reasons, in the manner of Ibn Ezra — namely, the Sabbath and the sacrifices.

The reasons for the mitzvah of the Sabbath

The Sabbath (*Commentary,* The Ten Commandments, Application 6) commemorates the creation of the world and the Exodus from Egypt, which testify to God's sovereignty in the world. It has another benefit of "perfecting the soul," for our troubling ourselves with our business prevents us from investigating the secrets of the world, through which we can come to know the reality of God. Because of this it is called "a Sabbath *to the Lord,*" and this benefit applies also to the festivals. However, the number seven teaches that God is the "seventh form,"* and perhaps because of this the Torah juxtaposed the mitzvah of Sabbath with the prohibition of idol worship.** Sabbath observance also has a "political" benefit (in Gersonides' words), for every working person will toil especially hard when he knows that a period of rest is near. Additionally, those who love God and who cleave to Him are immune on the Sabbath to the evil influences that come from the harmful stars on the seventh day, in accord with Ibn Ezra's view. Astrological explanations like these are not rare: Yom Kippur was fixed in the seventh month "when the sun enters the realm of the southern zodiac" and on the tenth day of that month "to teach that the number of separate intelligences is ten"*** (comment on Leviticus 16, end).

Gersonides' critique of Maimonides on the sacrifices

Regarding the sacrifices, Gersonides agrees with Maimonides that some of the mitzvot in the Torah were given in order to distance the people from idol worship; only with regard to the prohibition against men wearing women's clothing does he provide an ethical reason alone (comment on Deut. 22:5) without mentioning Maimonides' explanation. He explains (commenting on *Kedoshim*) the prohibitions of mixed fabrics and cross-breeding according to the rationale given in the *Guide*, and adds that these mitzvot were also given in order for us to distinguish between the Forms and thus recognize the Creator, Who apportioned them to His creations. Thus, his opinion is that although the explanation of the sacrifices in the *Guide* is not erroneous, it is one-sided (comment on *Tzav,* end):

> The Torah used one law to teach many lessons, as the Torah makes clear with respect to the Sabbath . . . ; indeed, one of its intentions was to wean them . . . from sacrificing to idols, as the Torah mentions explicitly in

* The lower forms are: (1) the form of the elements, (2) of composite bodies formed of the elements, (3) of plants, (4) of animals, (5) of human beings, and (6) of the Separate Intellects (see below). About other numbers that allude to God, compare Gersonides' Commentary on Numbers 28, Application 10. For another explanation of the number 7, see *Haḥodesh* (Exodus 12), Application 11.

** Commentary on Numbers 15:32. It is part of Gersonides' method to interpret "*semukhim*" (i.e., the juxtaposition of various topics in consecutive passages of the Torah, which are assumed to have been placed together for some special purpose). See his Commentary on Leviticus 19, and on Deuteronomy 23:18 ff. on the connection of the laws of interest and the prostitute.

*** The ten Separate Intellects are assumed by the medievals to govern the motion of the celestial spheres: the moon, the sun, the 5 planets visible to the naked eye (Mercury, Venus, Mars, Jupiter, Saturn), the stars, the 24-hour rotation of the entire celestial array, and a tenth thrown in for good measure — the Active Intellect, responsible for the transmission of divine rationality to the terrestrial realm. (IH/LL)

> Leviticus (17:7: "so that they should not bring their offerings to the goat-satyrs," etc.); therefore, it seems that this was one of the intentions in the creation of the Temple and in the appointment of the Priests for this worship. Nevertheless, it is not credible that these practices served no independent purpose as well, for in that case the Temple rituals would not have been spelled out in such detail . . . rather the Torah was wise enough to ensure that an independent utility would be served also, just as a good physician would do when he sees a sick person who has not accepted his regimen due to his misbehavior — he will endeavor to direct the misbehavior itself to bring the person towards health if it is possible to do so. For if he wanted to eat a food that was ill-advised for him because of his disease, the physician would combine with it things that would mitigate the ill-effect of that food and thus transform it in a way that heals his disease. For this reason God presented the sacrificial laws in this wonderful manner on which we have commented . . .

And after deliberating on the reason for the appointment of the priests, Gersonides concludes: "We give thanks to Him for revealing in His mercy and great kindness the reasons for these profound matters,[3] concerning which we have not found even an inkling of understanding in the books that came before us, but rather that which would discourage us from investigating these matters in this way."

This criticism is directed, of course, against Maimonides, who cautioned (*Guide* 3:26) against searching out the reasons for the details of the sacrificial laws. Maimonides believed that the Torah limited the laity's access to the Temple because the mitzvah of the sacrifices was less important in its view than prayer and other kinds of service that it permitted at all times. Gersonides counters this opinion through an incisive and interesting idea (in *Aharei Mot,* end) when he explains why it was forbidden to the High Priest to enter the Holy of Holies except on Yom Kippur: "whatever a person is habituated to see, he will not devote much effort to investigating its significance . . . you see, for example, in the matter of these wonderful prayers that the members of the Great Synagogue instituted for us, we are so habituated to them, by reciting them daily, that we make no effort to penetrate their secret meaning. You similarly find in the case of our entire Torah, that we are so habituated to it, we content ourselves with a simple reading of it and we do not search out its intentions in depth, to the point that many of our expert sages have no conception of many of its topics, such as the construction of the Tabernacle and its implements, the order of the sacrifices, the laws of purity and impurity, and the like."

The Reasons for the Implements of the Sanctuary

What, then, are the secrets and intentions for the above-listed mitzvot? Even the Tent of Meeting and the Temple, in their arrangement and their implements, have a deep reason (see *Terumah,* p. 104b). In the days of Moses our Master, philosophical education was so deficient (Introduction to Commentary on the Torah) "that the only one of the causes known to them was the material cause, and they were ignorant of the formal cause, the efficient cause, and the final cause."[4] "When the Torah wished to guide us to acquiring human perfection, which cannot be acquired except through attaining knowledge of existent things . . . it guided us to the belief that there are forms . . . and it started with the noblest form of terrestrial beings, namely that of the rational soul." Therefore it ordained that there should be two cherubim over the Ark of the Covenant which contained the Tables of the Covenant. The one cherub symbolizes the hylic (potential) intellect, while the other cherub symbolizes the Active Intellect*; "their faces are turned toward each other," as elaborated in Aristotle's treatise *On the Soul* . . . In the ark were the Tables of the Covenant, to teach that the attainment of prophecy is possible by means of these two cherubim[5]; this is a major principle and sturdy pillar . . . for without this belief, the Torah in its entirety would fall . . . therefore it says, "There I will meet with you, and I will speak with you from above the cover, from between the two cherubim" (Exodus 25:22). After speaking at length about the shape of the cherubim that symbolize the separate intellects, the text enumerates the other implements: the table symbolizes the nutritive soul**; the lampstand symbolizes the sensitive soul; the two altars symbolize the "privations," and thus mortality, for when it dies, every body will be resolved into the four elements that compose it, "and for this reason the altar has four corners."[6] Because the Temple signifies all these secrets of existence, the Torah ordained that we should worship God only in this place (Deuteronomy 11:26, Application 5), and it set apart a special family to deliberate on the secrets of this noble worship (*Koraḥ* Application 15).

---

* In the common medieval Aristotelian view, human ideas are acquired through the action of the "Active Intellect," which is one of the ten Separate Intellects, on the "hylic" or "material" intellect of the individual human being. (IH) (See the translator's Introduction to Book I of Gersonides' *Wars of the Lord* [translated by Seymour Feldman] for an account of the medieval concept of Active Intellect and its historical development from Aristotle's remarks on the topic. — LL)

** Medieval philosophy recognized a hierarchy of functions in the human soul corresponding to the taxonomy of life generally. "Nutritive" functions are shared by all living beings, even plants. "Sensation" and "locomotion" are common to all animals. The human soul includes a "nutritive" and "sensitive" component (in common with plants and animals respectively), but in addition a "rational" component unique to human beings. (LL)

Reasons for the Priesthood

The sacrifices also have important reasons. "Perhaps the intention for offering salt on each sacrifice was so that we should not regard the matter of the sacrifices as a bland matter without *ta'am* (pun: "taste" or "reason")! . . . Thus the rule about the salt accompanying the sacrifices should arouse us to seek their reason" (*Tzav,* end). Indeed, Gersonides found several reasons for the priesthood: (1) Together with the ceremony of the priestly blessing, the priests teach us concerning God's sanctity (*Shemini,* Application 2); (2) they awaken us to repentance, as the view of Ibn Daud (*Vayikra,* Application 1); (3) this action is reinforced by the ritual of Yom Kippur (on Leviticus 23:23); (4) they effect atonement, as the view of the Sages (*Vayikra,* 121, p. 4); and (5) they "are prepared and oriented for the arrival of prophecy" (Numbers 28, beginning). Even though Gersonides speaks only of the High Priest and of Moses,* his view here resembles that of Halevi.

Gersonides' explanation of the mitzvot is based on his philosophical method (even more than we emphasized in our brief survey), which has its foundation in the method of Aristotle and his Arabic commentators. After the collapse of Aristotelianism, those who came after him were not able to derive much benefit from his commentary. But there is great significance in the fact that precisely in the case of such a sharp and sober thinker, scientific philosophy did not diminish his valuation of the mitzvot but led him to find even more importance in their finer details.

---

* Because they achieve atonement (especially for the Golden Calf), they enable the Shekhinah to rest on Israel (Commentary on *Shemini,* Application 1).

Chapter 13
Ḥasdai Crescas

Defense of the Torah against Christian attacks

All Jewish philosophers are in a certain sense "guides to the perplexed," although the sources of the perplexity are different in different ages. Maimonides and Gersonides defended Judaism foremost from philosophical attacks, whereas in the days of Rabbi Ḥasdai Crescas the danger from Christianity grew stronger. Not only with physical force did the Church fight the religion of Israel, but also with spiritual weapons, and the political victory of Christians going from victory to victory in this era in their reconquest of the Iberian peninsula paved the way for their religious propaganda. Many among our nation were perplexed, especially with regard to the value of the commandments. It was toward these perplexed that Rabbi Ḥasdai Crescas extended his hand.

He was certain that the Aristotelian philosophy, which his predecessors had celebrated within Jewish thought, was philosophically deficient, and additionally endangered the defense of the Jews from Christian attacks. The view of the Jewish Aristotelians, that the primary intention of Torah was to implant truthful ideas in our minds, was interpreted by the Christians (including the Jewish apostates among them[1]) to mean that Judaism is not a religion but a philosophy! And as for the view that certain commandments were given as a safeguard against the weaker understanding of the common people, the Christians used this view to prove that the Torah was obsolete and its time had passed.[2]

The generation of the wilderness was not spiritually inferior

Thus the task that Crescas took on was not an easy one,[3] and he was repeatedly forced into blazing new trails. His proofs are aimed in three directions: he claims (1) that the generation of the wilderness did not stand on an inferior religious level; (2) that the Torah is "a religion of salvation" (and one may even say: "*the* religion of salvation") that redeems one from original sin and from the astral influences; and (3) that the Torah is a "law of love" that guides us to love of God, especially through its commandments.

Countering the students of Aristotle, though without quoting them directly, Crescas (in *Refutation of Christian Principles* 6:2) emphasizes that Abraham already had full knowledge of God, and that he "commanded his children and his household after him and they kept the way of the Lord." The Israelites in Egypt also held fast to the tradition of their earlier ancestor and did not accommodate to the religion of Egypt in order to "escape from servitude" (an allusion to the apostasizing Jews of Crescas' time!). Because they endured their affliction, God performed the well-known miracles and drew them close to Him to be His treasured people; therefore "one could not find a more thorough preparation in any nation to receive the commandments that lead to perfection."

Original Sin; salvation through circumcision and the Akedah

In contrast to all of his philosophical predecessors, but in agreement with the views of some Talmudic rabbis, Crescas acknowledged the doctrine of original sin (*Light of the Lord* 2:2:6).* Abraham was the complete opposite of Adam, as Adam was God's own handiwork and thus groomed for the highest perfection and yet he went bad, whereas Abraham grew up among idol worshippers but came to recognize his Creator "and was superlative in his love"; therefore, it was quite reasonable that God enacted with him a "new covenant" (*sic*!) in order to purify his children. This salvation was achieved by way of two commandments that were given to Abraham: the commandment of circumcision and the commandment of Isaac's binding. From here Crescas explains the wording of the blessing of circumcision with which he was familiar: "that he sanctified the Friend (= Abraham) from the womb . . . therefore, in reward for this the living God — our portion and our Rock — commanded to save our beloved ones of the holy seed, our remnant, from destruction for the sake of His covenant that He placed in our flesh"; to this destruction we would be "consigned by reason of original sin." And the deed of Isaac's binding was reckoned to the credit of Abraham our Father "as if he had sacrificed to God Isaac and all of his offspring"; therefore, it was an "inclusive sacrifice of the entire nation."** By virtue of it, Israel is called a treasured nation above all the other nations,

* Compare Paul's famous declaration: "As all men were made guilty through the sin of one man, thus through the merit of one man all men shall earn life" (Romans 5:18).

** This, apparently, was Crescas' response to Paul's words (Romans 6:4ff.), that all who believe in Jesus "were slain and buried with him." The difference between the two arguments, in favor of Judaism, is striking: it is hardly credible that all humanity were included in one man, and especially one who was not truly a man according to their belief (*Refutation of Principles of Christianity*, 20), whereas it is more reasonable to suppose that the whole people of Israel were included in Abraham and Isaac, to their merit, just as they were included in Adam to their detriment!

"to whom God apportioned judges in accordance with the constellations of the heavens and their movements."* Therefore, our forefathers offered two lambs every morning and evening, the offspring of the ram that Abraham sacrificed in place of his son, in order to indicate that the stars exercised no sway over the Jewish people, and the shofar, the horn of that ram, clearly attests that only God rules over us.

How are we redeemed through these two commandments?

How do these commandments, which Abraham our Father fulfilled and that recall his deeds, act upon us? The words of Crescas that we have cited up to this point give the impression that circumcision and Isaac's binding are the mystical causes of our salvation[4]; he emphasizes (*Refutation* 16) that the "theologians"[5] admit that through circumcision Abraham was saved from the punishment of hell. However is it possible that Crescas himself, who struggled to find rational reasons for mystical acts such as talismans and incantations (OH 4:5), and only after he succeeded in explaining them overrode the criticism that Maimonides leveled at them — that he Crescas, of all people, believed in such a mystical effectiveness of circumcision? On more than one occasion Crescas saw it necessary (in the manner of Maimonides) to conceal his opinion from the eyes of the multitude; according to his opinion, the Torah itself did not reveal the limits of free will in human beings (OH 48a; 2:5:3) because its "publication would harm the multitude," and Crescas followed suit.** It is possible, therefore, that he was being considerate of his readers, that they might believe in mystical actions and would be inclined to see the superiority of Christianity in this, and that it teaches that it is not by our merit but by the merit of someone else besides us that we are saved. In accordance with that view, he seems to say that we also have a "redeemer" whose merit stands for us, as is attested to by God's explicit promise, and who (it stands to reason) is more fit to correct the sin of Adam than Jesus, because the sacrifice of all Israel certainly was fit to atone for us.

The salvific power of all the mitzvot

Let us leave aside the question of whether Crescas believed in a special mystical power of these two mitzvot that were given to the patriarch

---

* Crescas is alluding to Deuteronomy 4:19, and relies also on the rabbinic saying that Israel has no *mazal* (i.e., no ruling astrological sign). The Christians, too, believed that their faith freed them from the influences of the stars (W. Gundel, *Sterne und Sternbilder*, 1922, 268).

** I.e., uniquely of all the medieval philosophers, Crescas was a philosophical determinist but cautious to announce it. (LL)

Abraham. Indeed, he believed without a doubt that all the mitzvot of the Torah contribute to our salvation, and he explained this effect in a psychological way. He cites (OH 38b; 2:2:6, beginning) the saying of the Sages: "When the serpent came upon Eve, he laid a pollution upon her; when Israel stood at Sinai, their pollution ceased" (*Yevamot* 103b, and elsewhere). He adds that this "pollution" was the "strong impression that resulted from Adam's inclination to materiality," an impression that brings destruction upon all his progeny after him, and that this pollution "ceased" once God gave us His Torah, which brings the human being to perfection "and subdues his appetites and annihilates his evil urge." On the one hand, the fulfillment of the mitzvot demonstrates the love on the part of the person fulfilling them, and on the other hand "acquires a quality and fixed attribute in the soul"[6] (2:2:4, beginning). In this way he interprets the trials that God brought upon our ancestors and on us; He is trying us, "to know whether you love the Lord your God — he did not say, whether you will love Him, for this He already knew," but just as He said to Abraham, "Now I know that you are a God-fearing man" (i.e., after the trial a new love was generated that previously did not exist in the heart of the one tried) "and this for me is the afflictions of love that are mentioned in the words of the Sages" (i.e., afflictions that arouse in us the love of the Creator). Perhaps these words appear sober and even overly intellectual. However, we may understand them in light of the events of that historical period, and in light of Crescas' own feelings. After his young son died a martyr's death he wrote, "I offered him as an innocent lamb for a burnt-offering; I accept the justice of God's judgment, drawing comfort from his good portion and his blessed fate."[7] This, I imagine, was Crescas' true view: it is not the "performed deed" (in the Christians' terms) of our ancestor that redeems us from the suffering of original sin, but rather our doing deeds like his deed: a deed like this is apt to generate in us the qualities that negate the "inclination to materiality" and to implant in us the attribute in which "Abraham excelled": unlimited love for our God!

The love of God is the pivot of faith

These words of Crescas cited above were written with his heart's blood. His age, like all ages of persecutions, was liable to cause the weak to surrender while it gave added strength to the knights of faith. Indeed, the power of knowledge increased in his soul no less than the power of faith. He fought valiantly to give a scientific formulation and to prove by way of decisive proofs that the Torah leads and educates us to the pure love of God, which is the center and axis of faith.

Why so many mitzvot?

In his apologetic treatise (*Refutation*, 68) Crescas already responded briefly to the criticism that the Christians directed at the large number of the Torah's mitzvot. Our intellect "is not always in a state of actuality," and does not control our appetites. Therefore the divine religion could not be content with the principles of the mitzvot, but had to add specific mitzvot, in order to be equal to the power of our anger and appetites, and to implant in us the true opinions that are required for our own sakes. This view, that the Torah should have an effect on our ethical qualities and on our ideas, is no different from the Aristotelians'. But in the philosophical work that he composed later *(Light of the Lord* 2:6) Crescas succeeded in deepening his outlook considerably, joining the explanation of the mitzvot to his general religious-philosophical outlook, which was completely different from that of his predecessors.

Primary purposes

Indeed, his preface is simply Aristotelian. Every action has a purpose, but one must distinguish among initial, intermediate, and ultimate purposes.[8] (For example: the thirty-nine kinds of work that were performed in constructing the Tent of Meeting were not performed for their own sake, but were means or sub-means to the erection of the tent, which was the ultimate purpose, "the end of work in prior thought.") Therefore we must investigate the proximate purposes of the Torah (its narratives and especially its precepts) as well as the ultimate purpose for which it was given.

Intermediate purposes

We can recognize the intermediate purposes according to the Aristotelian assumption that the good that flows from any thing is its purpose. And we see that from the Torah proceed four "goods" (in the original: "perfections"): it improves our ethical qualities and our opinions; it makes us happy in this world, and prepares us for the life of the world to come. Crescas explains in brief that the specific commandments come in order to achieve these goals (thus they become "initial goals"). In deliberating on improvement of the ethical qualities he emphasizes that there are mitzvot that apply between a person and himself. Therefore the Torah restricted sexual liaisons and forbade us to consume foods that generate "evil qualities in the soul . . . and extinguish the light of our reason" and guided us "to cautiousness and austerity." The laws of impurity come to cleanse and purify us and to guide us toward sanctity. The Torah also determined the relations of a man with the other members of his household ("his wife, children and slaves") and the Sages followed its example in their sayings and their enactments. It commanded us how to conduct ourselves with other persons (in Crescas' words: "when it says, 'with the men of his city,' it is not precisely limited to this"); and Crescas emphasizes that there is one mitzvah "that comprises all matters of interpersonal human dealings, namely the mitzvah of love, concerning which the Creator instructed us in saying, 'Love your neighbor as yourself'; and Hillel the Elder responded to the man who came to be converted, 'What is hateful to you, do not do to your fellow . . . the rest is commentary; go and learn!'" Crescas devotes only a few lines to the rest of the "goals." In discussing the improvement of our minds, he emphasizes that the festivals were established in remembrance of the miracles and wonders that prove the reality of God, His oneness, His knowledge, and His providence. In order to prove the benefit that the Torah brings us in this world (in the words of the source: "bodily perfections"), he hints at the promises that God pledged to our ancestors and also at the promises of reward for those who keep His mitzvot. However, only some of them have a relation to this world; even verses such as "Happy are you, Israel, who is like you," are explained by reliable tradition in terms of the reward that awaits us in the World to Come, "namely, that the souls survive after death and enjoy the Divine glory."

Our Eternal Lives Are Not Dependent on the Acquisition of Correct Opinions

From this short overview, we see that Crescas arrives at a formulation of the main question: What is the ultimate purpose of the Torah (52a)? Indeed, the four purposes do not stand on the same level. Three of them are time-bound, and one must view them as preparations for the fourth purpose: eternal happiness, which our soul receives in the World to Come. Additionally, our welfare in this world supports the activity of the soul, which utilizes "physical tools," and it goes without saying that our ethical purification and intellectual illumination will benefit our souls. However, one must beware of the opinion of the Aristotelians, who say that improving our virtues and perfecting our life circumstances are valuable only in that they perfect our *intellect,* and on that — that is to say, on the acquisition of true opinions — our eternal lives depend. It is easy, of course, for Crescas to prove how far this opinion is from the tradition according to which whoever does a single mitzvah is repaid with good. He is right to ask if the martyrs who gave their lives for the sanctification of God were distinguished by having sophisticated intellect, or, on the other hand, if informers or those who embarrass their colleagues in public (who do not have a portion in the world to come according to the tradition) were lacking knowledge. However, Crescas energetically and successfully attacks from a scientific perspective as well the psychological roots of this opinion — the opinion of those who say that by way of our effort we will merit "acquired intellect" and that, even though it comes into being during a limited time, it will last forever, whereas the "soul" is doomed to oblivion. Both the Torah and philosophy teach us about the immortality of the entire soul. But how should one explain that we arrive at the immortality of the soul with the help of performing the mitzvot?

Rather: The Ultimate Purpose of the Mitzvot of the Torah is Love and Fear of God

"When we investigated the Torah and its parts, we found in it a part small in quantity but great in quality that is not completely about knowledge and not completely about action: *Love of God and true fear of Him*" (53b). Crescas proves that eternal happiness and the love of God that brings it about are the ultimate purpose of the mitzvot of the Torah. Verses such as "What does the Lord your God ask of you but to fear the Lord your God, to walk in His ways and to love Him and to worship the Lord your God with all your heart and with all your soul" and others prove that the purpose the Torah requires us to aspire to is that we do God's will with the greatest eagerness (*ibid.*). One must prove scientifically and by relying on words of Scripture the belief that by way of this love we will merit life in the world to come. All love connects the lover with the loved. One of the earlier philosophers* taught that love is the foundation for all existence. We understand, then, that love — not logic! — strengthens the attachment between us and the source of real life. Even though "truth is its own witness," we must note that the statements of the rabbis also fit with the view that there is a connection between the love that we manifest and our reward in the World to Come, like that of Rabbi Meir: "At what point do children merit life in the World to Come? When they know to respond 'Amen,'" — that is to say, to express their gratitude and their love to God. Of course, we do not hold the love of God in high regard because of the accompanying reward (which would be "love dependent on an ulterior motive"); rather we see it as the purpose of our life, according to the words of the Sage, "Fear God and keep His commandments, for this is the whole of human existence" (Ecclesiastes 12).

* OH 55a. The thinker is the one called by modern scholars "Pseudo-Empedocles," probably dating in late antiquity, author of the treatise *The Five Elements*. On his influence, see D. Kaufmann, *Studien über Ibn Gabirol*, 1899, 4.

There are, then, apparently two purposes of the Torah: love of God, and life in the World to Come. Both have inherent value; that is to say the first is not the means to the second, and vice versa. Indeed, the rabbis truly said: "It is better to have one hour of repentance and good deeds in this world than an eternity in the World to Come, and it is better to have one hour of contentment in the World to Come than an eternity in this world," implying that the value of these two purposes is equal. We can affix their mutual relationship in this way: Love is the ultimate purpose from the perspective of the commanded one (the person who is performing the mitzvot), but from the perspective of the Commander (God, Who promises us a reward for our actions), the purpose is "acquiring good and eternal attachment to the Divine Presence" (OH 56b).

How Does the Torah Educate Toward Love of God?

Because love of God is the ultimate purpose, Crescas must prove that the Torah guides us to this purpose through its stories and mitzvot. He dedicated Chapter 2:6:2 to this task. He relies on what he has already proven: first, that the perfect person naturally loves the good (and there is no good greater than God), and second, that the Torah helps us to attain perfection of our thoughts and virtues. If we could all arrive at this double perfection, there would be no need for particular mitzvot to reinforce our love of God. However, the Torah took care to implant love "in the hearts of the perfect and imperfect alike," and particularly in the hearts of the latter. Crescas admits, then, without spelling it out, that the mitzvot were given first and foremost for those who have not reached perfection. Were it not that our appetites and the pursuit of honor and wealth have power over us, it would be enough for us "to recite the first verse of the Shema once a week" for us all to worship God out of love. But such is not the case. Therefore, the Torah took ingenious measures in order to destroy the desires and to strengthen the power of the intellect by way of its stories and mitzvot. It remains for us to survey what Crescas says about the role of the mitzvot in training us for this task.

The Reasons for Various Mitzvot

The Torah demonstrates to us the power and kindness that God has bestowed on us. The holidays and prayers remind us of both of these, but the social commandments are based on the memory of God's kindness as well. The Torah also imparts true opinions to us, to the extent of our power of comprehension. To do so, it employs the "allusions" that are connected to "the Temple, its vessels, the rituals of purification, the counting of days, the sprinkling of the blood, and the like."* Again, the Torah teaches us that God supervises Israel by means of a special providence. This supervision is recalled through all the commandments pertaining to divine service: the prayers, the fasts, and especially the service in the Temple, the sacrifices (on which he expatiates a bit), and also the Temple vessels, such as the seven-branched candelabra, which alludes to the influence of the light that emanates from God by means of His seven celestial "servants" [the sun, moon, and planets]. Within this section he mentions circumcision, the Days of Awe, and the rituals of Sukkot. (He alludes to what he wrote in 2:2:2 about Israel's redemption from original sin and astral influences.) He briefly remarks that the banishing of the scapegoat attests to the major principle that Israel recognizes no ruler but God alone. He attributes religious rationales to the commandments of the debt-release, the Jubilee, and the agricultural commandments (e.g., one must set aside the first fruit to God; however, the fruits of the first three years are not fit to be offered). Not only the counting of the Omer, but also the offering of two loaves connects the Feast of Weeks (Shavuot) to Passover, in order to impress on us that the ultimate purpose of the Exodus from Egypt was the giving of the Torah. Furthermore, the dietary and sexual prohibitions, which instill in us "health of body and soul" and protect us from bad traits (such as cruelty) and indulgence, demonstrate God's providence. The same applies to the laws of purity: that which they forbid us is harmful to our minds and morals or has an idolatrous aspect.** Sorcery, too, is forbidden because of its idolatrous character.

The Torah promises us reward and punishment. It includes "warnings to awaken slumbering hearts from the sleep of fools." Again he deliberates on the holidays that remind us of the wonders of God, and especially the Sabbath, which is the "root of all the wonders." Therefore the Torah is stringent concerning the Sabbath, and honors the number seven in the laws of the holidays. It set aside the fiftieth year as the year of freedom [the Jubilee], in order to remind us of the Sinaitic revelation, which took place on the 50th day after the Exodus from Egypt. It is easy for Crescas to amass examples in which the Torah exercised ingenuity or cunning, in order to awaken us from the sleep of apathy. We mention briefly that the sacrifices also

* Here Crescas adds remarks about the authority of the High Court, apparently to refute the view of the extreme allegorists who rejected the literal meaning. In *Refutation* 77 he also emphasizes that we are obligated to observe the mitzvot in their plain sense, just as Christians still observe immersion (baptism) in the literal sense, even though it has a symbolic sense as well.

** In *Refutation* 77 he speaks of mitzvot "by whose doing a person shall be called holy." Some of them keep one from bestiality and pollution and draw one near to God. Here, Crescas alludes to the rules of impurity governing a corpse, and may be associating to Deuteronomy 26:14: "I have not given [an offering of my produce] to the dead" (which would indeed be idolatrous).

"awaken a sense of submission" (58b). The burnt-offering comes to remind a person that he deserves to perish on account of his heart's evil thoughts, but by God's kindness the offering is credited to him for atonement. He also explains the laws of immersion in a symbolic manner: the impure person is likened to a dirty garment that cannot be cleaned except in soap-water; therefore we take ashes (and specifically the ashes of the largest animal because these ashes are very effective) and also cedar and scarlet-stuff that cannot produce fruit "in order to teach submission."[9] The commandment of the Sukkah reminds us of the miracles that were performed during the generation of the wilderness. Its details allude to the person: just as the body bears the soul, which (according to Aristotle) is the form of man and protects him, so too is the roof-covering (*sekhakh*) the essence of the sukkah and protects it. The roof-covering needs to be from the vegetative growth of the land in order to teach us submission; it cannot contract impurity, in order to caution us regarding the cleanliness of our souls. The prohibition of species-mixtures teaches that all of our actions should be directed to one purpose (in addition to the reason mentioned in the *Guide* 3:33, to distance us from idolatry). Finally, the Torah warns us to love God not only through explicit admonition, but also by means of the special commandments, among them the commandments of the sacrifices "which are a marvelous impression and symbolic enactment"* as they are "a ransom for our souls as if through them we will sacrifice ourselves to God's service." Therefore, there is hope that through them we will merit "the emanation of (divine) influence and attachment to the light of the perceptible and imperceptible divine presence."[10] Sometimes even fire fell from heaven. This attachment is also manifest in the fact that the priests (and to a lesser degree, the laity) consume a part of some of the sacrifices and thus "they partake from the table of the Most High." They are like guests whom God invited to His house out of affection and friendship. Also the Urim and Thummim [used in priestly divination] reinforce this attachment.

In this chapter, of course, there are shortcomings with regard to the presentation of the topics. They are not separated out from one another, and therefore Crescas is forced to repeat his words more than once. The proof that the purpose of all of the mitzvot is to awaken in us love of God is not demonstrated sufficiently. However, if one should take Crescas to task for this, he will be mocking the helpless. For did not death snatch his pen from his hand before he was able to enhance and edit his book?[11] Even so, he managed to make a great contribution toward understanding the reasons for the mitzvot.

---

* The physical act of bringing the animal is an acting out of the spiritual impulse, the love of the worshipper for God.

Crescas is the first who argues in a methodical and scientific way that the goal of the Torah is to guide us to pure love of God. Of course, this emphasis on and appreciation of love is no innovation; here, he relies explicitly on verses of the Torah, on the sayings of the rabbis, and, in all likelihood, on the "Chapter on Love" in Baḥya's *Duties of the Heart.** He also comes close to Halevi, who said that "the souls yearn for" the God of Abraham whereas logic alone leads to the God of Aristotle (4:16). But on the other hand, the Torah-verse that Crescas cites speaks primarily of fear. The rabbis surely admired the one who acts out of love, but it is difficult to decide whether for them the central place of honor rested with love or with deed, whereas Baḥya values submission and similar virtues no less than love, and Halevi believes that the ultimate purpose is not to guide us to religious and ethical virtues, but rather to raise us to the rank of the prophetic superman! As for the difference between Crescas and the students of Aristotle, we have nothing more to add or delete. In Crescas' view, the Aristotelians saw the final objective in "intellectual perfection" (which also holds the key to the World to Come). This view is based on *Guide* 3:27, especially the value it ascribed to rejecting idol worship and Maimonides' innovations on the explanations of the mitzvot.

However, we have already seen that Maimonides also emphasized the value of the love of God, and, especially in the *Guide* 3:52, he acknowledges that there is "one goal" of all the mitzvot in the Torah, and that is the pure love and fear — according to the verses that Crescas also cites! Should we say, therefore, that Crescas exaggerates the difference between himself and Maimonides? No! One does not judge a philosopher based on what he simply stated (or more precisely, what he conceded), but rather, on what he argued and brought out in a logical manner from the premises of his method. Indeed, Maimonides mentions the love of God many times, but only in a casual way; the displays of God's power awaken both our love and our fear of God (*Mishneh Torah, Book of Knowledge* 2:2). He emphasizes God's providence over His creations, and especially over His pious ones (*Guide* 3:18), but nowhere in any of his books do we find any explicit mention of God's love of His creations.[12] He mentions Hillel's words, that all of the mitzvot are nothing more than a commentary on "love your neighbor as yourself," only tangentially in his *Commentary on the Mishnah* (*Peah* 1:1). In the *Guide* he does not stress any relation between the mitzvot and the love of God.** By contrast, Crescas' teaching of love is central to his

---

* Perhaps Crescas is alluding to Baḥya when he says (2:6:1, 56a): "Until one loves nothing except for the purpose of this love and this service, as another writer has written at length." (See DH 10:1.)

** We have also emphasized above that Gersonides does not attribute any special significance to the command "Love your neighbor as yourself."

philosophical outlook. He opposes (1:3:5) the students of Aristotle who say that God finds personal satisfaction and, as it were, "joy" within the fact that He knows all. He asserts that we, too, God's creations, do not derive joy from our knowledge, but only in the acquisition of new knowledge; therefore accordingly (it is written). "God rejoices in his works" (27a), that is to say, in the works of His love, in that he "renews each day the works of Creation."

The theology of Crescas is thus completely in keeping with his anthropology*: in place of thought he locates feeling and the deeds that come from it, love of the Creator toward His creations, love of the creations to their Creator, and love of a man to his neighbor, "which includes all of the matters between man and his fellow man" (2:6:1; 52a). They constitute "a threefold cord that is not readily broken." This idea is confirmed by the entire stamp of Crescas' outlook. For Crescas, the perspective that *love* connects people to each other and attaches them to their Father in Heaven is no less scientific than religious. He cites the opinion of the Greek philosopher who says that love is the connection of all things, and indeed, who would avert his eyes from the great difference between the force that draws a man to a woman and the pure, untainted love that serves as an axis of Crescas' religious teachings! We will not think that his opinion is less correct or "scientific" because its basis is not a doubtful postulate of natural-philosophy, but rather a religious experience — the experience of Crescas' generation — those who risked their lives on account of their faith and precisely in their sufferings became acquainted with the love that is "as powerful as death," which is embedded in the heart of Israel since time immemorial.

This experience, confirmed in his view by science, serves as the basis for a *unified* explanation of all of the commandments of the Torah. But this monism, completely suitable to the teleological doctrine of Aristotle, is not inconsistent, certainly, with the acknowledgment of certain "intermediate objectives"; that is, it does not prevent Crescas from resorting to many explanations that his predecessors asserted, that indeed all of these reasons "speak to love" in a certain sense. He agrees with Maimonides that many commandments were given in order to distance us from idolatry; how will we love God without believing in His unity? Indeed, he attributes to all of these commandments, especially to the sacrifices, additional explanations, as Gersonides had done. His views also agree with Halevi, that certain commandments cause the Divine Presence to

* See OH 2:6:4 in which he demonstrates that the purpose of the world and the purpose of the Torah are the same: "production of good insofar as possible." See Joel, *Creskas philosophische Lehren*, 62.

rest on Israel, and thus is revealed the divine Providence that holds sway over us, arousing our love for our Father in Heaven. Crescas does not contradict those who believe in secret allusions in the Torah, though he does not elaborate on them. Only astrology does he treat with reserve. In contrast to Ibn Ezra and Gersonides, he maintains that the astral bodies govern the nations, but they do not govern Israel, and though the Torah differentiates specific times, such as the Days of Awe, nevertheless all times are equal before God, but not before man. The times that "were adorned in commandments" are important to us and they arouse us to repentance, submission and happiness; in addition to this we can say that Yom Kippur was chosen because on that day God became reconciled to Moses and because in that season the world is judged regarding water. We were commanded to take to God the species that have a relationship to water, but he passes over the astrological explanation of the month of Tishri and of the Sabbath in complete silence. He almost never mentions the utilitarian explanations that Saadia emphasizes and that Maimonides does not disparage, as the ordering of political and economical life is a necessary precondition for the development of spiritual life (*Guide* 3:27). Indeed, Crescas acknowledges (2:6:1) that the Torah facilitates our bodily perfection through certain commandments, but he devotes only one line to explaining these commandments, and he mentions only the promises connected to their fulfillment, not any hygienic or economic benefit that they cause directly. There is in this a certain one-sidedness, but it is not his monistic tendencies that caused it (it was easy for him to posit connections between the benefits that ensue from the commandments and our love of God who gave the Torah), but rather an apologetic motive. In his book *Refutation of the Christian Principles* (82) he emphasizes that material affairs are only the secondary intention of the Torah, and that the primary intention is to acquire eternal life.

Nevertheless this one-sidedness also highlights the purely religious character of his explanation. Nearly all of his predecessors seemed to grant equal value to various explanations: for example, utilitarian* (not only Saadia, but in another sense Ibn Ezra) and rational (that the Aristotelians also viewed as religious). Crescas recognized clearly that religion is not a philosophical outlook, but rather attachment to God, and that anyone who turns the Torah into a textbook of logic or science is in error. In this he agrees with Halevi. Nevertheless, Crescas speaks here of "the perfect individuals such as those who are *intellectually* enlightened or morally exceptional" (3:5:1, end). Even though he believes that science is incapable

* There may be a "utility" in being freed from astral influences by performance of the mitzvot, but Crescas does not explicitly give any such utilitarian reason for them.

of knowing and proving all of the principles of religion,* it is possible nevertheless to explain the intentions of the Divine Legislator, with the assistance of scientific research. Not only can science decide in favor of the Jews who affirm the commandments over the Christians who disparage them, but it can also assist us to observe them properly. Only if we know that their purpose is to instill in us love of God and that the fulfillment of them is in a certain sense human creatures' reactions to the Creator's love for us can we then serve our Creator from this same intention that He desires. The Aristotelians assigned religion the task of intellectual enlightenment; Crescas charges religion to take control of our entire soul (not our intellect alone), in order to purify and to elevate it, and science is capable of *assisting* religion by explaining the commandments. In this way Crescas arrives at a new definition of the relations between religion and science. This is an important fruit of the work of this thinker, who is perhaps the most original philosopher the Jewish people have ever had.

* For instance, in Crescas' view, it is impossible to prove philosophically that only one God exists (3:4).

Chapter 14
Joseph Albo

In Rabbi Joseph Albo's *Book of Principles* (*Sefer Ha-Ikkarim*),[1] the apologetic tendency is even more apparent than in Crescas' *Light of the Lord*. The attacks of the Christians were also directed, of course, against the observance of the mitzvot. Albo does not respond to these attacks by defending each mitzvah separately, but contents himself with defending certain mitzvot that the Christians specifically criticized, as well as giving a psychological explanation of the observance of the mitzvot in general.

The Reasons for the Sacrifices and Sabbath

The Christians first of all disparaged the "filthy" sacrificial worship (as contrasted with their "clean" communion service — see *Ikkarim* 3:25). But Albo responds that the sacrifices have sufficient reason: perhaps their purpose is to distance the people from idolatry (as per Maimonides); perhaps they serve to have an effect on the heart of the sinner (as per Ibn Daud and others). Perhaps the kabbalists were right (and, one should add, Halevi and Ibn Ezra) when they said that the sacrifices cause the Divine Presence to rest upon Israel. In giving a reason for the Sabbath (to prove that the seventh day is the true Sabbath), Albo also mentions the views of the kabbalists, who said that the ninth Sefirah called Yesod (Foundation) is also called "Sabbath" (2:11). He cites other reasons: the Sabbath, on which the Torah was given to Israel, attests to the continuity of the connection between God and the Jewish people (*ibid.*), and more broadly one may say that it recalls the continual providence of the Creator, not merely the creation of the world (3:26).

In attacking the observance of the mitzvot in general, the Christians argued (3:25 beginning) that (1) the Mosaic Torah requires only "correctness of action, not purity of heart, and (2) that it speaks only of "material prosperity," whereas Christianity emphasizes the life of the world to come and also "saves humankind from the doom of hell."

The Three Kinds of Laws and Their Value

Albo bases his defense on the classification of laws on which Jewish and Christian thinkers were agreed in principle.[2] There are three kinds of laws: natural, political, and religious.* Natural law (which already exists among certain animals) exists of itself and is directed only at the utility of the members of the group; political law is given to human beings by a legislator "in order to distance them from the despicable and bring them closer to the fitting"; religious law is given to people by a legislator, in order to guide them to achieving their perfection[3] and enable them to acquire the life of the world to come. Political law is superior to natural law, not only in its value but also in its extent, for it "orders people's affairs in a fitting manner," and religious law, of course, includes the functions of political law, but only (according to Maimonides) so that the lack of social order does not interfere with attaining our ultimate perfection (1:7). Therefore it (religious law) also lays down injunctions forbidding murder, theft, and the like. However, these laws in the Torah have a completely different meaning from similar laws in secular legislation (3:28).

Everything Goes According to the Heart's Intention

Whoever claims that the Torah requires only the "performed deed"[4] is completely in error. "You should adopt a cardinal rule regarding the performance of the mitzvot: Everything goes according to the heart's intention, as the rabbis said, 'God desires the heart.' Therefore, there can be a person who does many mitzvot and they have no worth or, at the very least, their performance is not enough to provide him with human perfection or even a recognizable part of it; and there can be a person who performs one mitzvah and through it acquires a great portion of perfection on account of his/her intention" (3:27). One may deduce from this that the "negative mitzvot" also bring a reward "even though it is astounding that a person can acquire any perfection while sitting idly"; and of course: One who does not eat pork because he does not desire it and has another kind of meat does not receive a reward, but one who encounters an occasion to sin but conquers his inclination out of the fear of God, that person demonstrates the proper intention no less than one who performs a positive commandment.** Albo goes on to explain the rabbinical statements that we have repeatedly mentioned: "A person should never say: I do not want to eat pork, etc." and "greater is the one

---

* He writes (1:7): "Law is of three kinds: natural, conventional, and divine." The last attribute is ambiguous. One can call this kind of law divine because it is divinely revealed, or because it leads one to be close to God. The latter quality is the essential one for Albo, and therefore I have termed it "religious law."

** This distinction applies to positive precepts also. The rabbis distinguished between one who eats the Paschal lamb for the sake of fulfilling the command and one who eats it to satisfy his appetite (*Ikkarim* 3:30:2.).

who is commanded and performs than the one who is not commanded yet performs" (3:27, 28). Perhaps because of his great appreciation for the heart's intention, Albo discusses at length the "service of the heart," that is to say prayer, whose nature is not to influence the will of the Creator (4:20 and below), but rather with repentance (4:18) it prepares us to be fit to receive the good influence that emanates from God. His understanding is reminiscent of that of R. Judah Halevi, who attributed to prayer greater educational value than utilitarian-practical value.[5] Not only is Judaism not worse than Christianity in its appreciation of intention, but it even surpasses it.

Judaism Surpasses Christianity in Its Appreciation of the Heart's Intention

Albo only hints at this, in his way and in the way of all Jewish apologetes of this period. According to our faith, there is no value to a sacrifice offered without the proper intention (3:36), whereas the Eucharist, which the Christians regard as a sacrifice, is effective in their view "from the moment of utterance from the priest's mouth, any priest, no matter whether he is righteous or wicked" (3:28). The Binding of Isaac was so important because the performance of this mitzvah depended on Abraham's will; the aggadah says that he could have responded to God: "Did you not say to me, 'through Isaac you will have progeny'?" Therefore the deed was counted to Abraham's credit but not Isaac's, even though (according to the Midrash) he was already thirty-seven years old, because he had no counter-claim, and for this reason we mention in our prayers only the Binding of Isaac and not the merit of the martyrs who died sanctifying God's name (3:36). Jesus' "merit," on which Christians rely, is not similar to Abraham's merit; Jesus was taken out to be killed against his will, and this kind of "sacrifice" has no religious value!

Practical value realized from keeping the mitzvot

However, in our appreciation of intent we should not begrudge the value of the actions themselves! Just as the majority of humankind are unable to maintain their bodily health without specified actions, so too we are dependent — and even so are the Intelligences that guide the planets* — on certain acts, in order to achieve spiritual perfection (3:31). But the actions that are effective for reaching this purpose are not known to us as a matter

* 3:4. The medieval belief in "separate intellects" (i.e., spirits that guided the movements of the stars and planets), was a legacy from ancient times.

of course (3:8); therefore, God sent us the prophets, whose principal role was not to reveal the future (as per the Christian view), but to admonish and encourage us to observe all of the commandments (3:8,12).

This is Albo's answer to the second Christian claim: through fulfilling the commandments we arrive not only at perfection, but also at life in the World to Come, not directly, but through the religious sentiments that are linked to their fulfillment: sentiments of fear and love, and in addition to these, joy.

Albo describes these feelings at great length; in this regard he surpasses all of the Jewish philosophers who preceded him,* and he diverges particularly from the method of Crescas, his teacher, who only speaks about God's joy and human beings' love for their Creator.

Levels of Feeling Connected to Fulfillment of the Commandments

These feelings have levels. There is love of reward and fear of punishment; one who fulfills the commandments because of reasons like these is called one who does commandments "not for their own sake" (3:32), whereas one who has love of God and fear of God is called one who "engages in Torah for its own sake" (*ibid.*). Albo especially emphasizes the value of pure reverence.** In the beginning of chapter 3:21, he even says that the sole purpose of all of these commandments is this reverence. Albo correctly points out the general demands of the Torah: for example, "to reverence this honored and awesome Name" (Deuteronomy 28:58), and the fact that Abraham is not called a "God-fearing man" until after he withstood all of his trials (3:34). This fear is not like the fear of other human beings: "Because one who is fearful because of a man or a king or a ruler stands constantly in fear and trembling, and this shortens his life; however, one who fears God, not only does such trembling not shorten his life, but rather his days are lengthened. Solomon says: 'Fear of God lengthens your days' (Proverbs 10:27) " (*ibid.*). Therefore, there is no contradiction between religious fear and joy, as the passage in Deuteronomy makes clear when

* On Halevi, see above, p. 72ff.; on Ibn Daud, p. 86ff.; on Maimonides, p. 105ff.; on Crescas, p. 33.

** The meaning of *yir'ah* can be "fear" or "reverence" or a combination of the two, depending on context. It is important in this connection to stress the difference between physical fear of external consequences and a more internalized fear, such as the fear within a positive relationship of disappointing the one with whom one is in relationship. The person in relationship with God is (on the higher levels of which Albo speaks) fearful not of what God will do by way of punishment if one acts badly, but how one's relationship with God will be adversely affected by one's performing below expectations. The term "reverence" is used among other things to express this internalized, sublimated kind of fear. (LL)

it says (28:47): "Because you did not worship the Lord your God with joy and with a good heart," because just as a person who is healthy in his body will feel his pain when he becomes sick and also fear entering his hand into fire, so too the fact that the soul is afraid of doing a disgusting thing is an indication of the health of the soul and it is fitting that we should rejoice upon it (3:23). Indeed, there are laws that are not agreeable to logic, such as the prohibition of eating pork. Of these David said: "I am resolved to follow your laws forever *ekev*" (Psalm 119:112), which is explained as "I have predisposed and compelled my logic because of the *ekev,* (that is to say: the reward) for which one must wait; and from the standpoint of the reward there is also reason to rejoice in their fulfillment (*ibid.*). Indeed, the last reason is fitting to explain this verse and other verses in the same psalm, but this is not consistent with Albo's criterion, that love for the sake of reward is not called perfect love. Therefore, he "broadens the discussion" and says that the burden of fulfilling the commandments is certainly unpleasant. However, when we remember its fruit, namely the pure reverence and recognition of God's elevated status, we are glad of the burden just as one who mines silver from its ore; and of this scripture says, "If you seek [wisdom] out as you do silver and search for it as for treasures, then you will understand the fear of the Lord" (Proverbs 2:4–5) (3:34). And one who fulfills this verse in the full sense — that is to say, one who does not feel the pain but does everything with joy in order to come to this pure reverence — his rank will be very exalted, and he is not only called "God-fearing" but also a "lover of God," a title specially apt for Abraham our Father. The rabbis similarly said, "Those who act out of love and find joy even in suffering — of these, scripture says: 'Those who love Him are like the sun rising in its might' (Judges 5:31)" (*ibid*).

Fear and love should not be seen, however, as different emotions in their essence, nor do they complement each other as per the view of Maimonides (*Mishneh Torah*, "Laws of Ethical Qualities" 2:2), but rather love is on the highest step of reverence, and we achieve it when we connect fear with joy.

The Relationship Between Religious Emotion and Fulfillment of the Mitzvot

What is the relationship between this three-sided religious feeling (fear, joy, and love) and the fulfillment of the mitzvot? We already know that from the days of Baḥya onward* the sages of Israel set a reciprocal connection between our deeds and our measure of religiosity. This religiosity

* See above, p. 57ff.

is both a cause of our deeds and is caused by them in turn.* Albo also believes in this double connection, even though he did not express this view explicitly. Indeed, on most occasions it seems that he does not think that the connection between deed and correct intention is necessary; rather, he *recommends* that we fulfill the mitzvot from within the correct intention, and he emphasizes that Abraham *demonstrated* his fear and his love by withstanding all of his trials. On the other hand, he writes that this attribute (fear) is achieved by way of keeping the mitzvot (3:31), and he expounds at length the verse: "What does the Lord your God demand of you? Only this: to revere the Lord your God, to walk only in His paths, to love Him, and to serve the Lord your God with all your heart and soul, keeping the Lord's commandments" (Deuteronomy 10:12). It was logical to require of the person that he should fear God and love God with all his heart and all his soul, but as this is very difficult, God was lenient and commanded the worshipper "instead of this, just to keep God's laws and commandments, and through this he would achieve the virtue coming to him as a consequence of his service with all of his heart and soul" (*ibid*). This sentence (and what follows it) is not worded precisely. If we accept it literally, it teaches that "the performed deed" is a *substitute* for correct intention — in contradiction to everything that Albo has asserted in the psychological chapters that we surveyed.** But it would seem that in this sentence it is also his intention that "the attribute of reverence, by which human perfection is achieved, is consequent on the fulfillment of the mitzvot of the Torah"[6] — that is to say — reverence follows on the fulfillment of the mitzvot and results from it (*ibid.*). This is consistent with the rabbinic dictum (cited in 3:32): "From doing the mitzvah not for its own sake, one comes to do it for its own sake," as well as with the explanation of Albo that we expounded above.[7]

Not by Intellectual Understanding but Rather by Reverence for God Do We Earn the World to Come

In any case there is a strong connection between the fulfillment of the mitzvot and religious emotion, whose foundation is reverence. This emotion opens for us the gates of the World to Come as well. For thus it is written: "How great is Your goodness that You have in store for those who fear You" (Psalm 31:20). And what if the inquiring person would ask: How

* Note: this reciprocal relation is similar to the triangle of "externalization, objectification, internalization" described in Peter Berger, *The Sacred Canopy*, Chapter 1. (LL)

** Especially the start of 3:27: after he had emphasized that "everything follows the intention of the heart," he continues: "All the commandments of the Torah are a means of acquiring human perfection."

is it that reverence brings eternal life, and not intellectual understanding (according to the view of Maimonides and Gersonides)? Here he cites Ecclesiastes as evidence that philosophy only aids a person "to be happy and to do good *in his life*," that is to say that with its help we achieve good and moral life only in this world, but that which is done out of reverence, "it shall be forever" (see Ecclesiastes 3:12–14*); "and since His wisdom thus decrees, we need not be over-wise and ask, how can reverence guide one to human perfection?" (3:33).

What is the difference between Crescas and Albo?

The ideas of Albo that we have reviewed are sufficient to demonstrate the difference between him and Crescas, his teacher. Indeed Crescas defended the Jewish faith, especially its commandments. He also argued against the Christians that the commandments are capable of gaining us entry to the World to Come, but his argument is theoretical; he teaches in detail in what way the 613 commandments guide us to the love of God, and he relies on the Greek philosophers in order to explain that love connects us to our Heavenly Father. By contrast, Albo does not explain the relationship between the commandments and the emotions scientifically, or between the emotions and eternal life; rather he relies on scriptural verses, or more exactly, on the midrashic interpretation of these verses. This divergence from his teacher's method derives from the essential difference between them:** that Crescas remained a philosopher even in his apologetic writings, whereas Albo was first and foremost an apologete. Perhaps he was justified in thinking that midrashic interpretations based on philosophical premises would interest his readers more than abstract proofs, and that they would be more fitting to demonstrate the truth of the Jewish faith, as his Christian opponents also acknowledged the authority of the Bible.

---

* The deduction follows from the two assertions in verse 14: "Whatever God has brought to pass will be forever;" and "God has brought to pass that men revere Him." Hence, the fruits of reverence will stand forever. (LL)

** Perhaps there is a difference — not in kind but in degree — also in the fact that Albo emphasizes more the authoritative character of certain commands. He acknowledges explicitly (3:24) that there are mitzvot "whose reason is not known, such as the prohibition of pork and mixed fabrics and seeds, the red heifer, etc. which are the King's decree," "and they tell us nothing except that this is God's will." He passes in silence over all the attempts to find reasons even for these mitzvot, and he praises (3:27) those "who do not try to second-guess the Lord but follow His instruction in all innocence." He interprets honoring father and mother as an injunction to follow "the tradition of the fathers and the sages of the religion" (3:26), for "his purpose is not to justify Judaism but to refute Christianity" (Tänzer, *Dioe Religionsphilosophie Joseph Albos*, 1896, 77), or more precisely, to deflect the Christian attacks on his own faith.

The Value of Albo's Method

Even though the apologetic factor is prevalent in the book (and we should not disparage anyone who stood up to the prevailing current of Christianity and the wave of baptism in this time period), there is also educational (that is to say "religious-practical") and scientific value in his explanation of the commandments. However, the field in which he showed his greatest strength is not the purely theoretical (i.e., philosophy), but rather the descriptive-scientific: psychology. In his description of the relationship among reverence, love, and joy, Albo was unrivalled in his generation, and among those who came after him as well. Indeed, that branch of modern science called "psychology of religion" uses more subtle analytical techniques than those of the Middle Ages, but even now the central questions are capable of solution only through introspection and exhaustive research of religious literature. It appears even in our time that Albo's ideas, with their emphasis on the common denominator between fear and love, are truer to religious experience and the spirit of the Bible than the view of Rudolf Otto, which emphasized precisely their opposition, as stated in his very influential book *The Idea of the Holy*. Albo thus makes a major contribution to the understanding of our religious-spiritual experience.

Chapter 15
Don Isaac Abravanel

Categories of the Torah's Commandments

In his commentary on the Torah,[1] Rabbi Isaac Abravanel paid great attention to the explanation of the mitzvot. He speaks in many places about the primary question: whether there are reasons for all of the mitzvot. In the introduction to the portion *Mishpatim*, he distinguishes among: (1) Testaments (*edot*), "which are the mitzvot that testify about the true beliefs and the wonders of God, like the Sabbath, the mitzvah of Pesaḥ, matzah, the holiday of Sukkot, and the like, whose reasons are known"; (2) Statutes (*ḥukkim*), "whose reasons are elusive and unknown" and which we accept as "the edicts and decrees of the King"; and (3) Civil Laws (*mishpatim*), which are "laws pertaining among fellow human beings." His essential intention is to prove that this third category is also different from the laws of non-Jews.

There is an Intrinsic Value to the Mitzvot of the Torah

Abravanel does not seek to decide if it is possible to find reasons for the *ḥukkim*. He certainly knows that there are commentators who completely reject investigation into the reasons. In the introduction to Portion *Shoftim* (the 5th doubt) he asks why we are obligated to follow the words of the great court "even if they say that the left is the right and the right is the left; for behold, that would justify the opinion of the one who says that there are no reasons for the mitzvot and that they are all according to the Divine will (that is to say that God's will is their only reason); and therefore, since God wants us to follow the Sages of the generation, and we have already done His will, this causes no harm. But according to the one who says that whatever the Torah forbade harms our souls and causes an evil effect in us, even though we do not know its reason . . . behold, when the Sages of the generation are in agreement in saying that an impure object is pure, shall we say that eating that object will not harm our souls and that it will not act according to its nature" just as it is obvious that a doctor's mistake is liable to harm us, even if all the doctors of the generation agree about it? We will not discuss Abravanel's answers to this difficulty; it is enough for us to emphasize that he explains that it is our duty to rely on the traditions of our Elders, on their explanations, and on their enactments, as they all are consistent with the essentials of the Torah (introduction to Portion *Shoftim*, Note 8). In other words, he rejects the assumption of those who say that there is no intrinsic value to the mitzvot of the Torah. In accordance with this, he asks (in his comment to Gen. 17): "What is the reason for the mitzvah of circumcision, since all of God's actions come out of His wisdom and they necessarily have a specific purpose, as Maimonides explained (*Guide* 3:23)?" Indeed there are "the King's decrees"*; but still we may ask about their reasons (in his introduction to Portion *Aḥarei Mot*, Question 17): "Since God wants the High Priest to perform the holy service on [Yom Kippur] in white garments, why did the Torah not command that he spend the entire day in them . . . and if it were a decree of the King that some of the worship would be in golden garments and some in white garments," why did it not enact that he first complete the worship in the golden garments and afterwards the worship in the white garments, and instead commanded that he switch the garments several times?

There is No Uniform Purpose for All of the Mitzvot of the Torah

Many of our nation's Sages have said that there is not only a separate reason, available for our investigating, for each mitzvah, but that there is also a uniform purpose to the entire Torah: it leads — either directly or indirectly — to knowledge of God (*Guide*), or to love of God (Crescas), or to the pure reverence of God (Albo). According to Abravanel, too, the mitzvot of the Torah are not separate domains. The verse is precise: "All of the *mitzvah* which I command you" — and not all of the *mitzvot*; the Rabbis equated the mitzvot of the Torah with our 248 limbs in order to indicate that the unity of the Torah is similar to the unity of our body (comment to Deuteronomy 8); because of this, even the mitzvot that we are unable to perform now should be important to us (comment on Exodus 26, end). But Abravanel does not affix a specific and uniform purpose to all of this "mitzvah." On the contrary, in the abundance of reasons that he brings for several mitzvot, some of them contradict one another, as if he is trying hard to defend the mitzvot at any price and in any possible way. However, Abravanel rejects or at least limits as much as possible the value of two ways of explanation used by earlier commentators:

---

* We observe the prohibition of mixed species and certain other laws "because they are the king's decree, not because of intellectual judgment" (Introduction to Portion *Kedoshim*).

Abravanel Objects to Utilitarian Reasons for the Mitzvot

(1) Abravanel is wary of reasons that contain any material utility (economic, hygienic, etc.).[2] Of course, he cannot deny that the law of divorce, which he defends against attacks by the Christians, was given for our benefit, but he also explains the permission to divorce and the prohibition to return the divorcee who was married (Deuteronomy 24) in a symbolic way: the man signifies form, the woman matter "in the parables of the prophets and their riddles."* Just as matter does not receive or retain form unless it is ready for it and the heavenly factors support their union, so too is the human union not compatible unless the characters of the man and woman are compatible and they have God's added help; and just as the form will separate from the matter that is not compatible with it and will never return to it, so too is it with a man and his wife. In opposition to "many commentators," Abravanel completely rejects the hygienic reason for the forbidden foods (in Leviticus 11), "for if it were so, the book of God's Torah would be on the level of one small book of the many medical books that are short in their words and explanations, and this is not the way of God's Torah or the depth of its intentions."** He rejects the opinion of Maimonides that the incense was ordained to neutralize the bad smell of the slaughtered meat (on Exodus 25:39). Indeed, he admits that the performance of the mitzvot liberates us from the sway of the astral bodies[3] (on Deuteronomy 4:19, 270c etc.), not in a magical way, but because God, Who desires our worship, annuls the power of His servants (on Exodus 12, before verse 15). He emphasizes the reward for the mitzvot and sees in the conferring of reward an essential difference between the laws of the Torah and all of the secular laws (introduction to Portion *Mishpatim*), but these results, even though they are "useful,"*** do not blur but rather highlight the religious character of the Torah.

Abravanel is Sparing with Social Reasons for the Torah's Mitzvot

(2) Even though Abravanel is very interested in the social question and the development of social differences, social explanations are surprisingly rare in his commentary. Indeed, to give a reason for the festival pilgrimage

* On the basis of Plato, who compared matter to the female (*Guide* I, 17), Maimonides interpreted the evil woman and good woman in Proverbs as two kinds of matter (III, 8), and many (such as Gersonides) followed his example.

** This statement is opposed first of all to the views of Maimonides (see above, p. 109) and Gersonides (above, p. 121). Of course Abravanel cites scientific evidence in support of his own views; he emphasizes, for example, that the Torah did not forbid any plants, though some of them are quite harmful.

*** Abravanel speaks of the spiritual and moral "usefulness" of mitzvot in many places.

he points out that it is liable to facilitate peaceful interpersonal relations because people are dependent on each other (end of *Re'eh,* Application 4). But the primary significance of the sabbatical-release and Jubilee years refers to "the two great kindnesses that God wrought in His world": the original Sabbath of creation, and the giving of the Torah fifty days after the Exodus from Egypt (beginning of *Behar,* "the First Way"). On the basis of this idea he interprets all the details of these mitzvot, adding a psychological and cosmological explanation as well. Abravanel nearly passes over in silence the command "love your neighbor as yourself." One should perhaps understand this according to the purpose of his book: to remove stumbling blocks and refute objections.* It is nevertheless strange that he did not emphasize the value of this mitzvah, even though the appreciation of love is so prominent in the works of Crescas and Albo, as well as in the *Dialogues of Love* of his son, Judah Abravanel, and the Sages called this "the major principle of the Torah."**

Abravanel's Method of Interpreting the Mitzvot

The ways Abravanel followed in order to explain the mitzvot of the Torah are three: fulfilling the mitzvot reinforces the tie between Israel and their Heavenly Father because (1) they teach us the correct and desirable way to express our religious feelings; (2) they impart important ideas — cosmological, psychological, historical — on which our religious outlook is based; and (3) they direct us to lead holy and pure lives.

Some mitzvot incorporate two or all three of these objectives; we shall address these first.

The Reasons for the Sacrifices

In discussing the purpose of the sacrifices (Introduction to Leviticus, p. 183d) Abravanel mentions the view of Maimonides, who said that these mitzvot were not given for their own sake ("primary intention") but only to distance us from idolatry. He rejects Naḥmanides' criticism of this notion. According to Abravanel, only on the basis of Maimonides' method can we explain why the Torah limited access to the sacrificial service (but not to prayer), and why the prophets condemned exaggerated valuation of this form of worship. Some rabbinic sayings also support

* It is interesting that Abravanel explains the lulav and etrog (in Leviticus 23) only briefly, perhaps because satisfactory explanations were already well known among the people.

** He opposes other explanations not out of methodological scruples, but because the scientific ideas that formed their basis were garbled, and relying on them was like "relying on a broken reed" (Introduction to Portion *Terumah,* 155c).

Maimonides.* But the sacrifices also have another significance, "that a person should draw near to God, submit to Him, and believe in God's existence, unity and providence." It is for this reason that Adam and Noah[4] offered the sacrifices to which Naḥmanides alluded (184b). This was also the view of Gersonides[5]; however Abravanel does not accept his explanation of the sacrifices. He attributes different purposes to different sacrifices in accord with their detailed rules: the burnt-offering suggests that just as the animal in its death unites with the fire on the altar and ascends as a sweet fragrance to God, so should the person making the offering ascend to God after his death. Therefore it is called an *olah* (something that "goes up"); not only does it express our hope, but it immediately causes our souls to cleave to God, and for God to imbue us with the spirit of prophecy[6] (184c). The laws of the meal-offering and libation that are brought with the burnt-offering accord with this explanation: the fine flour, food fit for humans (unlike the barley or animal fodder that the suspected adulteress brings), and the oil signify our pure intellect, whereas the wine is a symbol of the people of Israel, who are compared to a vineyard and a vine.

He explains the purpose of the sin-offering and guilt-offering by analyzing their detailed rules. For example, the monetary expense that these offerings occasion for us is liable to make us wary of any carelessness; the innards of the sin-offering offered on the altar signify our inner purity, for we did not transgress the mitzvot maliciously (184d).

The peace-offerings come to express our thankfulness for the past or our prayers for the future; the intestines and kidneys, offered on the altar, allude to our thoughts (he also adds other reasons); the priests participate in eating the peace-offerings, so that they will also participate in the thanksgiving of the offerer and his prayer (185c, and see comment on Leviticus 6:12).

---

* Abravanel attached great significance to the dictum of R. Phinehas in the name of R. Levi (Leviticus Rabbah 22:8); however, Rabbi David Hoffman, in his Commentary on Leviticus I, 82, correctly emphasized that this passage was transmitted incorrectly. The midrash reads: "A parable of a son of the king whose appetite got the better of him and he got in the habit of eating non-kosher meat. The king said, 'Let this (i.e., similar meat, but kosher) be served regularly on my table, but let them be forbidden to him.'" In Abravanel's commentary, he cites it as: "Let him eat them regularly on my table" — as if the king is feeding his son the non-kosher meat and hoping thereby to convert him from his evil habit!" Hoffman is of the opinion that Abravanel was unaware of the corruption of the text, but rested his argument on it nevertheless. In my opinion the fault is with the copyists or printers of Abravanel's work. Abravanel would not liken the sacrifices to eating non-kosher meat. He only relies on the fact that the king invites his son, not because he desires his company, but to wean him from sin, and this is Maimonides' theory of "second [indirect] intention" regarding the sacrifices.

Abravanel displays considerable effort in his commentary on the public offerings. We have seen that Maimonides rejected the question of why the Torah commanded to offer a ewe rather than a ram, seven ewes rather than eight, though he did not himself refrain from explaining some of these details[7]; whereas for Abravanel, these fine details of the mitzvot are extremely important. For example, "the numbers found in the divine Torah, whether in connection with the sacrifices, the festivals, or the purification rituals"[8] — they all have their reasons, and were instituted with a specific intention (272a). Therefore, he goes on at length to explain the sacrifices listed in Portion *Pinḥas* (Numbers Chapters 28–29): the two daily offerings symbolize the giving of the Torah (which took place in the morning) and the Exodus from Egypt (for the Paschal lamb was slaughtered at twilight); a *kebhes* (sheep) is offered because we are "subdued" (*nikhbashim*) before God*; and the meal-offering recalls the manna. He is even more persuaded of the cosmological explanation: the daily offering alludes to the double progression of the sun over the visible surface of the earth and its hidden side**; for the day and night "overtake" (*kobeshim*) the world (253a). The two lambs offered on the Sabbath recall the creation of the world and the Exodus from Egypt (253b). The seventy bullocks of the festival were instituted to represent the seventy nations of the world, as per the view of the rabbis, as well as the seventy years of a normal human life-span (comment on Numbers 29:12). In this manner he finds reasons for all the festival offerings.

The Reasons for the Shofar

Abravanel finds a wide variety of reasons for the mitzvah of the Shofar (see on Leviticus 23:24):

1. Just as the blowing of the horn during the Jubilee year announces the emancipation of the slaves, so on Rosh Hashanah it proclaims that we are not enslaved to the astral powers.
2. Just as it was blown during the enthronement of King Solomon, so do we blow the Shofar in accepting God's sovereignty over us.
3. "Shall the horn be blown in the city and the people not tremble?" Thus the Shofar "confounds Satan" (i.e., our own evil impulse) and awakens us to repentance.

---

* Etymological homilies are found occasionally in the Bible (*kayitz/ketz* [summer/end] in Amos 8:2, *shaked/shoked* [almond/take care] in Jeremiah 1:19), and quite frequently in the rabbinic lore (as *kappot/kafut*, connecting the palm frond [lulav] to Isaac, in Leviticus Rabbah 30:10).

** This recalls Philo's explanation (in *The Special Commandments* I, 269) that the daily offering symbolized God's mercies that persist by day and night.

4. It recalls the Binding of Isaac.
5. It recalls the gathering of the people at Mount Sinai.
6. It alludes to the ingathering of the exiles and the resurrection, at which time the great Shofar will be sounded.

These examples suffice to explain that the mitzvot serve as an expression of our feelings — feelings of thanksgiving, repentance, and submission. But we should add a few words about the pedagogic and moral value that Abravanel attributes to the mitzvot.

The Pedagogic Value of the Mitzvot

The mitzvot teach us about religious, historical, natural-scientific, and psychological matters. Not only do the sabbatical-year, the daily offering, and the Shofar allude to the giving of the Torah, but the Red Heifer does as well. It is a symbol of our Torah, and therefore it is introduced by the phrase: "This is the statute of the Torah." The two goats of Yom Kippur, as well as the sounding of the Shofar, also have a historical value. In the rabbis' view they recall Esau the *se'ir* (hairy one/goat) and his brother Jacob the *tza'ir* (younger one — comment to Leviticus 16:5). The commentary on the Tabernacle is similar to that of Josephus,[9] which he quotes: "The Tabernacle and its implements allude to the shape of the earth and its parts" (as well as the upright path that a person should choose — comment to Exodus 25:10). For the garments of the High Priest he suggests a cosmological explanation (see on Exodus 28:10, and the "Third Way") on the basis of the Greek assumption that the world in its arrangement and connection is like a single body: the diadem is a symbol of the upper world, the world of intellect; the turban symbolizes the constellations; the rest of the garments symbolize the terrestrial world; the "four elements" correspond to the four materials out of which the garments were composed (blue, purple scarlet yarns, and twisted linen)*; and the two precious lazuli stones on which the names of the tribes of Israel were inscribed are a sign that the Jewish people is prepared to accept the prophetic inspiration. However, to this explanation he prefaces two others that are partly or wholly anthropological. According to the first (on Exodus 28:6, 162b) the garments of the ordinary priest allude to the deeds of our limbs that they cover: the robe that covers the body cautions us concerning the perfection of our deeds in general, the breeches and sash signify modesty, the turban signifies faith. The garments of the High Priest are to be explained in another fashion: the ephod indicates the

* He also (like Gersonides) found a cosmological reason for the fringed garment (on Numbers 15:37).

superior rank of the people of Israel, the tunic signifies divine providence, the breastplate and diadem point to prophecy. The second solution matches all the garments to our limbs: the turban corresponds to the head, the breastplate to the heart, the ephod to the liver, the robe to the reproductive organs (and of course they all symbolize the virtues connected to these parts of the body), the tunic is like the skin, the breeches correspond to the flesh, the turbans to the bones, the sash to the sinews.

Ethical-Religious Explanations of the Torah's Commandments

The anthropological explanations serve as a transition to ethical-religious ones. The view that the Torah comes to redeem us from the pollution of original sin[10] does not occupy an important place in Abravanel's explanation of the mitzvot. He notes that it is the purpose of the Torah to guide us to a unified stance, ethical and religious, by means of all its injunctions; for this reason it combines — in the Ten Commandments, in *Mishpatim* (the Covenant Code: Exodus 21–23), and in *Kedoshim* (the Holiness Code, Leviticus 19–20) various mitzvot that are apparently quite dissimilar,* such as: forbidding vengeance, limiting the appetites, and dietary rules, so that we shall be "abstinent from every dishonor, lowliness and evil action." Because they generate evil qualities in our soul, in discussing the foodstuffs that the Torah prohibits (on Leviticus 11), he writes, in language similar to the Mishnah (end of Tractate *Niddah*): "Caution leads to abstinence, and abstinence leads to sanctity."

Abravanel learns important ethical lessons from the laws of the Passover on the basis of a commentary that he found "in the words of a certain sage of the gentiles" (on Exodus 12:15, 122c). The six days of the festival followed by a day of cessation of work correspond to the six days of creation followed by the first Sabbath, and both of these remind us of the days of our life amounting to seventy years: for sixty years a man should labor in the world and be productive, whereas in the last ten years "he should not engage in material concerns but rather in attachment to his God." God brought about the Exodus from Egypt not only on the model of the creation of the world, but also on that of the birth of the infant who comes out into the world amidst pain and suffering. The prohibition of leaven cautions us that we must abolish "the leaven in the dough,"[11] namely the evil impulse in ourselves; for this reason, it is also forbidden to offer honey on the altar. "At twilight on the fourteenth day" we inspect for leaven by the light of the lamp (or candle) "which represents the soul," because a person is not

* Abravanel is also prone to interpret the juxtapositions of portions and the continuations of verses.

punishable for his sins until his fourteenth year. He piles on these symbolic explanations of the mitzvot and customs of Pesaḥ ad lib. (His explanations of the other festivals are similar in character.) If these mitzvot arouse us to ethical reflection, the commandment of circumcision operates on us more directly through its very fulfillment. Not only do we carry in our body the king's banner, but circumcision also reduces the animal urge, and therefore all our children are begotten in sanctity, the daughters no less than the sons (on Genesis 17:9).

The Religious Influence of the Mitzvot

The influence of the mitzvot is religious, not just ethical. We have already seen that the sacrifices were prescribed in order to distance us from idolatry; in particular, our ancestors were commanded to offer a lamb when they left Egypt, to demonstrate that "they turned their back on the worship of that astral sign (Aries) and became attached to God" (on Exodus 12:3), for the Egyptians were supposed to have worshipped the ram. Other mitzvot (the prohibition of meat-with-milk: Exodus 23:19, and of hybrid species: Leviticus 19:19) were also given so that we should not perform abominable rituals that were customary among other nations, as Maimonides interpreted. The sacrifices cause the spirit of prophecy to rest on the people of Israel, as per the view of Halevi (Numbers 28). However, even though Abravanel agrees with Halevi in regard to the value of the Land of Israel and the mitzvot connected with it that prepare us to receive the influence of the prophetic spirit,[12] Halevi's view that all the "hortative" mitzvot have the purpose of raising us to the level of the "superior type" of prophetic man plays no recognizable place in Abravanel's explanation of the mitzvot.

All the Mitzvot Speak to Us in Allusions and Symbols

After reviewing the modes of explanation that Abravanel rejects, and those that he particularly prizes, we should note that in his view, too, the whole Torah is unified, but its unity is not so much integral as methodical (i.e., not all the laws are directed to a single ideal — such as knowledge or reverence — but the majority speak a common language: the language of allusion). In this language they recall for us the secrets of eternity, the elements of our human and Jewish existence, and the lives of the ancients. There are very few mitzvot for which he has not found a hidden reason,* and there are many for which he labored to find a new allusion,

* For instance, certain mitzvot in Portion *Kedoshim* (Leviticus 19–20), whose intention is to keep us from idolatry (see his Commentary to Leviticus 19:23).

not resting content with the clear and simple reason that the Torah itself offered for them, such as the commands of the sabbatical-release year, Pesaḥ, and the garment-fringe. Perhaps we sober moderns will say in hindsight that the explanations Abravanel carved out for himself with regard to several mitzvot are "broken cisterns," but the mystical veil that he draws over our mitzvot was appropriate to its time, when the symbolic and even the allegorical approach was in the ascendancy, as we see in the kabbalah[13] and in the sermons of that time.[14] However, we need not judge all his explanations of the mitzvot as being limited only to their time. The dichotomy between the "classical" tradition, striving for clarity and simplicity, and the "romantic," which values allusiveness and mystery in their own right, has not ceased and perhaps will never cease. It is worth remarking that to the extent that the romantic spirit has influenced the interpreters of religion, they have come closer to Abravanel, knowingly or unknowingly. Rabbi Jehiel Michael Sachs, in his German translation of the Mahzor, prefaced the Shofar-blowing service with an explanation that may be seen as a paraphrase of Abravanel's many-faceted commentary on that mitzvah. Rabbi Samson Raphael Hirsch, who interpreted most of the religious mitzvot symbolically, decked out our religious life in a mystical and allegorical garb such as Don Isaac Abravanel imparted to the mitzvot of the Torah.

Chapter 16
Summary of the Medieval Thinkers

In the previous chapters, we clarified the differences of opinions among the philosophers of the Middle Ages. Now we will show their common elements.

The Difference Between the Hellenistic and Medieval Thinkers' Explanation of the Mitzvot

These philosophers continue the Hellenistic endeavor. They, too, strive to build a bridge between the scientific life-outlook of the Greeks and our Torah. But the two disadvantages from which Hellenistic Judaism suffers are not to be found in the explanations of the commandments of the sages of the Middle Ages. They had expert familiarity with the Bible in the original, as well as rabbinic literature. We have already shown, for example, how Ibn Daud and Maimonides drew on the prophets and the rabbis for their explanation of the sacrifices. And even though they did not accord the aggadah the same authority as the halakha, the midrashim provided them with ammunition to take a stand against the Greek spirit. Furthermore, most of them had better scientific training than Philo and Josephus. Greek rhetoric did not spoil them at all, whereas their spirits were disciplined by love of investigation and science. Maimonides and Crescas were independent thinkers in the full meaning of the word, not just men of letters who used illustrations from science to explain the tradition of their fathers. Their level of intellectual explanation of the commandments, therefore, was superior to that of the Hellenists. (As for the rabbis, it was never their purpose to provide a general systematic explanation.)

Balance of Autonomous and Heteronomous Reasons

The above-mentioned philosophers benefited from the influence of Jewish literature and philosophy. The devotion to their ancestral heritage was joined in their hearts with the scientific "eros" of the great Greek thinkers. Thus they tended to seek the golden mean in their explanation of the commandments. The Tannaim and Amoraim had emphasized the heteronomic reasons, and paid attention to the autonomous reasons only in order to awaken the emotions of morality and piety. The Hellenistic thinkers, on the other hand, took it upon themselves to present the commandments of the Torah as commentary on the universally accepted natural law, and they neglected the theonomic reasons. The medieval thinkers based the fulfillment of the commandments on our obligation and our decision to carry out wholeheartedly the will of the divine Creator-Legislator; this theonomic reason establishes the religious character of performance of the mitzvot.* But they all agreed that it is possible for us to clarify the will of the Creator with the assistance of philosophy, which discovers the ways of God's activity in nature and explains the ethical requirements. On the question of which method should be given preference, the external way of authority or the internal way of reason and conscience, their views differed. But even the authoritarian Halevi explains the influence of the commandments with recourse to medical science, which demonstrates the influence of drugs on the body, whereas the rationalist Maimonides enunciates, even in the *Guide*, that the divine Torah requires a method of explanation quite different from that used in interpreting ordinary human laws. The philosophers of the Middle Ages gave equal weight to theonomous and autonomous reasons, to scientific understanding of religion, and the traditional ways of knowing God.

We said earlier that the commandments are "rational from the perspective of the Lawgiver and irrational from the human perspective."[1] Indeed, this difference "from the perspective of the Commander and the commanded" is explicitly emphasized by only one of the medieval thinkers, namely Crescas,[2] and his formulation bears the stamp of his personal outlook. But in a certain sense he speaks in the name of all his colleagues.

Crescas teaches that the purpose of the commandments from God's viewpoint is to train us for eternal perfection; so far, his view is the same as that of all the other philosophers. Some additionally attributed material utility to the commandments. Even Saadia, who harps on this utilitarian aspect more than his peers, agrees that at the very least the "hortative" commandments were given to us to earn our eternal reward. Maimonides (*Guide* 3:27) assigns primacy to "intellectual perfection" over "ethical perfection," as only the first is "the reason for eternal life."[3] The definition of this goal — preparation for eternal salvation — is based on three

* That is why the concept of *avodah* ("service") is prevalent in the rabbinic lore, and the term *oved* ("to serve") in the philosophical literature. But Philo also speaks frequently of *therapeutai theou* (i.e., "the servants of God").

assumptions: (1) the eschatological hope (i.e., the faith in the immortality of the soul or the spirit) that was held in common by all the religions that use the Bible and the later Greek philosophers from the days of Plato onward; (2) the principle of eudaemonism (that all our actions are directed at our happiness and our perfection), which is rooted in the human heart and which received its scientific expression in Greek philosophy; and (3) on Greek theology, which Crescas expounded more thoroughly than his colleagues, and which says that every created entity (including every law in the world) has a purpose for which it was created, and that only by uncovering this purpose is it possible to understand it and to prove its worth. The explanation of the mitzvot with the help of this triple thread is characteristic of the medieval thinkers; the eudaemonistic idea, which is very common in Philo's writings (and which should not be identified with this idea in the Middle Ages or in the modern period*), does not serve as a reason for the Hellenistic writers in their explanation of the mitzvot of the Torah.

The Creator's Wisdom is Recognized in His Mitzvot

Many of the philosophers emphasized (and none disputed) that obedience to the mitzvot is itself sufficient to arouse God's favor, which imparts to us eternal life and frees us from the rule of the astral powers (Ibn Ezra, Gersonides). If that is so, one should not interpret the substance of the mitzvot on the basis of the Creator's eschatological will. However, all the philosophers acknowledge not only that God's commands are an indication of His wisdom and justice (this was a common belief of all our great thinkers), but also that it is possible to a great extent for us to know and demonstrate the qualities of the Legislator from His laws. They especially tried to demonstrate the proof of those mitzvot that appeared pointless in the eyes of the scientific community. In this systematic explanation they are close to the Hellenistic thinkers; but whereas the latter first proved the worth of the mitzvot and deduced from this that they were "divine," the medieval thinkers relied on the faith common to all the religions, that the Torah was divinely revealed, and from it they derived the conclusion that the mitzvot were not given for naught. The Creator's wisdom is recognized especially in the power of the mitzvot to guide us to intellectual or moral levels. Some of the thinkers found a causal connection between this pedagogic intent and the eschatological one that we discussed earlier; our

* The Greek concept of "*eudaemonia*" combines pleasure and tranquility with obedience to the "daemon" that dwells within our conscience. (See my *Poseidonios' metaphysische Schriften* I, 64; II, 76.)

ascent to the rank of the "elect,"* through the knowledge or love of God, already connects us in this world by an unbreakable tie to the true Source of life.

We Must Observe the Mitzvot Even If Their Reasons are Hidden From Us

The power of the mitzvot to enable us to acquire our eternal reward serves as a basis for explaining the mitzvot only from the standpoint of the Commander, for we should see him not as a tyrant who imposes his will on his servants, but as a father who wishes his sons to earn their merits. This does not work from our standpoint as those commanded (i.e., we should not be as servants who serve the master in order to obtain a reward, whether temporal or eternal). Indeed, Maimonides[4] attacked Antigonus of Socho on pedagogical grounds for revealing his view to the ordinary masses without considering that they will do the good only if one shows them the reward, like the schoolchildren who must be won over by the incentives of reward and punishment.But he also agrees with Antigonus in his *Commentary to the Mishnah,* which is a book that was not written only for the elite. Rabbi Joseph Albo expressed the view of his colleagues when he said that only one who acts out of love and fear of God is called one who engages in the Torah "for its own sake," not as one who loves the reward and fears the punishment. Pure love and fear motivate us to fulfill all the mitzvot, even those whose special reasons we do not understand.** In this respect one may say that the fulfillment of mitzvot is "irrational from the standpoint of the doer." But this irrationality, which the rabbis emphasized even more, is mitigated by all the philosophers through their demonstration of the value of the mitzvot — scientific, ethical, and pedagogic. These demonstrations, which occupy such a considerable place in the philosophic literature, are important not only in order to explain the mitzvot from the standpoint of the wise and just Creator, but so as to deepen their fulfillment from the human side. For in the view of all the philosophers from Saadia onward,*** the love of truth and right is implanted

---

* "Elect" — the Arabic term *safwa* is used by Baḥya and Halevi. On the Aristotelians, for whom knowledge was the elevating principle, or Crescas and Albo for whom it was love, see above, pages 102, 137, 144.

** See my discussion of this idea above in connection with Ibn Daud (p. 87), Maimonides (pp. 96ff.), Albo (p. 142), and Abravanel (p. 149).

*** Indeed, Maimonides and his followers attributed to knowledge (and indirectly to virtue) an eschatological value, but there is none who will say that the scientific "eros" burned in him less fiercely than in Saadia. In his view ethical virtue was merely the health of the soul, and it was natural for us to strive for it.

in our hearts, and the more we recognize that the Torah enlightens our eyes and purifies our hearts, the stronger grows our love of the mitzvot and the love of the Creator who wishes His creatures' perfection.

The Love of God, Not Pursuit of Happiness, Enables Us to Fulfill the Creator's Mitzvot

As is known, the sage S.D. Luzzatto[5] attacked the Spanish-Jewish thinkers for their admiration of the Greeks, who had prescribed "personal enjoyment and success by worldly standards." Proponents of Hellenism acknowledge that eudaemonism (to which the Jewish thinkers approached) "causes egoism, to which the majority of the Greek thinkers succumbed."[6] However, our survey has demonstrated that the accusation of egoism is not justified at all in the case of our medieval thinkers: first, because eschatological eudaemonism serves as a basis of a pure and exalted ethical doctrine even in Greece (as in the teaching of Plato); and second, because the factor that motivates us to the fulfillment of the ethical and religious commands is not the pursuit of our happiness but love of God and love of the good. For that reason, the modern attacks on eudaemonism (Kant, Nietzsche) do not affect these Jewish thinkers.

The Individualistic Direction in Explanation of the Mitzvot

However, even if there is no egoism in their method, there is indeed individualism.* These philosophers are directed first and foremost to the perfection of the individual person and his happiness, and they even attribute the communal promises in the Torah primarily to individual interests. In Maimonides's view,[7] the good reward that the Torah promises to the people of Israel refers to eternal reward, for it is what facilitates every individual to perform the mitzvot with a willing heart. Halevi indeed emphasizes the difference between the promises of the Torah and the description of paradise in other religions,[8] but he adds that the consciousness of the "finger of God" and the closeness of God, to which the history of our people testifies, is apt to arouse in the soul of the inquirer the yearning to liberate himself from the yoke of this world,[9] and the confidence that we can be close to God, even in this world. This individualism is found not only in Greek thought, but also in connection with the eschatological

---

* Indeed, Halevi portrays the individual person as a limb of the body of the people, in order to explain the value of communal prayer (3:19). For more on his attitude to individualism, see the annual *Kenesset* 1942, 278.

hope — in Christianity* and in certain streams of Islam. It follows that the social motive** in the Middle Ages, unlike the Hellenistic period, occupies a very limited place: not the perfection of the world under the rule of justice, but guiding the individual to the next world was considered to be the most important objective for all religions in this period.

Of course, some will find fault with this individualism and with the corresponding eudaemonism despite its limitation. However, we should recognize that every outlook must compromise, one way or another, between the "categorical imperative" and every person's aspiration to happiness and salvation, between our feeling of connection to the community and our striving for personal fulfillment. We certainly do not share all our predecessors' assumptions; we shall address this in the final chapter. We should note here that they did not lower the traditional standard of Jewish ethics by drawing closer to Greek thought. They tried and succeeded in drawing on the scientific idealism of the Greeks in order to explain and strengthen the religious idealism of Judaism, even when deliberating on Judaism's unique identifying characteristic: the mitzvot of the Torah. The three factors that we elaborated in our introduction — the apologetic, the theoretical, and the pedagogic — influenced all these thinkers to various degrees. They defended the mitzvot against the attacks of philosophers, Christians, and apathetic Jews who did not recognize their manifest and hidden value; they explained the mitzvot on the basis of a God-concept that was in agreement with tradition and the philosophy of the times; they deepened the sense of piety by rejecting any mechanical performance of the mitzvot that contained no heartfelt intention; and they discouraged superstition. Their conclusions are not ours, although many of their explanations are important to us as well. By their methods, they set an example for everyone imbued with love of science and faith in their tradition.

---

* Perhaps it is no accident that the notion of "salvation" in its eschatological sense is not to be found, evidently, except in the books of the later philosophers, who occasionally resorted to the terminology that was in currency among Christian theologians. The translators of the early philosophers [bearing in mind that Saadia, Baḥya, Halevi, and Maimonides wrote in Judeo-Arabic and were translated into Hebrew by the Ibn Tibbons — LL] speak rather of "eternal life." Klatzkin's *Thesaurus of Hebrew Philosophical Terms,* which neglects post-Maimonidean thinkers, does not even mention this idea. The lexicographer Ben Yehuda cites instances only from the later thinkers, such as Albo, Shem Tov Ibn Falaquera, and Isaac Abravanel.

** We must make a distinction, however, between the *social motive* for observance of mitzvot in general and the *social idea* as addressed in such mitzvot as *tzedakah*. The latter was indeed very important. See above, p. 110 on Maimonides, and see the book of Dr. Yehuda Bergman, *Ha-tzedakah be-Yisrael*. (IH/LL)

Chapter 17
Principal Conclusions

When we set out on our journey, we had two objectives: historical and principled. Up to this point, we have dealt primarily with the historical investigation. We have tried to extract from the teachings of our great thinkers psychological findings that attest not only to their intellectual creativity but also to their character as human individuals and as Jews. If we have succeeded in illuminating the portraits of our spiritual leaders from a new viewpoint, our foray into this branch of Jewish literature will not have been in vain.

However, the question of principle is no less important. Indeed, our predecessors wrote what they wrote not to demonstrate their intellectual prowess, but to offer instruction to anyone interested in the reasons for the mitzvot, especially their coreligionists, who felt the need for an explanation because of the three factors that we explained above (in the latter part of Chapter 1), in whole or in part. There is no doubt that in previous times, the vast majority of those who read these classic Jewish thinkers did so only because of their present relevance to them. Does this kind of relevance of the explanation of the mitzvot apply in our own time?

In our consideration of each of these thinkers we have already raised this question, but only by way of allusion. Now, as we conclude this first volume of our work, we should recognize that the various individual answers offered to our problem by the classic Jewish thinkers do not stand in isolation. Despite the divergence of views that we highlighted in our historical survey, we have before us a single movement, with a unified objective: to defend the mitzvot and bring their value into the light of day. Many ideas recur repeatedly in the different schools. What, then, is the timeless and enduring value of this whole movement?

In order to give an answer, we must first arrange all the ideas in a systematic order, setting chronology aside, and we shall see how they are dependent on the spiritual situation of the past and the characters of the thinkers, and to what extent the facts themselves gave rise to their ideas and how meaningful they are for us as well.

(A) A Systematic Arrangement of the Answers to the Problem

Some of the explanations are heteronomous and some are autonomous.

All the thinkers believed (the Hellenistic Jews and Albo[1] were explicit on this point) that one should make a distinction between the law of nature, common to all humanity, and the laws of states and religions that are given by legislators. The law of nature can be proved by the aid of our intellect in the same way that we prove the laws of mathematics, whereas human laws are only susceptible of being *interpreted* by the intellect, as we interpret, for example, the laws of grammar. Thus we cannot base our obligation of obedience on rational proofs alone. This principle underlying the mitzvot was not expressed by any of these thinkers in so many words, but they all intuited it. Therefore we do not find a single one who parts company completely with heteronomic reasons. Whereas the Hellenists, in explaining heteronomic motives, emphasized particularly the national reasons that the Greeks also acknowledged,[2] the rabbis and medieval philosophers relied on the theonomic idea (that we perform the Creator's explicit will) that confers a religious character on all our actions. It is Rabbi Judah Halevi who says, particularly of the precepts characteristic of Judaism, that it is impossible to arrive at the divine matters except through the word of God. He did not differ from his colleagues on this point, but only gave their common view a particularly sharp formulation.

The Differences Between the Two Types of Reasons

The difference between the two explanations — appropriate to two different kinds of laws — engendered an important difference between two kinds of mitzvot: those that are simply a part of natural law, common to all human beings and susceptible of rational proof, and those specific to the Torah, which reason can only interpret. With regard to the latter, we cannot dispense completely with heteronomic motives. The formulation of this difference, of which the Torah gives only the merest hint,* takes on different forms in the thought-systems of its interpreters: the rabbis distinguished between *ḥukkim* and *mishpatim*, Saadia distinguished between "rational" and "revealed" ("hortative") commandments. Ibn Daud, Maimonides, and Albo also recognized this difference, but used these terms with some qualification. This difference is not found in the writings of those thinkers who paid no attention to autonomous reasons, or in the Hellenistic literature, which assigns no religious value to the heteronomous explanation.

* See my discussion above, p. 5, on the two sources of our religious life.

Every heteronomous explanation is irrational, for reason cannot prove the heteronomic mitzvot but can only interpret them; however, reason can explain and interpret the value of heteronomy itself. It is precisely Ibn Daud, the rationalist par excellence, who emphasized the religious value in our obedience when he said that the patriarch Abraham proved his fidelity by observing those mitzvot whose reason eluded him.* Maimonides also justifies the abundance of the mitzvot (alluding to the saying of Rabbi Hananiah ben Akashya) — to wit, the addition of the arbitrary mitzvot, in addition to the rational — with the explanation that they give us the opportunity to show the love of God. We should not be surprised, therefore, that Albo and Abravanel praised those who observed the mitzvot without any "rationalization" (i.e., second-guessing the motives of the legislator). This idea, that precepts that are hard to justify from the standpoint of the Commander but are nevertheless important and dear from the standpoint of the commanded, and the value placed on obedience for its own sake, differentiate the rationalism of the Middle Ages from that of Hermann Cohen and Abraham Geiger.

We should add that some of the rationalists even recognized the danger latent in the investigation of the reasons for the mitzvot. Maimonides cautions explicitly against neglect of those mitzvot whose reason we could not find, citing the rabbinic saying that the Torah refrained from revealing the reasons for the mitzvot publicly; and in the *Mishneh Torah*, which was written also for the laity, he is sparing in giving reasons. But if knowledge of the reasons is not a necessary condition for performing the mitzvot, what was the purpose of the spokesmen of Judaism in delving so deeply into their explanation?

We mentioned the three factors leading to these investigations (Chapter 1). Now we should ask: To what extent did these factors motivate these Jewish thinkers?

The Apologetic Factor

The *apologetic* factor is not found at all in the Torah, and is not especially prominent in the rabbis' explanations. They "deflected with a reed" those who challenged the mitzvot, without expressing their true views to them. But to the extent that our ancestors encountered the surrounding culture, they had to defend the mitzvot to them, and were even able to use the ammunition of their opponents in their defense. Their method of defense

* In the rabbis' view, Abraham demonstrated his limitless love by holding steadfast through many trials. Baḥya, Halevi, and Crescas also emphasized this theme. Philo, too, stresses that Abraham's obedience was testimony to his piety (Philo, *On Abraham* 62, 170).

is instructive. The challenger who says, "Your precepts do not fit the standards of the culture" can be answered in two ways: either by showing that the misfit is imagined, or by arguing that these criteria are not absolute. We can see how much these criteria changed in the course of time. We thus tend to prefer the second route. Two of our classic thinkers adopted it: Rabbi Judah Halevi, when he said that the Aristotelians' opposition to religious ritual can be explained in terms of their general outlook, to wit, their conception of God, which was religiously defective, and Rabbi Ḥasdai Crescas, who used sweeping psychological proofs to refute the intellectualism his contemporaries had absorbed from the method of Aristotle and his interpreters. Though they were critical of some points of the prevailing outlook, the remaining thinkers did not go so far, which is understandable. It is, of course, easy to argue that the Jews are a unique people with different applicable standards than other peoples,* but it is hard to refute the prevailing wisdom by convincing demonstrations and to establish new assumptions in its place. Furthermore, not only the Jews believed in the compatibility of the Torah's precepts with prevailing views, but to a limited extent some non-Jews agreed with them. There were Greeks who identified the Mosaic religion with a scientific faith.[3] It was Philo's view that such views ought not to be contradicted but extended by proving that even those precepts that they did not approve conformed to Jewish religious principles that were acceptable to those same gentiles. To be sure, Christianity maintained that it alone provided redemption from original sin, but Augustine admitted that circumcision also had that power.** Should one be surprised that Crescas cited his argument and expanded on it in explaining the power of the Akedah and the giving of the Torah? On the basis of these facts, Jewish thinkers believed that there was no ground for withdrawing from and avoiding the attacks of opponents, but they should be countered by broadening the assumptions found in world literature, thus fortifying the belief in the value of the mitzvot.

The Theoretical Factor

The theoretical factor also has an apologetic intention. Even philosophic thinkers such as Maimonides and Crescas gave reasons for the mitzvot not just from a scientific standpoint, nor did they try to give them any causal explanation, but they sought to justify them on the basis of their faith in the Creator's wisdom. For if the Creator were to give us mitzvot

* Perhaps Rashi would have answered in this fashion to the attacks from the Christian side, which his grandson Rashbam definitely took into consideration.

** See also what Thomas Aquinas wrote on circumcision: it mitigates lust (*Summa* I 102:1, 5), and it demonstrates obedience (III, 37:1) and faith (III 70:4, 5).

that had no purpose, would not mankind, who acts purposively, be more perfect than his Creator? Abravanel deduced from this, "Since all God's actions proceed from His wisdom, they must necessarily have a certain purpose." We ought not deduce from this that mortal humans have the ability to understand all the secrets of the Torah, just as there are phenomena in nature whose purpose we do not comprehend, but as these are exceptions, so is the case with the mitzvot. Does not the Torah itself state explicitly that we have "perfect laws and rules," as even the nations of the world recognize? (Ibn Ezra and Maimonides, citing Deuteronomy 4:8). Why, then, should we refrain from recognizing our Creator's wisdom from our Torah?

The Practical Factor

This question jumps out even more in connection with the *practical* factor. Only it — not the apologetic or the theoretical — is perceptible in the rabbis; it grows in importance in the explanations of Baḥya and in Maimonides' *Mishneh Torah,* and its influence is noticeable also in the thought-systems of Halevi and Abravanel. All of them emphasize the ideas and emotions that are apt to be aroused in us by the love of the mitzvot. The rabbis spun interpretations of the mitzvot, as of the narratives, in order to teach us a way of living, and not simply ethics. Baḥya cautions us about the intention of the heart, so that we shall merit our eternal reward; Maimonides tries to rid us of any superstition. All of them made the mitzvot dearer to our hearts, and thus fulfilled the theoretical and apologetic needs, for no way will be accepted as reasonable for understanding and justifying the mitzvot unless it proves to have a beneficial influence in the human arena.

The motives for explaining the mitzvot are nearly all *religious.* Before we summarize the explanations, we should specify the subject of the proofs and their methods.

Different Views Concerning the Reasons for the Commandments

The subject of the explanations, in general, is the Torahitic mitzvot, not the rabbinic ones, because the reasons for the latter are mostly clear. Only Ibn Daud and Crescas declared briefly that the rabbinic ordinances were advanced "as if Torahitic"; Maimonides gave reasons for Purim in the *Mishneh Torah;* Halevi addressed the formulation of the prayers at great length. In explaining the mitzvot of the Torah, our predecessors took into account (Albo in fine detail) that they are based on divine law (i.e., on a law that proceeded from God and leads to God). In particular, Philo,

Halevi, Maimonides, and Albo tried to prove the superiority of the Torah in comparison to other laws and religions. Because the content of the laws and their order were of divine authority, the rabbis and some later commentators (Gersonides and Abravanel) also tried to find reasons for the placement of one law next to another, in order to derive important ideas and to draw conclusions about the relations of the mitzvot to each other.

Among the methods of explanation, there are three whose status was the subject of dispute. Some of the rabbis interpreted the mitzvot using the same midrashic method of fanciful exegesis that was the custom in interpreting narrative. Maimonides saw this method as contradictory to a scientific approach and avoided it. He also restricted the recourse to symbolic interpretations, such as one finds among the rabbis, the Hellenistic writers, and the "romantics" such as Ibn Ezra and Abravanel. He introduced the "historic" method,* interpreting the mitzvot with due consideration for the spiritual level of the generation of the Exodus and the customs of neighboring peoples. Naḥmanides criticized this method on principle, ** as did Jacob ben Asher (author of the *Tur*); even Gersonides did not consider it sufficient to interpret the sacrifices, and Crescas undermined its basis by arguing that the generation of Moses was not on such a low level as Maimonides and Baḥya imagined.

But all the commentators agreed that the mitzvot may be interpreted by a logical method and by examining their consequences.

The *logical* way is clearly based on the rabbinic principle of "measure for measure," which the Hellenistic thinkers and medieval philosophers also adopted: the punishment should fit the crime. On this basis Philo and Maimonides interpreted the maxim "eye for an eye." Also logical is the answer that Hillel gave as the principle of the ethical commandments: those deeds which you condemn when others do them to you, you may not justify when you do them to others. Of course, logic requires that one repay good, or at least express gratitude, to our benefactor. To some extent one may regard, in Saadia's view, all our ritual and obedience as an expression of thanks to our Creator. According to Crescas and Abravanel, one can invoke this principle to explain some of the laws of the sacrifices. Baḥya adds that to the extent that God's kindness was generous to a particular

* However, Saadia had already emphasized (ED 6, L 259) that "the Torah had consideration for the needs of the people to whom the Torah had been given" in order to explain why the Torah did not make extended mention of the reward of the World to Come.

** Naḥmanides Commentary on Leviticus 1:9; and see R. Y. Uno, *Rabbi Moshe ben Naḥman* (1942) 42. And yet Naḥmanides also wrote (on Leviticus 2:11): "The reason for the prohibition of leaven and honey is likely what Maimonides wrote in the *Guide*. He said that he found in certain books that it was an idolatrous custom to bring their offerings with leaven and to mix honey in all their sacrifices, and so therefore God forbade these practices."

community, its obligations increase: it is for this reason that more mitzvot were given to the Jewish people than to other nations, and that more were given to the priests than to the ordinary tribes of Israel.

Another logical principle is the doctrine of "the golden mean." The rabbis invoked this principle in opposing extravagant vows (including the Nazirite vow).[4] It was invoked in its philosophic form by the followers of Aristotle, such as Philo in his explanation for the dietary laws,[5] and Maimonides in his ethical doctrine. Baḥya also discussed it, in setting limits to asceticism. More energetically, Halevi exclaimed that God desires our religious joy no less than our submission through fasts (*Kuzari* 2:50).

Consequences of the Mitzvot

The *consequences* of the mitzvot fall into the categories of utilitarian, pedagogic, and ethical-religious.

The *utilitarian* consequences in the narrow sense — to exclude consequences that themselves are the means to an ulterior end — are divided into two classes. There are utilitarian consequences that have no intrinsic causal connection with the mitzvot themselves, but God's will has decreed that we shall receive reward for our deeds in this world and even more so in the world to come. This is the view of the rabbis. Saadia Gaon taught that God gave us the mitzvot (especially the hortative ones) so that we may earn our eternal reward through our deeds. Similar to this view is Albo, who said that through our reverence we shall merit eternal life by God's decree. This idea, which occupies an important place in the Aggadah and in the philosophic literature of the Middle Ages (but not in Hellenistic thought!), serves as an explanation for the giving of the mitzvot from the *Creator's* viewpoint; on the other hand, we are enjoined not to be like servants who serve the Master in order to receive a reward (we have discussed this at length above).

Inasmuch as we receive a reward for performing the mitzvot, it is impossible to explain the essence of the specific mitzvot in this fashion, but only the fact of their being given, in general. It seems plausible from the standpoint of the adherents of astrology (Ibn Ezra, Gersonides, and Abravanel) that performance of the mitzvot should free us from the dominance of the astral powers, in agreement with the rabbinic maxim "Israel has no *mazal.*" This method allows for explaining why certain prohibitions and sacrifices were instituted for particular days, because of the astral dangers attendant on them.

Whereas this method is based on the assumption that God overrides the power of His servants — the stars — as a reward for our service, there is also the view that our actions operate directly, in a causal and mystical way, on the upper realm. This view is found among the rabbis regarding the sacrifices, and Gersonides expressed agreement with it in his commentary. A similar mystical power was attributed to circumcision. Such views were even more widespread among the masses. The translators of the Septuagint called the tefillin "phylacteries" (i.e., prophylactic devices or amulets). Maimonides vociferously opposed those who used tefillin to exorcise demons. We know that the belief in magical practices found fertile soil in the kabbalistic tradition.

On the other hand, several of our rabbis believed that particular mitzvot *necessarily* cause beneficial effects in this world. The Sages recognized, for example, the beneficial effect of our rendering assistance to our enemies. Saadia found sober reasons for certain hortative mitzvot: marrying one's relatives, for instance, is forbidden so that even homely women should find their mates. The Hellenistic thinkers attributed a hygienic advantage to circumcision; Rashbam and Maimonides did the same for certain dietary laws and Ibn Ezra did so for the laws of leprosy, Gersonides for the dietary laws and family purity, and Abravanel protested against every attempt to demote our holy Torah to the level of a medical textbook.* We may also classify as utilitarian Halevi's account of the role that the blessings play in adding to our pleasures and joy.

All these utilitarian advantages apply only to the individual. The sociological viewpoint — the recognition that the mitzvot safeguard the survival of the people — is apparently to be found only in the outlook of the Hellenists and in the commentary of Ibn Ezra.

And yet, the utility that the mitzvot generate directly pales in comparison with the fact that they serve as the teachers and educators of the Jewish people.

The view that the mitzvot teach us is more prominent among the medieval philosophers than in the earlier literature. First of all, the mitzvot teach us a proper view of God. Maimonides in particular emphasized that certain mitzvot have the purpose of distancing us from idolatry. His observation was accepted by some of his successors. His view that the sacrifices were instituted so that the people would not bring offerings to idols was also agreed to by Gersonides, Albo, and Abravanel, even though they did not regard it as sufficient to explain all the details. The philosophers emphasized that the Sabbath recalls the creation of the world, and Crescas, in saying that the festivals attest to God's providence with which Israel was privileged, expresses their common view. The blessings also recall God's beneficences (see Halevi). The cardinal prin-

* This harks back to the rabbinic view, "The mitzvot were not given for enjoyment" (see above, p. 15).

ciple is that through the mitzvot the remembrance of God is imprinted perpetually on our souls (see Ibn Daud, Maimonides) and thus they elevate their adherents above the terrestrial world and its petty pleasures and cares. This view of God (that the mitzvot bequeath to us) is connected with a cognate view of nature and history. The Hellenistic thinkers and Ibn Ezra emphasize that the Torah is in accord with the laws of nature and enlightens us concerning the role of the numbers that play a dominant role in the world, such as the number 7. From the symbolic interpretation of the Tent of Meeting and the priestly garments we can learn about the order of nature that demonstrates the wisdom of the Creator. The mitzvot serve us both as a "Book of Principles" (catechism — in the words of Samson Raphael Hirsch[6]) and a "Book of Memories"; not only were certain days instituted "so that your generations shall know" (Pesaḥ, Sukkot,[7] Shavuot, according to the rabbis), but there are historical associations even with the High Holy Days. In the view of Philo and Abravanel, the shofar commemorates the giving of the Torah; even Maimonides, who is not in love with such allusions, acknowledges that Yom Kippur commemorates the day that Moses came down to the people to tell them that their repentance had been accepted.

Some mitzvot have a *psychological* value. According to Gersonides, the cherubim allude to the difference between our intellect and the cosmic "active" intellect; some rabbinic homilies speak of how the mitzvot teach us the course of human affairs (for instance, whoever marries a beautiful captive woman will eventually despise her, etc.).

Such homilies provide a transition to *ethical* explanations. The Torah addresses our moral awareness and even more our moral emotions, and all the commentators emphasize its objective of educating the people of Israel through its injunctions. In the view of Hillel, which that was cited in his conversation with the pagan who came to be converted, all the mitzvot are nothing other than a "commentary" on the essential ethical mitzvah. This agrees with several rabbinic sayings. The Hellenistic thinkers are sure that the mitzvot guide us to the four cardinal virtues of Greek ethics. All the medieval philosophers emphasized the pedagogic value of all the mitzvot of the Torah; if moral perfection ranked lower than intellectual perfection for the Aristotelians, was it not still the case that breaking free of the tyranny of bodily desire was an absolute condition for the correct knowledge of God?

This ethical educational objective was widely encompassing. Philosophical ethics never had a precept as far reaching as the prohibition against coveting (Ibn Daud). The prohibition of leaven tells us to rid ourselves of the "leaven in our own dough" (Abravanel). The sacrifices and the confessional connected with them reveal to us the weight of our sins, and together with this they protect us against the despair that sin not infrequently causes (Ibn Daud, Saadia). Indeed, the mitzvot have two special objectives:

1. They distance us from *bodily appetites*. Philo wrote a whole treatise on this subject. It includes not only the sexual prohibitions but also the commandments of fringes (according to the rabbis), circumcision (according to Philo, Ibn Ezra, and Maimonides), and purity (according to Gersonides).
2. The dietary laws lead to a life of satisfaction (Philo, Baḥya). In considering this line of ethical influence, Crescas and Abravanel taught that the mitzvot free us from the sin of Adam, which was the fruit of desire.

Social values (such as are found in the laws of debt-remission and the Jubilee) are especially emphasized by the Hellenistic writers. Maimonides and Gersonides allude to them as well. In the view of Targum Jonathan, Philo, Rashbam, and Maimonides, some of the dietary laws also allude to the principle not to inflict pain on animals.

Of course, the primary objective of education through the mitzvot is religious. All the philosophers from Baḥya onward agree that there is a reciprocal relation between fulfillment of the mitzvot and religiosity of the heart; our obedience is a sign of our religious feelings and an important factor in their development. Even the Aristotelians admit that the mitzvot lead us not only to knowledge of God but also to the pure fear of Him (which is different from any fear of mortals — see Ibn Daud) and to the love of Him (Maimonides).* Crescas went further in claiming that the love of God is the highest purpose of all the mitzvot of the Torah "from the standpoint of the one commanded." His student Albo followed him in explaining the value of fear and the relation between it and love. Our thinkers also tried to depict the character of the religious experience that we are privileged to experience as a result of performing the mitzvot, even at the moment of performing them. According to Albo, prayer prepares us to receive the supernal flow; by the influence of the sacrifices is born in us "another spirit" (Halevi); and Ibn Ezra is very close to the view of the kabbalists, who emphasize that "an added soul" is active in us on the Sabbath day.

According to all the views, the religious experience brings about a new existence and raises one up above the throng who are trapped in the chains of this world. The right kind of enlightenment not only enriches our

* Of course the rabbis and Hellenists also agreed on the value of love. This is not the place to discuss this further, despite its importance; however, they did not teach explicitly that religious love is the purpose for which the mitzvot were given.

intellects, but (according to the Aristotelians) fashions a lasting connection between us and the higher world that we attain by the power of our ideas; the same is the case with love, according to Crescas. In Halevi's view (*Kuzari* 1:109) the mitzvot enable us to ascend to the level of the prophets and draw us nearer to God in this world and in the world to come. All these thinkers believe, then, in a causal connection between the fulfillment of the mitzvot and its spiritual results and earning eternal life. From this aspect, there is a synergy between performance of the mitzvot and the study-with-elaboration of the books of the Bible, according to most of the philosophers. The "Doreshei Reshumot" taught (*Sifrei Ekev* 11:22): "Do you wish to know the One who spoke and brought the world into being? Study Aggadah!" Halakha and Aggadah — particularly the description of the patriarch Abraham serving his Creator out of love, and the allegorical interpretation of the Song of Songs describing the love between Israel and their heavenly Father — worked together on the interpreters of the mitzvot in setting up religious "types" as exemplars, hovering before their eyes.[8] In their formation of these types, some of them added the mystical and philosophical ideals as well. Indeed, the author of the *Tur,* who recognizes only the heteronomic explanation, begins with a depiction of such a type: "Be strong as a leopard and fleet as an eagle . . . to do the will of your Father in heaven." But in Baḥya's view it is precisely reason that attests to the radical opposition between "religion" and "this world,"[9] and whoever fulfills the mitzvot of the limbs and above all the mitzvot of the heart on the basis of this recognition ascends to the class of the "chosen" who are citizens of the world to come while they yet dwell on this earth. According to Halevi, the "chosen" are those who approach the level of the prophets, and fulfillment of the mitzvot assists us both in meriting the influence of God's presence while we are yet in exile, and in becoming like "kings," whose ascetic disciplines and pure enjoyments are desired by our Creator. Maimonides is generous in his praise of the one who does not let his attention be distracted at all from God and divine matters (*Guide* 3:51) but who "engages in Torah," wrapped in his tallit, crowned with tefillin, and in all matters does more than the strict law demands — such a one has sanctified God, and of him the verse says, "And He said to me, 'You are My servant, Israel in whom I glory' (Isaiah 49:3)." (*Hilkhot Yesodei Ha-Torah* 5:11). Even though he expressed the purpose of the mitzvot in an intellectual formula, he knew that in point of truth all the influences of the mitzvot among which we have drawn distinctions — the pedagogic, the ethical, the religious — do not come separately, but operate together so that we may perform the mitzvah "between us and ourselves" (see Crescas above): to sanctify ourselves in our thoughts, our feelings, and our deeds in accordance with the command of the Torah.

(B) What Can We Learn from the Classic Jewish Thinkers' Explanation of the Reasons for the Mitzvot?

Some readers will reject out of hand the question that we have just posed, not only because our period is extremely different from that of our predecessors in every aspect, but also because of the differences of views that we have expounded. If the teachers were in disagreement with each other on such important points, what can a student learn from them, other than that such a question is insoluble and whoever deals with it is "pursuing the wind"? But precisely the many aspects of our predecessors' views — their agreements as well as their disagreements — can illuminate the nature of the question.

The Subjective Factor

There are completely "objective laws," such as the Pythagorean theorem, and there are questions that lend themselves to "subjectivity," where it is impossible to decide among the contenders, such as the question of optimism, in which the answer depends on the character of the responder and his experience. Then there are matters that stand between these two categories, matters in which it is possible to discuss them and each person can learn from the views of his opponents, but the final decision depends on the predilection of the decisor. Questions that have to do with world-view, approaches to spiritual phenomena (such as the essence of "Hellenism," the creative style of Plato and Goethe, and — it should go without saying — the Bible) are all counted in this last group. Our survey shows that another question in this category is that of the "reasons for the mitzvot."

The subjective factor is easy to recognize on the basis of this historical survey. Three groups of thinkers stand before us: the concerns of the first are practical, of the second intellectual, and the third (among whom we may include the kabbalists) are drawn to feeling and mystery. The first are very frugal in their explanation of the mitzvot (e.g., the rabbis), and some of them rejected any autonomous explanations (e.g., the *Tur*); the second sought utilitarian reasons (e.g., Saadia) or rational reasons, and also promoted the "historical" method; the third preferred a symbolic or mystic explanation. We need hardly add that their disagreements were caused not only by the personality of the thinkers, but also by the currents that influenced them: the rabbis took consideration of popular syncretism; Philo learned from Pythagoras, Plato, and the Stoics; Maimonides borrowed from Aristotle, and so forth.

Despite this, it is impossible to say that they ignored each other or spoke different, mutually incomprehensible languages. The differences in character among these thinkers should not be exaggerated. In hinting at the reasons for the mitzvot, the Torah itself appeals to our obedience, our considered judgment, and our sense of the mysterious. Each of the Jewish scholars-builders whom we have discussed was composed of different aspects — practical, intellectual, and sensitive-emotional in an integrated personality. They differed only that in one of them a certain aspect predominated, in another a different aspect. Therefore those who chose to explain the mitzvot understood the reasons for those who refused to do so, whereas the rabbis, who are to be counted among the pragmatists, did not shut the door against the pursuit of reasons, and Maimonides had much to offer to the mystics who took a different path after him. Nor did the differences in historical periods and external influences interpose an iron partition between the thinkers. Even Maimonides, who rejected the absolute authority of Aggadah, relied on rabbinic exegeses; Philo's explanations turn up in the teachings of his medieval successors (especially Ibn Ezra), though they were not acquainted with his works. To be sure, they differed on important issues, but the faith that the mitzvot of the Torah were given to enlighten our eyes and perfect our virtues was common to nearly all Jewish thinkers, and the paths they pursued to arrive at their objective are not so far apart in principle.

A grasp of the historical perspective helps us to understand the situation in our own time. The differences in the personal preferences of the thinkers are a variable independent of time: there is never any shortage of those with a historical approach, who (in Baḥya's words) "set tradition over theory," or of the "classical" type, who seek intellectual clarity, or of the "romantics" in love with mystery and esotericism, in the very broad sense. As in the past, so is it in the present and so will it be in the future. It is very difficult, and in most cases perhaps impossible, for a person to succeed through proof and argument in changing his fellow-thinker's personal disposition, the personal idiosyncratic ground out of which the fruits of his spirit grow; therefore a person of independent judgment is not able to accept another person's explanation of the mitzvot without modification. But there is the hope that every many-sided view may prove illuminating and provocative even to those who do not agree with the author's approach. Modern writers like Samson Raphael Hirsch, Franz Rosenzweig, and R. Abraham Kook were able to influence a wide audience of readers, including some who stood outside the outlook common to their predecessors, and all of them believed in the supreme value of the divine mitzvot. For this reason and in this sense it is possible for all of our contemporaries to learn from the ancients — not because we should belittle the magnitude and value of what has changed with time, but on the contrary, because we believe it is possible to distinguish between what has changed with time and what is based on objective fact and is of lasting value for all time.

This applies (1) to factors that motivated our predecessors to investigate the reasons for the mitzvot, (2) their methods, and (3) the results of their investigations.

The Value of the Explanations

As for the *value* of investigating the reasons for the mitzvot, there are controversies that last to this day. We, too, have our "pragmatists" who feel no need to find autonomous reasons.* Indeed, we should note that the advocates of explanation agreed with the rejectionists in appreciating the obedience that Abraham, for example, exhibited in upholding the divine command whose reason was hidden from him. In this regard the rationalists acknowledged to their opponents that it is impossible to base the authority of the historical law (as opposed to the natural law) on intrinsic reasons alone, but one must also recognize the value of heteronomic reasons, which are valid precisely for a given community. Indeed, the appreciation of obedience and heteronomy contradicts, if not "the spirit of modern times," at least the spirit of liberalism, with which Judaism is to be identified, according to the view of some of our friends and all of our enemies! In truth, the sensitive and knowledgeable Jews of our age have struggled to mediate between the tendency of freedom and the tendency of obedience, both of which are rooted in the hearts of our spiritual visionaries. Nietzsche's aphorism (from *Zarathustra* I): "There is one who lost half his value, on the day that his servitude ended"** (which applies especially to some of today's Jews!) teaches that appreciation of the right kind of obedience is not at all characteristic of periods whose time has past! Also, the dangers envisaged for this obedience from a *one-sided* investigation of the reasons for the mitzvot — dangers about which Maimonides warned — surely apply in our day!

However, even the factors that motivated the intellectuals and romantics to find *autonomous* reasons for the mitzvot did not become obsolete with time either! To be sure, defense of the mitzvot changed its approach

* B. H. Auerbach, in *Geschichte der Gemeinde Halberstadt* 209, writes that ultra-Orthodox Judaism regards the mitzvot, given to us from Sinai, not as a means to communicate exalted ideas but as ends in themselves, testifying to our absolute obedience to our Father in Heaven.

** Nietzsche was alluding to Homer's *Odyssey* 17:322: "A man loses half his value on the day of his servitude." The list of three pilgrims at the start of Nietzsche's *Thus Spoke Zarathustra* (who are compared to a camel, a lion, and a child) imply an opposition to Kant's view that heteronomy is unworthy of a free person.

with the change of the attackers, and one may ask whether the methods of defense of our predecessors are appropriate to our day. However, as the attacks have not decreased, the need to counter them is not past. The same applies to the "theoretical" factor, which motivates us to interpret the mitzvot with the help of new material, which is found precisely in our day (see below). The same applies to the "pedagogic" factor. Surely we are not over the danger, to which Baḥya in particular attended, that those who "set tradition in place of investigation" are obsessed with the smallest of details "and they ignore the duties of the heart" and the cardinal principles of the Torah. We should add: every place where the light of science has not penetrated has been enshrouded in the shadows of superstition. Almost seven hundred years after Maimonides wrote the *Mishneh Torah,* we can find people who consider the mezuzah an amulet to keep away the demons . . . therefore it is not superfluous even today to teach the true reasons for the mitzvot.

Just as the passing of time has not rendered obsolete the arguments of the proponents of explaining the mitzvot, so is the case regarding the *methods* that the explainers have employed.

As for the value of the authority of *aggadot* (maxims and lore), nothing has changed. The value of the historical approach has increased greatly, thanks to the discovery of ancient pagan law-codes. The comparison of Hammurabi's Code with the Torah's laws proves to us especially what the Torah changed from the pre-existing law, and why; thus we can recognize more clearly the ethical and social content of its precepts. But we should not reject the symbolic method either, inasmuch as psychology has proven how popular were allegorical descriptions — including symbolic ones — even in most ancient times.*

The Apologetic Method

The *apologetic* method deserves special consideration. To the argument of the attackers, who said that the mitzvot are inappropriate by the criteria of world culture, most of the defenders responded that they are indeed appropriate. Only a few, such as Halevi and Crescas, dared to criticize the criteria themselves. And here we especially welcome the fresh wind that blows through their books. The view of Abravanel, who said that the Aristotelian philosophers rely on a broken reed, was confirmed by later history that dethroned him from his pedestal. It is easy, therefore, for us to proclaim that the God of Aristotle is not the God of Judaism, as Hermann

* In recent times, Samson Raphael Hirsch favored the symbolic method. See my *Altjüdische Allegoristik* 9.

Cohen said,[10] but it is very difficult to deduce from this the *methodical* conclusion that it is naïve to identify the eternal criteria of Judaism with the transient ones of our own age. History encourages us to hold on firmly to our criteria even if they do not agree with those of the age. Go and learn: how much did the Hellenistic Jews struggle to defend the Sabbath, which the pagans saw as a sign of our "laziness,"[11] and here "the stone that the builders rejected has become the cornerstone" even in the view of others whose outlook is completely different from ours.

We should consider the passing of time in coming to deal with the question of what value there is in the *answers* that our predecessors gave to the reasons for the mitzvot. The historical survey proved that every age was forced to carve out its own path for understanding the mitzvot on the basis of its own assumptions, and could only adopt the insights of its predecessors insofar as they agreed with its own outlook. We may deduce from this, on the one hand, that we cannot ignore the extent to which our outlook has changed from that of previous times; we need not do battle with astrology, nor does the Christian doctrine of salvation pose a danger to Judaism. But on the other hand, we should know that just as some of the challenges have passed into history, so the aid that our predecessors enjoyed from their enemy's camp is not there either: the common belief in a divinely revealed Scripture and a common eschatological hope are not so widely accepted in modern culture as to provide the basis to mount a defense of our tradition on them. It goes without saying that the picture of the world on which the philosophers based their symbolic interpretations and the Aristotelian teleology have lost their authority. Conversely, we have the experience of several centuries that reveals the fruit of keeping the mitzvot and the effects of their neglect; this experience can be put to good use by the *sociological* method that is so popular in our time.

The Sociological Method

There is no need to list here the reasons whose value has been vitiated by what we have just said. We do not wish to deliberate on specialized questions, whose answer has only limited validity even today (e.g., Maimonides' method in explaining the sacrifices). It is enough to point to certain explanations that have value and that we ought to accept, especially after we translate them into the language of our own time.

The explanations of the mitzvot that we discussed are almost all individual. The Sages asked: Why has the exile come upon Israel, and by what virtue were our ancestors redeemed (and, by implication, may we be redeemed as well)? But their answers were mostly based on a heteronomic explanation: our sins and merits act on the will of the Creator, who decreed these events. In most cases there is no natural-causal connection between our deeds and our fortunes. We dealt at length above with the philosophers' individualism. Only the Hellenistic thinkers and Ibn Ezra emphasized that the performance of the mitzvot *causes* the survival of the people. If they themselves did not highlight this explanation, it is very important in our own view. There is no doubt that the character of Judaism as a "religion of law" was a factor in its survival, which has been seen as a miracle in the eyes of the gentiles: "let our enemies be the judges!" (Deut. 32:31). After a lecture in which Hermann Cohen denigrated Judaism's alleged "one-sidedness . . . that wishes to dominate every area of our lives," his friend Wellhausen expressed the view that "enforcement of the traditional law was the cause of Jewish survival."[12] Perhaps the Christian scholar was referring only to those laws that are a safeguard against assimilation, such as the dietary laws. But we Jews know how much our "Jewish awareness" and community feeling are dependent on observance of the mitzvot and strengthened by it. The father who brings his son into the covenant of Abraham sees himself not only as fulfilling the command of his Creator but also as connected with the multitude of his kinfolk in whom the seal of the holy covenant is impressed in the flesh, and with the more than three thousand years of past generations. Even the free-thinkers in our midst, to the extent that they do not want to write themselves out of the Jewish people, feel the "social" value of certain mitzvot.

From a sociological outlook we can consider the words of our predecessors, that the mitzvot are the *teachers and educators* of the Jewish people. Their proofs are nearly all individualistic, especially those of the philosophers. They teach that the individual person acquires intellectual views, ethical values, and the right religious feeling by observance of the mitzvot. All these proofs are generally based not on philosophical views whose time has past, but on the religious experience common to our predecessors and to us. Whatever is not a product of a particular time is not outdated with the passing of time. Some details are disputable, but the general outlook is still valid and respectable. We can even say that the mystical kabbalah deepened our religious experience to a significant degree, especially with respect to observance of the Sabbath, and that modern psychology has enabled us to give it more exact expression. However, the "individual" perspective must now be complemented — not neglected, as the modernists would do! — by a "collective" orientation. Experience — and especially the experience of our age — teaches that it is possible to influence the spiritual state of any community not only through theoretical instruction, but more especially by common activities, which create a common base of knowledge and common ideals that are dear to the heart of a group of people, not through abstract teaching, but by presentations, parades, and celebrations that create a "spirit of community."* Popular leaders recognized this method of education from ancient times to our own (we should add: for destructive ends as well!) more than the ideologues. Such education was particularly necessary for our people, "the smallest of the peoples," whose individual leaders were influenced by the currents around them even when they dwelt on their land (in the days of Elijah the Prophet and the period of the Hasmoneans), and how much more so in the Diaspora! Here the mitzvot have come and guided the Jewish people on a united path: the calendar — which is a pedagogic book in its own right — not for abstract principles alone (as Hirsch would have it), but also for the history of the people, by whose knowledge our historical consciousness is fortified. Performance of the mitzvot generated (and by their neglect, undermined) ethical traits that the nations of the world see as characteristic of our people, such as sobriety, generosity, and family-feeling; on this ground grew that religiosity that Halevi described so beautifully, infused with seriousness and joy together, which enabled our people to find encouragement and fortitude throughout all its afflictions.

These short notes will suffice to demonstrate that it is possible to avail ourselves of our predecessors, and in what way it is possible to do this in order to find a basis for performing the mitzvot of the Torah that will be valid in our own age. We have departed from the way of the medieval philosophers inasmuch as we have limited — but not rejected — their individualism, whereas the thinkers of the 19th century, with some exceptions,** enlarged on it. Our retracing our steps in this manner is but a "return" (*teshuvah*) in the full sense of the word. The Torah itself says, in order to reconcile us to the dietary prohibitions: "You shall be holy to Me because I the Lord am holy; and I have separated you from the nations to be Mine" (Leviticus 20:26). This idea, that the entire people is separated by the mitzvot to be a holy nation, was alive and well in the rabbinic mind. They demonstrated this not by their explanations but by their enactments, in which they continued the educational work of the Torah in organic fashion: they set up a defensive shield around our national life (as through those enactments — on ordinary wine, etc. — that had the stated intent

* Most of the medieval philosophers (see Baḥya, p. 59, Maimonides, p. 100, Crescas, p. 139) thought that the mitzvot were addressed primarily to the naïve masses rather than to philosophically educated, independent-minded individuals. This view was based on an individualistic assumption. From a sociological standpoint one may say that educational differences are apt to create class divisions among the people (see for instance Mommsen, *History of the Romans* II, 423, 428), whereas common observance of religious laws and customs can help to alleviate this danger.

** S. D. Luzzatto opposed this tendency; and this opposition was a right-minded motivation for his excessive and wrong-headed attack on the imagined "eudaemonism" of the philosophers whom we discussed above (p. 163).

of discouraging intermarriage), instituted days of national mourning and rejoicing in order to perpetuate historical memories, and certainly became "partners to God" by enriching the experience of the already-designated festivals and their pedagogic function through establishing the special holiday liturgies. They were joined in time by their "children-builders" — the liturgical poets and the innovators of customary practices. They thus developed the powers latent in the mitzvot of the Torah in accordance with the Torah's intention: they all believed — whether they expressed it explicitly or not — that this intention was to unite and sanctify the entire Jewish people; for the preservation (*kiyyum*) of the people in the full sense of the word, its life and vitality, were dependent on the performance (*kiyyum*) of the mitzvot and on understanding their purpose.

Abbreviations

BT	Babylonian Talmud
DH	*Duties of the Heart* (Baḥya Ibn Pakudah)
ED	*(Sefer) Emunot ve-Deot* (= Saadia *Book of Doctrines and Beliefs*)
HUCA	*Hebrew Union College Annual*
JPS	Jewish Publication Society
JQR	*Jewish Quarterly Review*
JT	Jerusalem (Palestinian) Talmud
L	Landauer (edition of Saadia *Sefer Emunot ve-Deot*)
MGWJ	*Monatsschrift für Geschichte und Wissenschaft der Juden*
OH	*Ohr Ha-Shem* (= Crescas *Light of the Lord*)
PRK	*Pesikta de-Rav Kahana*
REJ	*Revue des Études Juives*
SUNY	State University of New York
YD	*Yoreh De'ah* (Part II of the *Shulḥan Arukh*
YM	*Yesod Mora* (= Ibn Ezra *Foundation of Faith*)

Notes

Notes to Chapter 1: The Nature of the Question

1. BT *Avodah Zarah* 35a. See also BT *Shabbat* 83b, concerning "a Mishnah whose reason was not revealed," and BT *Pesaḥim* 25b ("what does the topic of the murderer have to do with the topic of the maiden?") where they did not regard the words of the verse as a logical reason.
2. There is in addition the tendency to rest content with the description of well-known facts and to dispense with any inquiry into their underlying causes. See, for instance, Strabo *Geography* p. 104.

Notes to Chapter 2: The Biblical View

1. There were indeed some thinkers in antiquity who argued that the prohibition of the Tree of Knowledge was due to divine jealousy, in other words, that it was for a non-moral consideration. (See my article in MGWJ 1938, pp. 389ff.) But we need not take account of this view, (1) because even many freethinkers rejected it; (2) because it is our primary task to expound the mainstream views of traditional Jewish thinkers, who needless to say did not entertain such a view; and (3) because all agree that such motives played no part in the later normative Jewish commandments.
2. See Leon Roth, *The Reasons for the Commandments* (Hebrew), Jerusalem 1946, p. 10.
3. One may find additional examples in Joseph Wohlgemuth, *Das jüdische Religionsgesetz in jüdischer Beleuchtung*, Berlin: H. Itzkowski, 1912, and in Michael Guttmann, *Beḥinat kiyyum ha-mitzvot (Differences in Observance of the Commandments between Traditional Judaism and Jewish Sectarians in the Late and Post-Second Temple Period* [Hebrew], Breslau, 1931, p. 30.
4. I have found this judgment of Rosenzweig (from Buber & Rosenzweig, *Die Schrift und ihre Verdeutschung*, Berlin: Schocken 1936, p. 248) voiced also among Christian scholars. It is only true with some qualifications.
5. See also Exodus 22:26: "I will hear for I am gracious."

Notes to Chapter 3: The Views of the Rabbis

1. I have discussed the "creative philology" of the rabbis in my book, *The Ways of the Aggadah* (Hebrew, Jerusalem: Magnes Press 1948), 1948, Book Two.

2. Concerning those ancients who were called "servants" by themselves or by God, see *Sifri* on Deuteronomy 3:24.
3. BT *Shabbat* 10a; *Mekhilta Ki Tisa* 1 (Horowitz Rabin 343). See also BT *Shabbat* 119b: "Whoever recites the passage 'The heavens and the earth were finished' on Sabbath evening is counted by Scripture as if he were a partner with God in the work of creation."
4. BT *Bava Kama* 97a; see also BT *Bava Kama* 38a and *Avodah Zarah* 3a.
5. Similar rabbinic utterances: Leviticus Rabbah 7:4: "Noah's sacrifices are comparable to those of Israel, except that from the fact that God commanded Israel to perform them, we know that those of Israel are preferable." Also JT *Shabbat* 1:1 (3a): "Hezekiah said: Whoever is not commanded yet performs an action is regarded as simple." We shall explain Kant's theory of autonomy in Part II, Chapter 2.
6. See BT *Bava Metzi'a* 58b; *Sifra* to Leviticus 19:14 § 32, 25:17 § 43; and also Lazarus, *Ethik des Juentums* (Frankfurt: J. Kaufmann 1898–1911) 406 (though I disagree with his interpretation); see also HUCA IV, 161.
7. More sources are cited in the article of Israel Lévi, REJ 13–29.
8. BT *Ḥullin* 92a. See also Leviticus Rabbah 9:7: "Customary ethical norms (*derekh eretz*) preceded Torah by 26 generations." On *derekh eretz*, see Meir Friedmann's Preface to *Seder Eliyahu*, p. 104 and Gottlieb Klein *Der älteste Christliche Katechismus* (Berlin: G. Reimer 1909) 61ff.
9. "One is not punished unless one has been admonished." BT *Sanhedrin* 56b. Some scholars such as Michael Guttmann (*Das Judentum und seine Umwelt*, Berlin: Philo Verlag 1927, 99ff.) have paid insufficient heed to this distinction. (See also Stephen Schwarzschild, "Do Noachites Have to Believe in Revelation?" JQR 1962, reprinted in *The Pursuit of the Ideal: Jewish Writings of Stephen Schwarzschild*, SUNY 1992. — LL)
10. On this entire topic, see Max Kadushin, *Organic Thinking*, Jewish Theological Seminary 1938, 108ff.
11. See the commentary *Minḥat Yehudah ad loc.*, citing parallel passages and their formulation. As for the gentile's gods rejoicing in their temples, see my *Ways of the Aggadah* p. 83 n. 10.
12. Cited in *Tanḥuma (Buber) Shemini* § 12.
13. See my *Altjüdische Allegoristic* (1936) 72, 78, and my final chapter of *The Ways of the Aggadah* on homilies that stand on the border between serious thought and artistic play.
14. A shorter version of this homily occurs in BT *Yoma* 67b, with the variants: "against which Satan counter-argues" and "you have no right to question them." The continuation shows that "questioning them" is identical to what the Sifra calls "arguing against them." It would not have occurred to them to condemn honest inquiry into the commandments and their reasons, but only such skeptical questioning as proceeds from rebellious and prideful motives.
15. PRK Chapter 4, 40b.
16. This answer is fully in keeping with our previous citation from the Sifra. The pagans and the evil inclination unceasingly argue against certain commandments that have no logical basis but are based on God's will, whose authority the pagans do not recognize.

17. R. Samson Rapahel Hirsch listed the Talmudic Sages' explanations for the mitzvot in his commentary to Deuteronomy 24:18.
18. See my article in *Tziyon* 4:280ff. and Judah Bergmann, *Jüdische Apologetic in Neutestamentlichen Zeitalter* (Berlin: G. Reimer 1908) 94ff.
19. See also Naḥmanides' commentary on Deuteronomy 22:6.
20. See Wohlgemuth 96; M. Guttmann 19, 26, 34.
21. In a different vein, Noah was said to have sought the reasons for the mitzvot: he deduced from the number of the clean animals rescued from the Flood that he ought to offer some of them as sacrifices (Genesis Rabbah 34:9, 26:1).
22. Michael Guttman cites many more examples in *Beḥinat kiyyum ha-mitzvot* (31, et al). On the appreciation of "measure for measure" in the aggadah and the difference between it and "eye for eye," see *Ways of the Aggadah* 64ff., especially 69ff.
23. See Michael Guttmann, דומלתה חתפמ (Csongrád, Hungary 1906–30), entry *Asmakhta*, 29ff.
24. Bacher, *Aggada der babylonischen Amoraim* (Strassburg: Trubner 1878), 70; Max Grünbaum, *Gesammelte Aufsätze zur Sprach- und Sagenkunde* (Berlin: S. Calvary 1901), 17.
25. On these two types, see J. M. Guttmann, *Beḥinat kiyyum ha-mitzvot* 32. The pedagogic value of the mitzvot was emphasized even by the Church fathers against the Gnostics (Judah Bergmann, p. 63, n. 17).
26. BT *Menaḥot* 43b. This passage tells of a Jew who was saved from sin by the fringes on his garment, which also brought about the repentance of the courtesan with whom he was involved (*Sifri*, end of pericope *Shelaḥ*). The story is also told of a vineyard-keeper who was saved from adultery by the mitzvah of immersion (JT *Berakhot* 3:4, 6c).
27. In support of this, see my article in *Tziyon* 4:63, and my book *The Ways of Aggadah* 199.

Notes to Chapter 4: The Views of the Hellenistic Jews

1. Josephus, *Antiquities* I, 182, III, 259.
2. See my book *Philons griechische und jüdische Bildung* (Breslau: M & H Marcus 1932), 475 and *Tziyyon* 5:187. Philo wrote a treatise *On Reward and Punishment.*
3. *Antiquities* III, 81; *Against Apion* II, 161.
4. See the references in Note 2 and also Josephus *Against Apion* II, 184.
5. For the criticism that the Greeks leveled at Jewish claims of revelation, see IV Maccabees 5:18; Josephus *Antiquities* III, 81. In addition we should mention that the philosophers criticized claims to revealed law in their own nation; see Plato *Laws* 624a and 634c on the allegedly divine laws of the Cretans.
6. BT *Sanhedrin* 82a; Philo, *On the Special Commandments* I, 79.
7. On Panaetius (of Rhodes, c. 185–110 BCE) and the development of "humanism" see my article "Humanitas" in *Paulys Realencyclopädie der classischen Altertumswissenschaft* (edited by Georg Wissowa and Wilhelm Kroll: Stuttgart: J.B. Metzlersche Verlagsbuchhandlung, 1931), Supplementary Volume V, pp. 282–310, esp. pp. 293ff.

8. *On the Embassy to Gaius Caligula,* 210, 277. I have explained these and similar passages in accordance with the Greek outlook in my *Education of Philo,* 470ff. On Josephus, see also Schlatter, *Wie sprach Josephus von Gott?* (Gütersloh: C. Bertelsmann 1910), 67.
9. *Embassy to Gaius* 301; *Education of Philo* 473; P. Kruger, *Philo und Jusephus als Apologeten des Judentums,* 59.
10. *Migration of Abraham* 89 et al. I have commented on this source and on the disagreement between Philo's view and that of the rabbis in *Education of Philo* 463ff.
11. Jeremiah 2:11: "Has any other nation renounced its gods . . . ?"
12. BT *Ḥullin* 13b. And yet the fidelity of Jews to the Torah was viewed by the rabbis as a sign of its effective action — Judah Bergmann, *Jüdische Apologetik* 107.
13. In my book *Altjüdische Allegoristik* 42ff. I have cited other examples and have also explained the profound difference between them and the places in which the rabbis explained the details of the mitzvot "by way of parable" (such as "they shall spread the bed-garment," Deuteronomy 22:17).
14. What the scholars have written about other allegorists, specifically about the allegorical interpretations of "Aristobolus," is based on an imprecise notion of "allegory." See the *Memorial Volume for Johanan Levi* 46ff.
15. See *The Education of Philo* 58 on Philo and Josephus; Optowitzer *Tarbitz* 2:137ff.
16. Philo, *On the Special Commandments,* I, 262; *Education of Philo* 73.
17. Much of what I allude to briefly here I have treated at greater length in *Education of Philo* 110ff.; 140ff.; and compare also Staehle, *Die Zahlenmystik bei Philon* 1931.
18. I here cite briefly Philo's remarks in *On the Special Commandments* IV, 230ff. which I have explained in *Education of Philo* 346ff. on the basis of other passages.
19. *Ibid.* III, 181ff.; *Education of Philo* 350ff.
20. See for instance Cicero, *De Legibus* II, 15.
21. *Against Apion,* II, 146 and especially 163, etc.
22. I give here only a brief summary of his argument in this chapter.
23. On this view, found also in Philo's *Hypothetika,* see *Education of Philo* 353, and Belkin, *The Alexandrian Halakah* 18.
24. *Education of Philo* 491.
25. See Franz Geiger, *Philon als sozialer Denker* (1932).
26. *Education of Philo* 142ff.
27. On Josephus' idealization of the ancients and the idyll of primitive life, see *Tziyon* 5:192.
28. See my article on Philo in the Pauly-Wissowa-Kroll *Encyclopedia,* V, 2344.
29. See my article in Wohlgemuth's *Jeshurun,* 1921, 108 et al.
30. See my article, "Was beim Übersetzen verloren geht," *Jüdische Schulzeitung* IV (1935) 1. Josephus certainly knew Hebrew; but he relied on the views of the Alexandrians in his interpretation of the mitzvot.
31. See *Education of Philo* 64.

Notes to Chapter 5: Views of the Medieval Philosophers

1. Rashbam, commentary on Genesis 26:5. See David Rosin, *R. Samuel ben Meir als Schrifterklärer* (Breslau: F. W. Jungfer 1880) 120 et al.

2. On the opposition that such views encountered, see Dr. A. Gottesdiener, פרג האריי בחכמי, 113, 126.
3. Baḥya ibn Pakudah, *Duties of the Heart*, Zifroni edition, Jerusalem 1928, p. 13.
4. Solomon Ibn Gabirol, *Shirei Ḥol*, ed. Bialik-Ravnitzky, 8:37: "How shall a man unbind the harness of intellect and understanding, rebelliously undo his armor?" 8:107: "How shall a man rebel against his heart's knowledge, and descend to the level of forest vegetation?" See my *Die Lehre von der Zweckbestimmung des Menschen* (Breslau: M. & H. Marcus 1926), 55. One need not even mention Maimonides and the other philosophers. Wiener said correctly: "Religious philosophy was their heart-felt faith" (*Devir* 2:176).

Notes to Chapter 6: Saadia Gaon

1. For the history of medieval Jewish philosophy, many standard works are available:
   Frank, Daniel & Olver Leaman, eds., *History of Jewish Philosophy*, Routledge, 1997.
   — *Cambridge Companion to Medieval Jewish Philosophy*, Cambridge, 1997.
   — (and Charles Mannekin), *The Jewish Philosophy Reader*, Routledge, 2000.
   Guttmann, Julius, *Philosophies of Judaism*, (tr. David W. Silverman), Holt, Rinehart & Winston, 1964.
   Husik, Isaac, *A History of Medieval Jewish Philosophy*, Macmillan, 1916, reprinted 1973.
   Lewy, Hans, & Alexander Altmann & Isaak Heinemann, eds. *3 Jewish Philosophers*, Toby Press, 2006 (reprinted from 1946 Oxford original editions by JPS and Atheneum in 1960s and 1970s).
   Scholem, Gershom, *Major Trends in Jewish Mysticism*, Schocken, 1946, 1995.
   Schweid, Eliezer, *The Classic Jewish Philosophers*, Brill, 2007.
   Sirat, Colette, *A History of Jewish Philosophy in the Middle Ages*, Cambridge, 1985.
2. See Rau's article in MGWJ 1911, 524ff.
3. See Saadia ED III, L[andauer edition] 132. [All references to Saadia's *Sefer Emunot ve-Deot* refer to the standard Landauer Arabic edition. The full English translation (Rosenblatt, *Book of Beliefs and Opinions*, Yale, 1948) refers to the Landauer pagination by angled brackets in the middle of the text; thus on the last line of page 162 of Rosenblatt, the notation <132> refers us to the current passage. — LL]
4. See also my article on Saadia's rationalism in the collection *Rav Saadia Gaon*, ed. Fishman, 1943. (IH)
5. S. Horovitz, *Die Psychologie bei den jüdischen Religionsphilosophen*, 48–90.
6. ED L 133; Jacob Guttmann *Religionsphilosophie des Saadia*, 133.
7. ED L 139. On Arab thinkers who understood the Indian view this way, see P. Kraus, *Riv. Degli Studi Orientali* XIV 335.
8. I here summarize briefly the beginning of Chapter III of ED.
9. Ignác Goldziher, Richtungen der Koranauslegung 136 "Fiqh" — *Enzyclopedia Islam* Abh. Gött. Ges. 1907. 22.

10. On our obligation to "serve" God by performing the mitzvot, see Rau, MGWJ 1912, 181.
11. Compare Altmann's article in the collection *Rav Saadia Gaon* (1946)
12. See above, Chapter 1.
13. This was recognized also by the Catholic scholar Engelkemper, *De Saadiae Gaonis Vita* (1879), 15.
14. See above, start of Chapter 3.

Notes to Chapter 7: Baḥya ibn Pakudah

1. Citations of *Duties of the Heart* are based on the Yehudah Arabic edition and the Zifroni Hebrew translation. There are two standard English versions of the work available: by Moses Hyamson (out of print) and by Menahem Mansoor (available in paperback). Book 3 is particularly crucial. See G. Golinsky, *Das Wesen des Religionsgesetzes in der Philosophie des Bachja* (1933); Georges Vajda, *La théologie ascétique de Bahja*, Paris 1947.
2. DH 3:9 (and see also 9:1).
3. See Goldziher, *Vorlesungen über den Islam* 169; Obermann *Der . . . Subjectivismus Ghazalis* (1921) 93.
4. Goldhizer, *Kitab Ma'ani al nafs* 24.
5. See, for example, the eighth rank of students of Torah.
6. On hypocrisy, see 5:4 ("idolatry is better than hypocrisy"); on pride, 7:9.
7. Introduction (Zifroni p. 13).
8. Introduction of Yehudah edition 105ff.
9. See also 3:6, beginning.
10. For instance, in 3:3 (6th reason for the advantage of the awakening of reason), which we have cited; also 3:5 beginning.
11. DH Zifroni edition p. 11 (cited earlier).
12. See DH Chapter 2, and what the Hebrew translator called *tzipiyah* (observation of nature), Zifroni 50; David Kaufmann *Gesammelte Schriften* (Frankfurt: J. Kaufmann 1908–10), II 82, 84.
13. See Chapter 3, above.
14. DH 1:10; Kaufmann II, 81. Compare also my book *Zweckbestimmung* 43 on appreciation of the mystical.
15. See Chapter 3, conclusion.
16. This similarity was rightly stressed by Golinski, *op. cit.* 251, n. 51.

Notes to Chapter 8: Rabbi Judah Halevi

1. See my article "*R. Yehuda Halevi Ha-Ish ve-Hoge ha-De'ot*" in *Knesset* 1942, 270.
2. On the influence of the Hermetic writings (attributed to the Greek God Hermes), see my *Zweckbestimmung* 39 et al., especially 45.
3. In the original: *Wajab*. However Halevi does not believe in a mechanical relation between cause and effect; see the end of the cited passage.
4. On the phenomena to which Halevi refers here, see Goldhizer, *Kitab ma'ani al nafs* 40.

5. Poem יה אנה אמצאך. (Brody III, 150) Compare Hillel's saying, "If You come to my house, I will come to Your house" (Tosefta *Sukkah* 4:3).
6. Even the Sabbath poem *Deror Yikra* (by Dunash Ibn Labrat?) is only tangentially related to the core notion of the Sabbath day itself.
7. From the poem יקר יום השבת תגדיל.
8. We have not the space here to deal with Abraham bar Ḥiyya, who preceded him somewhat in this regard.
9. See Dienburg's article, "R. Judah Halevi's *aliyah* to the Land of Israel" in *Minḥah le-David" (Festschrift* for David Yalin), esp. 24.

Notes to Chapter 9: Abraham Ibn Ezra

1. For a general overview of Abraham Ibn Ezra, see: Rosin, "*Die Religionsphilosophie Abraham ibn Ezras*, MGWJ 42–43; on his sources, see 42:27ff.; on his classifcation of the mitzvot, 43:85ff. On his rejection of the allegorists, see my article in HUCA XXIII Part I 621ff.
2. Compare what Ibn Ezra says in his introductions to his Commentary on the Torah (Rosin, *Reime und Gedichte des Abraham Ibn Ezras*) and his commentary on Leviticus 1:1.
3. Rosin, *Poems of Ibn Ezra* 35. This description is reminiscent of Baḥya (especially the colloquy between the mind and the soul in 3:5 and elsewhere) and the mystics who preceded him. (*Zweckbestimmung* 41).
4. Introduction to the complete commentary (Rosin, *Poems* 35).
5. Introduction to his incomplete commentary (Rosin, *Poems* 59).
6. Yesod Mora 7 (where he speaks of the ethical value of circumcision).
7. I have added explanations in parentheses, especially in accordance with Kreiznach's translation.
8. On the "houses of the moon" see Rosin, *Poems of Ibn Ezra* 44, 6.
9. See Rosin MGWJ 42:308, reading כשביעי in place of ושביעי.
10. Rosin deals at length with the significance of other numbers such as 1, 8, and 10 (MGWJ 1898 42:244, 309).
11. On the Christians, see Wilhelm Gundel, *Sterne und Sternbilder* 268.
12. These two verses were composed at the end of the ancient period (Gundel, *ibid.*) and were still influential in the subsequent period (Troels-Lund, *Himmelsbild und Weltanschauung* 222).
13. See Rosin MGWJ 43:237. Whereas Halevi emphasizes only the religious and moral instruction that we derive from prayer (see previous chapter, p. 71).
14. Rosin deals with all these details in MGWJ 42:360, 394 et al. On the relation between Ibn Ezra and the Talmudic rabbis, see Rozin 249.
15. Bouché-Leclerq, *L'astrologie grecque* 1899) 283.
16. Short commentary to Exodus 25:4 (Prague edition, p. 81).
17. Rosin, MGWJ 42:206ff., dealing with this in great detail. He cites the longer commentary to Exodus 26:1 and Yesod Mora 9.
18. Rosin, *Ibid.* 356. They symbolize the parts of the world and are a means of determining the horoscope. See also what Rozin says about the bronze serpent (208) and the atoning power of circumcision (359).
19. "Several mitzvot have many reasons" Rozin 42:359.

20. Troels-Lund, *Die Religion in Geschichte und Gegenwart* 12, 226; and see also 596: astrology paved the way for religious symbolism.
21. See above, start of this chapter, p. 76.
22. See above, Chapter 3, p. 16, and my book *Altjüdische Allegoristik,* 42ff.
23. On the difference between the Hellenists and the rabbis, see the references cited in Chapter 4, Note 17 above.
24. On the symbolic explanation of the Tent of Meeting among the Church Fathers, see Siegfried, *Philo*, 345, 369.
25. See my book *The Education of Philo,* 498.

Notes to Chapter 10: Abraham Ibn Daud

1. I do not summarize the entire chapter from Ibn Daud, except insofar as it pertains to our central topic; Jacob Guttmann (in *Die Religionsphilosophie des Abraham ibn Daud,* 214ff.) has explained it and brought important proofs concerning Ibn Daud's sources.
2. "Hermann Cohen, *Maimonides,* 1908, I, 80.
3. In the printed text ומהם, should be read ומה גם ("all the more so").
4. The "Moslem sage" whom Ibn Daud cites here is Ghazali (see Kaufmann, *Attributenlehre* 21, 348.
5. See my *Zweckbestimmung* 59ff.
6. The original text proves that Baḥya was referring to the Holy Scriptures and not to matters of piety in general.
7. The question, whether Baḥya had recourse only to Ghazali's Arab philosophical sources, or to Ghazali's works themselves, does not interest us here; with regard to their shared views, the experts are of a common opinion.
8. Kaufmann (*Attributenlehre* 241) and others are of the opinion that Ibn Daud knew the *Kuzari* but refrained from listing Halevi (whose poems he praised) among the thinkers who preceded him, in order that he should not have to contradict him openly. Kaufmann's evidences are not entirely convincing, but they are plausible. In any case we must assume that Halevi's basic approach was not unfamiliar to Ibn Daud.
9. The interpretation of the story of Zipporah, with which Ibn Daud expresses disagreement, is not found in either of Ibn Ezra's extant commentaries. Ibn Daud does not mention Ibn Ezra's scientific works, but as he was familiar with Jewish astrologers, it is unlikely that he was ignorant of the greatest of them.
10. On the views of Aristotelians see F. Boll *Sternglaube und Sterndeutung* 25, and see also Maimonides' views (next chapter).
11. What he writes on p. 79 on the Paschal blood and its reward is merely explicating what the Torah itself declares.

Notes to Chapter 11: Maimonides

1. Especially important is the second half of Part III of the *Guide* (from Chapter 26 onward). See Chaim Neuburger, *Das Wesen des Gesetzes in des Philosophie des*

Maimonides, Danzig 1933. [And of course in our day one should appreciate Isadore Twersky's extensive work on the legal aspect of Maimonides' thought, especially *A Maimonides Reader* and *Introduction to Maimonides' Mishneh Torah*. — LL]

2. And yet he explains, incidentally, those rabbinic commands that are closely connected with the Torahitic law, as in III, 37.
3. Maimonides cites this rabbinic passage also at the start of *Guide* III, 26. See my discussion of it in Chapter 3, p. 20.
4. This, too, he cites at the start of *Guide* III, 26. See above, p. 15.
5. See Neuburger, note 191.
6. See *Hilkhot Me'ilah* 8:8 and compare also *Hilkhot Temurah* 4:13.
7. Neuburger 33, with notes. He emphasizes the difference (which Maimonides himself apparently did not scrupulously observe) between the specifying details of the law and its component parts, and he alludes to the Introduction to the *Guide* where Maimonides warns against excessive precision in interpreting the parables in the Bible.
8. Amending בהכרח to בחברה (see Munk's note).
9. Neuburger cites other places (61).
10. See *Responsa of Maimionides*, ed. Lichtenberg, Vol. 2, V–1.
11. Julius Guttmann, *Philosophy of Judaism*, Hebrew edition 169 (German edition [referring to "religiöses Bewusstsein"] 205; English edition 182); compare his remarks in the collection *Entwicklungsstufen der jüdischen Religion* 89, 127.
12. Approximately at the start of the last third of the Introduction; Hamburger edition 50. See my book *Zweckbestimmung* 61ff.
13. See Ernst Hoffmann, *Die Liebe zu Gott bei Moses ben Maimon*, 1937. We need not dwell here on the different formulations (sometimes love is almost identified with knowledge, sometimes it is its fruit).
14. Laws of Mezuzah 5:4. For a list of mitzvot that Maimonides passed over in silence, see I. Kinkelscherer, *Maimunis Stellung zum Aberglauben* (1894).
15. BT *Niddah* 61b; Hamburger, *Realenzyclopaedie für Bibel und Talmud*, Supplement II, 47, 51.
16. Neuburger 68ff.; compare especially the introduction to *Perek Ḥelek* to the 9th of the 13 Principles (with Holzer's note on the textual variant); *Guide* II, 39; and *Mishneh Torah*, end of *Hilkhot Megillah*.
17. See above on III, 44; but on the Sabbath he speaks only briefly (III, 43) because its reason is well known.
18. See my article, "Maimuni und die arabischen Einheitslehrer," MGWJ 1935, 102.
19. This description is from his Introduction to *Perek Ḥelek* (Holtzer edition, p. 10).
20. And see above, page 101. Neuburger 26 demonstrates that statements such as this are a regular occurrence for Maimonides. [But Leo Strauss raised the probing question, whether such statements represented Maimonides' personal view, or only the public view that he thought should be encouraged among the non-philosophical portion of the believing Jewish population. — LL]
21. Such a criticism was also leveled at Maimonides' God-concept (see Fritz Bamberger, *System des Maimonides* 1935, to which I responded in MGWJ 1935, 197).

Notes to Chapter 12: Gersonides

1. All citations to Gersonides' Torah commentary are based on the Venice edition, with each *daf* (double-sided page) divided into four *ammudim* (columns).
2. On the importance of the final cause, see Commentary on the Torah *Yitro* Application 1, *Aharei* Application 8. On the four causes, see below.
3. Similarly at the end of his commentary to Numbers Chapters 28–29, Gersonides expresses his thanks to God, after giving his explanation for the festival sacrifices and the numbers specified in them.
4. Aristotle had similarly said: "The ancients were only able to discern the material cause in things." (See Leon Roth, *Moreh derekh bafilosofia ha-yevanit* 95ff.)
5. See Guttmann's chapter on Gersonides for Gersonides' theory of prophecy.
6. On the altars, see also his commentary on *Aharei* I, 157.

Notes to Chapter 13: Ḥasdai Crescas

1. On Abner of Burgos, see Baer, *Korresp. Blatt der Akademie für die Wissenschaft des Judentums* 1927, 27 (and also Colette Sirat's *History of Medieval Jewish Philosophy*, pp. 308ff. — LL).
2. See Julius Guttmann, "John Spencers Erklärung der biblischen Gesetze in ihrer Beziehung zu Maimonides," *Festschrift Simonsen* 259ff. Of course Spencer extends Maimonides' position considerably!
3. I have used the Deinard-Karni edition of Crescas' *Refutation of Christian Principles* and the Vienna 1859 edition of *Light of the Lord.* As the latter edition is quite corrupt, I have also resorted to the Ferrara edition and Munich manuscript, which have been sent to me in Breslau.
4. D. Neumark, *Crescas and Spinoza* 1909, 18.
5. Especially Augustine. All the views are cited in Thomas Aquinas, *Summa Theologica* III 70:4,5.
6. Page 37b. See Aristotle, *Nicomachean Ethics* 1114a, 9ff.: "The deed generates the quality."
7. The letter was published in Wiener's edition of *Shevet Yehudah.*
8. Aristotle's hierarchy of purposes is explained in Überweg-Prächter, *Philosophie des Altertums* 382; Zeller, *Philosophie der Griechen* 2, 320, 2, 326.
9. Crescas alludes here to the liturgical poems of Kalir, apparently to the *silluk* to Shabbat Parah, in which the poet cites several symbolic homilies: the hyssop alludes to "those who are oppressed as hyssop"; the cedar to "the one who rises proudly like a cedar over the haughty."
10. The same view of the sacrificial act is expressed in *Light of the Lord* 2:2:6, 39b (end).
11. See Wolfson, *Crescas' Critique of Aristotle* (1929) 18.
12. This is emphasized by Enrst Hoffman, *Liebe zu Gott bei Mosxe ben Maimon* 78.

Notes to Chapter 14: Joseph Albo

1. I quote here from the Husik edition (JPS, Philadelphia 1930).
2. Husik, HUCA II, 386ff.
3. On the purpose of life according to Albo, see my *Zweckbestimmung* 83ff.
4. *Opus operatum* in Christian language (see above, p. 127).
5. See above, p. 15.
6. Husik's translation implies the same thought here.
7. See also 3:16 where he comments on the rabbinic dictum: "Sin diminishes a person's soul."

Notes to Chapter 15: Don Isaac Abravanel

1. I quote this book according to the Hanow edition, counting 4 columns for each two-sided page.
2. See my article in MGWJ 1938, 398, where I allude to other researches.
3. Isaac Arama also subscribed to this view (*Akedat Yitzhak*, introduction to *Va-etḥanan*).
4. On Adam's sacrifice, see Genesis Rabbah 34:9 and other places.
5. See above, p. 122.
6. See also his introduction to the sacrificial portion in Numbers 28.
7. See above, p. 99.
8. For example, the number 7 (Commentary on Exodus 12:15, end).
9. Abravanel refers to Josephus as "Yosef ben Gorion" (Jacob Guttmann: *Die religionsphilosophischen Lehren des Abarbanel* [1916], 24).
10. Guttmann, op. cit., 103, referring to his explanation of the Binding of Isaac.
11. See my *Allegoristik* 39.
12. See Abravanel's book *Ateret Zekenim*, Chapter 13 (beginning), and Jacob Guttmann, *op. cit.* 56.
13. Guttmann documents the appreciation accorded Abravanel by the kabbalists (p. 13).
14. Schmiedl, *Studien zur Geschichte der jüdischen Religionsphilosophie* (1869) 217; D. Kaufmann, *Zunzfestschrift* 143. Both of these writers remark on the influence of Christian preachers, who were known to Abravanel and influenced his symbolistic commentaries.

Notes to Chapter 16: Summary of the Medieval Thinkers

1. See above, pages 6 and 13, where I speak also of the limits of this principle.
2. See above, p. 134.
3. On Halevi, who is apparently an exception to this rule, see below, p. 163, note 8. As for Baḥya, Ibn Daud, and the post-Maimonidean philosophers, what we said above will suffice.
4. Introduction to Chapter *Ḥelek,* Holzer p. 7; he expresses his own view in pp. 4–6.

5. In *Kerem Ḥemed* 3:182 he speaks only of the poets, but he includes among them Halevi and Solomon Ibn Gabirol, and his view on Maimonides is well known.
6. Wilamowitz-Moellendorf, *Der Glaube der Hellenen* II, 1, 179.
7. Introduction to *Ḥelek*, Holtzer edition 15.
8. *Kuzari* 2:107–109. D. Z. Benet rightly emphasized, in the annual *Kenesset* 1942 326, that Halevi stresses the eschatological consideration less than his Jewish and Moslem colleagues.
9. Perhaps these thinkers were also influenced by distinctive notions such as *dunya* (see above, p. 57), and *saeculum*.

Notes to Chapter 17: Principal Conclusions

1. See above, pp. 38ff. and also p. 142.
2. See pp. 37ff.
3. See my article on "Anti-Semitism" in the Encyclopedia of Pauly-Wissowa-Kroll, Supplementary Volume, 24, 32.
4. See the Sifrei on Numbers 6:11 ("when any soul has sinned").
5. *On the Special Commandments* IV, 102. He was influenced by the Pythagorean doctrine of harmony.
6. See above, p. 27; *Writings* Volume 1 p. 1.
7. For additional historical reasons in the Torah, see above, p. 9.
8. See above, pp. 12ff. on the "unifying purpose" of the mitzvot.
9. See above, p. 57 on the difference between *din* and *dunya* in Baḥya's thought.
10. In the German collection *Maimonides* (1908) I, 81.
11. Philo, *On the Special Commandments,* II, 60; and see my note to the German translation.
12. Hermann Cohen, *Jüdische Schriften* I, 26, II, 466.

Glossary

Adonai	"The Lord"; personal name for God in the Bible, conventional vocalization of "YHWH." Interpreted by Halevi as referring to God encountered in personal experience, as opposed to philosophical speculation. See Elohim.
Aggadah	(1) Collective: The whole body of rabbinic lore and wisdom, inclusive of tales, proverbs and occasional sayings. (2) Singular: A particular tale or rabbinic saying.
Amora	(*pl.* Amoraim) — a rabbinic authority of the Talmudic period, ca. 200–500 C.E.
Autonomous	Self-governed: describing the stance of a moral actor basing the authority of ethical or religious obligation on his own self or reason, or rules accepted on that basis. (See Heteronomous.)
Elohim	"God"; generic name for God in the Bible. Interpreted by Halevi as referring to God known impersonally through philosophical speculation. See Adonai.
Etrog	Citron: An aromatic tropical fruit, waved together with the Lulav (*q.v.*) in observance of Leviticus 23:40.
Eudaemonism	The view (associated with Aristotle) that happiness (whether this-worldly or other-worldly) is the goal of human endeavor, including religious practice. Contrasted with the Kantian view that the good should be performed or sought for its own sake, regardless of personal consequences.
Halakhah	(1) Collective: The whole body of rabbinic law, or the discipline of studying rabbinic law. (2) Singular: The decided rabbinic law in a particular case.
Heteronomous	Governed by another: describing the stance of a moral actor accepting an outside authority (God, human ruler, tradition or community) as a source of ethical or religious obligation, or rules accepted on that basis. (See Autonomous.)
Hortative	(Hebrew: *Shim'iyot*) — describing those mitzvot accepted on the basis of divine command, not clearly derivable from reason. In Saadia's schema, all mitzvot are either rational (*muskalot*) or hortative (*shim'iyot*). NOTE: I have coined the term "hortative" in search of a word suggestive of the varied meanings of the Hebrew root *ShMA'*: "hear" and "exhort." Other translations of Saadia refer to these as "religious" commandments or "commandments of revelation."

ḥukkim	(sing. *Ḥok*) In rabbinic parlance, laws that are not obviously rational, for instance, dietary laws or the details of the sacrifices. (See *mishpatim.*)
Kabbalah	(1) Tradition generally. (2) Mystical traditional teaching, especially of the Zohar and its associated literature.
Kosher	Fit, especially ritually fit for consumption (in the case of food) or use (in the case of other ritual objects such as Sukkah, Lulav, Tefillin).
Lulav	The palm-frond, bound with myrtle and willow twigs and waved ceremonially together with the Etrog (*q.v.)* in observance of Leviticus 23:40.
Matzah	Unleavened bread, eaten especially on Passover, in commemoration of Exodus 12:39 and 13:3–10.
Mezuzah	A doorpost ornament containing parchment with scriptural verses, in observance of Deuteronomy 6:9 and 11:20.
Midrash	(1) A characteristic rabbinic form of teaching in which ideas or lessons are presented in the form of interpretation of Biblical verses. (2) An example of this form of teaching. (3) A literary compilation of teachings in the midrashic form.
Mishnah	(1) The code of legal teachings assembled from previous oral traditions by Judah the Patriarch around 200 C.E.; the core of rabbinic law. (2) A single paragraph or law from that collection.
mishpatim	In rabbinic parlance, laws that are obvious to reason, such as the basic ethical code prohibiting murder, theft, etc. (See *ḥukkim.*)
Mitzvah	(pl. "mitzvot") — commandments, specifically, the rules and precepts of Jewish religious practice conceived as commanded by God.
Nazirite	One who takes on the "Nazirite vow" to abstain from wine and hair trimming, as described in Numbers 6:1–21.
Orlah	(1) The foreskin, removed in circumcision. (2) The fruit of the tree in its first three years, forbidden for eating, as described in Leviticus 19:23–25. (3) Figuratively, a moral encumbrance ("the foreskin of the heart" — see Deuteronomy 10:16, Jeremiah 4:4).
Pesaḥ	Passover, observed Nisan 15–21, in the Spring. (See Leviticus 23:4–8, Deuteronomy 16:1–8.)
Rosh Hashanah	New Year (1st of Tishri, in the Fall). This designation of the festival is post-Biblical. It is identified with the Day of Remembrance described in Leviticus 23:23-25.
Shavuot	Feast of Weeks, observed Sivan 6, in the late Spring. (See Leviticus 23:9–22.)
Sha'atnez	Mixture of linen and wool, forbidden by Leviticus 19:19.
Shekhinah	The Divine Presence or Indwelling of God in the world (based on Exodus 25:8: "that I may dwell [*ve-shakhanti*] in their midst," of central significance in rabbinic and mystical theology.
Shofar	The horn of a ram, blown ceremonially on Rosh Hashanah in observance of Leviticus 23:24 and Numbers 29:1.

Sukkah — An informal ceremonial hut, used for eating and other dwelling activities during the Feast of Booths (Sukkot), in observance of Leviticus 23:42-43.

Sukkot — Feast of Booths, observed Tishri 15–21, in the Fall. (See Leviticus 23:33–43.)

Talmud — (1) Either of the two major corpuses of Jewish law and lore (Halakhah and Aggadah), *viz.* the Bablyonian Talmud and Jerusalem Talmud, compiled in the 5th century C.E. based on rabbinic discussions of the Mishnah. (2) The enterprise of legal exegetical discussion and religious learning represented in these works.

Tanna — (*pl.* Tannaim) — a rabbinic authority of the Mishnaic period, ca. 1–200 C.E.

Tefillin — "Phylacteries" (so-called): The black leather ornaments containing parchment with scriptural verses, worn in observance of Deuteronomy 6:8 and 11:18.

Torah — (1) The Five Books of Moses, containing most of the Biblical laws of the Jewish religion. (2) The totality of all authoritative Jewish religious teaching, comprising Halakhah and Aggadah (*q.v.*).

Tzitzit — Garment fringe: The fringe worn on the corners of the garment in observance of Numbers 15:37–41.

World to Come — (1) The eschatological age of terrestrial world history inaugurated by the coming of the Messiah. (2) Spiritual immortality in the hereafter.

Yom Kippur — Day of Atonement (10th of Tishri, in the Fall). Described in Leviticus 16:29–34 and 23:26–32.

Index

A
Aaron, 7, 26, 61 (note)
Aaronid priests, 61
Abaye, 103
Abel, xix, 28
abomination, 11
Abraham, 26, 59, 71, 83, 105, 115, 128, 128 (note), 143, 144
  faith of, 91, 91 (note)
  leaving homeland, 5, 7
  living to an old age, 26
  not second guessing God, 6, 88
  obedience of, 97, 167 (note), 178
  showing love of God, 58, 106, 128–29, 130, 146, 167, 167 (note), 175
    see *also* Isaac
Abravanel, Isaac, 108 (note), 149–58, 162 (note), 164 (note), 167, 169, 170, 171, 172, 173, 174, 179
  books by, 152
  commentaries on *Mishpatim*, 149, 151, 156
  commentaries on *Re'eh*, 152
  and Gersonides, 153, 155 (note)
  influence of Christianity on, 195 n15:14
  and Maimonides, 152–53, 154, 157
  and Philo, 173
Abravanel, Judah, 152
abrogation, 14, 35–36, 77
absolute obedience, 178 (note)
abstinence, 43, 60, 82, 156
Abulafia, Joseph ben Todros, Rabbi, 113 (note)
actions
  and purposes, 131–32
  tensions with regard to, 104–5
    ethical actions, 105 (note)
  vs. virtures, 103
Active Intellect, 123 (note), 125, 125 (note)
Adam, 26, 66, 77, 128, 128 (note), 130, 153
"added soul" active on Sabbath, 174
admonishment, 27, 70, 185–86 n3:9
Adon 'Olam (poem), 47
Adonai [Lord], 106 (note), 197
adultery, 187 n3:26
  adulterous women, 28–29, 53, 153
Against Apion (Josephus), 41
Aggadah, xii–xiii, xv, 16, 70–71 (note), 143, 159, 171, 175, 177, 197, 199, 187 n3:22
    aggadic explanations, 108–9, 111
Aggadot ha-Bavliyim (Becher), 67 (note)
aggadot [maxims and lore], 179
agricultural commandments, 39, 112, 135
Aḥa, Rav, 21
Ahad Ha-Am, 66 (note)
Aḥarei Mot, 124
    Portion *Aḥarei Mot*, 150
Akedah, 128, 168
Akiva, Rabbi, 21
Al Parashat Derakhim , 66 (note)
Albeck, Chanoch, 109 (note)
Albo, Joseph, 106 (note), 141–48, 150, 162, 162 (note), 164 (note), 166, 167, 169, 170, 171, 172, 174
    books by, 89 (note), 141, 142 (note)
    and Crescas, 147, 152
    and Ibn Ezra, 141
    and Maimonides, 141, 142
    and Philo, 170
Alexander the Great, 22
allegories, 26–27, 39, 46, 56, 56 (note), 77–78, 135 (note), 158, 179, 188 n4:14, 191 n9:1
    Christian allegorists, 77, 83–84
    Greek allegorists, 83, 84

Endnotes page numbers show both chapter and note number, i.e., 185 n1:2 is chapter 1 note 2 on page 185.

allusions, 5, 35, 128, 134, 139, 157–58, 173, 194 n13:9
almond/take care *[shaked/shoked]*, 154 (note)
Also sprach Zarathustra (Nietzsche), 178, 178 (note)
Altjüdische Allegoristik (Heinemann), 179 (note)
Amalek, 16
Amidah, 68
Amoraim, 15, 23, 160, 197
Amorites, 112
Amos the prophet, 6
'amr ilahi, 67 (note)
amulets, 108, 142, 172, 179
animals, 65, 88, 121
  animal cruelty, 110, 122, 174
  animal hybrids (mixed species), 11, 40, 136, 150 (note), 157
  clean animals rescued from the Flood, 187 n3:21
  forbidden animals, 54
  purity in, 44, 81 (note)
  and sacrifice, 136 (note), 153
  soul of, 23
anthropology
  and Abravanel, 156–57
  and Crescas, 138
anti-Semitism, 35
Antigonus of Socho, 162
Antiochus Epiphanes, 44
Antiquities of the Jews (Josephus), 40, 44, 83
aphorisms, 178
Apollo, 36
apologetic reasons for the mitzvot, xviii, 3, 45, 141, 147, 148, 164, 167–68, 169
  apologetic method, 179–80
appeal to authority, 8
Arama, Isaac, 195 n15:3
Arba'ah Turim (Jacob ben Asher) *see Tur, The* (Jacob ben Asher)
arbitrary mitzvot, 167
  see *also* hortative *[shim'iyot]* mitzvot
arel [uncircumcised], 78
Aries, sign of, 78
Aristaeas, 83
Aristeas, 35, 44
"Aristobolus," 188 n4:14
Aristotelianism, 48, 63, 74–75, 85, 92, 102, 103 (note), 125 (note), 126, 127, 131–32, 139, 162 (note), 168, 173, 174, 175, 179, 180
Aristotle, 37, 50, 63, 84, 93, 105, 105–6 (note), 120, 125 (note), 126, 128, 136, 137, 138, 168, 171, 176, 179, 197, 194 n12:4, 194 nn13:6,8
Ark of the Covenant, 125
ascending to God, 153
ascensions, virtues *[ma'alot]*, 61 (note)
asceticism, 29, 71, 77, 171, 175
asmakhta [casual supports], 108
assimilation, 22, 44, 83, 181
astral powers, 80, 191 n9:12
astrology, 78, 79–80, 80, 80 (note), 81–82, 82 (note), 83, 86, 88, 93, 117, 123, 129 (note), 139, 157, 161, 171, 192 n9:20, 192 n10:9
  see *also* cosmological explanations
atonement, 26, 96, 110, 126, 126 (note), 136
  lechaper [to atone], 81
attributes of God, 117–18
Auerbach, B. H., 178 (note)
Augustine, Saint, 168
authoritarian/authoritative reasons for the mitzvot, 12–13, 45
autonomous ethic of the Greeks, 36–37
autonomous reasons vs. heteronomous reasons, 55, 159–61, 166–67, 178, 197
autonomy, xvi, 186 n3:5
  of rabbis, 28 (note)
Avodah service, 12
avodah [service], 160 (note)
awakening
  intellectual awakening, 59, 92
  of reason, 59, 59 (note), 62, 190 n7:10
  of the Torah, 59, 59 (note), 62, 92
awareness
  "Jewish awareness," 181
  moral awareness, 173
axioms, 51, 67

B
Babylonian Talmud, 199
Baḥya ben Joseph Ibn Pakudah, xiii, 49, 57–64, 145, 167 (note), 169, 170, 171, 174, 177, 179, 182 (note), 191 n9:3, 192 n10:6–7, 196 n17:9

and Crescas, 137, 137 (note), 164 (note), 167 (note)
and Gersonides, 137 (note)
and Halevi, 74, 162 (note), 164 (note), 167 (note)
and Ibn Daud, 92–93
and Ibn Ezra, 76 (note), 77, 87, 91
and Maimonides, 106, 115, 118, 119, 170
and Philo, 118, 174
and Saadia ben Joseph, gaon, 62–64
Balaam, 79
beards, removing of, 2, 79, 98–99, 112
Behar, 121, 152
behavioral laws
"behavioral" commandments, 68
mitzvot influencing behavior, 27–28
rationality of, xvii–xviii
Beit Yosef (Caro), 112
believers, kinds of, 117–18
Ben Yehuda, Eliezer, 164 (note)
Benet, D. Z., 196 n16:8
Berger, Peter, 146 (note)
Bergman, Yehuda, 164 (note)
betrothal, 9, 12, 68
Bible, 21, 46, 52, 56, 113, 121, 147, 154 (note), 161, 176, 193 n11:7
Binding of Isaac, 6, 97, 143, 155
bird's nest, 23, 28, 97
blasphemy, 53 (note)
blessings, 68, 172
blind obedience, 97
blindness, 17
body, 60
bodily appetites, 173, 174
life of the body in parallel with life of the soul, 69–70
perfection of the body, 100–101, 132, 139
and soul, 136
Book of Beliefs and Opinions (Saadia ben Joseph, gaon) [translated by Rosenblatt] *see Book of Doctrines and Beliefs, The* (Saadia ben Joseph, gaon)
Book of Doctrines and Beliefs, The (Saadia ben Joseph, gaon), 49, 53 (note), 57
Tenth Article, 51
"Book of Love" (Maimonides), 116
"Book of Memories," mitzvot serving as, 173
"Book of Principles," mitzvot serving as, 173
Book of Principles [Sefer Ha-Ikkarim] (Albo), 141
Book of Proof and Argument in Defense of a Despised Religion see Kuzari: A Book of Proof and Argument in Defense of a Despised Religion (Halevi)
"Book of Sanctities" (Maimonides), 115
Book of Tradition [Sefer ha-Kabbalah] (Ibn Daud), 92
branches *[kappot]*, 26, 154 (note)
"broken cisterns," 158
bronze serpent, 191 n9:18
Buber, Martin, 71 (note)
bullock-offering, 113 (note), 154
burnt offerings, 81, 113, 130, 136, 153

C

Cain, xix, 5, 28
calendar, Jewish, 27–28, 78, 182
sabbatical year, 121
Caligula (emperor), 37
Cancer, sign of, 78
candelabra, 82 (note), 135
Caro, Joseph, 112
Cassuto, Umberto, 82 (note)
casual supports *[asmakhta]*, 108
catechism, 27–28, 173
"categorical imperative," 164
cause and effect, 190 n8:3
"Cause of Causes," 50
caution and reasons for the commandments, 98–99
Cebes, 36
cedars, 109, 194 n13:9
celestial spheres, 121, 123, 123 (note)
challah, 26, 26 (note)
cherubim, 70, 125, 173
Children of Israel, 9, 13, 39, 69
Christianity, 92–93, 147
and baptism, 135 (note)
criticisms of mitzvot, 131, 140, 141, 144, 151, 164
attacks on the Torah, 127, 168 (note)
doctrine of salvation, 180
influence of, 195 n15:14

and influence of the stars, 129 (note)
and intentions, 143
and original sin, 168
refuting of, 147 (note), 148
circumcision, 27, 30, 77, 128, 129, 135, 157, 168 (note), 174, 198
arel [uncircumcised], 78
episode of Zipporah, 88
and gentiles, 44 (note)
of the heart, 39, 44, 77–78
importance of, 89 (note), 90, 172
mitzvot for, 5, 6, 19, 44, 68, 109, 121
power of, 168, 172, 191 n9:18
citron *[hadar]* tree as symbol, 26–27
civil laws *[mishpatim] see mishpatim* [rational commandments]
clarity, intellectual, 177
"classical" vs. "romantic" traditions, 158
cleanliness and cleansing rituals, 49, 71, 109, 121, 131–32, 136, 139, 151, 172, 187 n3:21
Cohen, Hermann, xv, 95–96 (note), 167, 179–80, 181
Cohen, Yehezkel, 115
Commander and the commanded, 134, 160, 162, 167
"commandments of the limbs," 57, 60–62
commemoration of historical facts, 110–11
commentaries *see* specific authors
Commentary on Exodus (Cassuto), 82 (note)
Commentary on Leviticus I (Hoffman), 153 (note)
commonly held *[mefursamot]*, 85
communal prayer, 163 (note)
community, spirit of, 182
compassionate God, 32
confessional prayer, 16
conscience, 5, 13, 17, 29, 61, 160, 161 (note)
good acts commanded by, 17
as source of correct behavior, 5–6, 7–8, 21
Torah amplifying voice of, 8
voices of, 7, 18, 19, 37, 52, 63
listening to, 36 (note)
consequences of the mitzvot, 171–75
conventional law, 142 (note)
corpses, 12, 135 (note)
cosmological explanations, 111, 121, 143 (note), 154
cosmos celebrated by the Torah, 40–41, 41 (note)
of fringed garments, 155 (note)
of garments of the High Priest, 155–56
and Separate Intellects, 123, 123 (note)
symbolism of Temple, 40, 56 (note), 70, 83
see *also* astrology
Covenant Code, 156
coveting, 48, 86, 173
creative philology, 185 n3:1
creativity, intellectual, 165
Creator-Legislator, 56, 160
Creator's wisdom, 54, 66, 71, 89, 161–62, 168–69, 173
see *also* God
Crescas, Ḥasdai, 127–40, 150, 159, 160, 161, 162 (note), 168, 169, 170, 174, 175, 179, 182 (note), 194 n13:9
and Albo, 147, 152
and Baḥya ben Joseph Ibn Pakudah, 137, 137 (note), 164 (note), 167 (note)
books by, 128, 128 (note), 129, 131, 133 (note), 135 (note), 139, 141
death of son, 130
and Gersonides, 139
and Halevi, 138
and Ibn Ezra, 139
and Maimonides, 137, 138, 139
and Saadia ben Joseph, gaon, 139
Creskas philosophische Lehren, 138 (note)
Crete, 187 n4:5
cross-breeding in the vineyard, 40, 112, 119, 123
curses, 26, 53
customs
of ancestors, 1, 22, 37, 103
value of, 37, 38

D

daemon, 161 (note)
see *also* eudaemonism
daily offering, 154, 154 (note), 155
Darkhei Ha Aggadah [Ways of the Aggadah, The] (Heinemann), xv, 71 (note)

Das jüdische Religionsgesetz in jüdischer Beleuchtung (Wohlgemuth), 89 (note)
date-palm trees as symbols, 26–27
davar [essence/matter], 67 (note)
David (king), 96, 145
Day of Atonement, 110, 199
Day of Remembrance, 198
Days of Awe, 32, 135, 139
dead, contact with, 12, 135 (note)
debt-release, 135
decision making, 56
decrees, 2, 24, 28, 44, 56, 147, 149
 King's decrees, 149, 150
 vs. mercies, 23
 "of the text," 24
deeds, 78, 106, 121, 138, 145–46, 155, 170, 171, 175, 181
 and faith, 91 (note), 92, 145
 God's deeds, 71, 102
 good deeds, 27, 116, 134
 "performed deed," 142
 quality of, 194 n13:6
 value of, 92
demons, 9, 172, 179
derech eretz [universal standards of common propriety], 49
derekh eretz [ethical norms], 186 n3:8
Deror Yikra (poem by Dunash Ibn Labrat?), 191 n8:6
devotion, 3, 63, 88, 96, 116, 159
Dialogues of Love (Abravanel), 152
Diaspora, 182
dietary laws, xvii, 30, 44, 69, 151, 153 (note), 156, 171, 172, 174, 181, 198
 forbidden foods, 48–49, 96, 114, 142, 145, 147 (note)
 kosher and non-kosher, 16, 153 (note), 198
 prohibitions, 11, 19, 39, 43, 49 (note), 56, 79, 83, 110, 121, 135, 182
din and dunya, 57, 57 (note), 63 (note), 196 n16:9, 196 n17:9
Die Religionsphilosophie Joseph Albos (Tänzer), 147 (note)
discipline *[mishma'at]*, 53
divine authority, 170
 yoke of, xvi
"divine Chariot," 103, 103 (note)
divine commandments, xviii, 2, 6, 12, 53 (note), 66–67, 68, 85, 93, 178
divine jealousy, 185 n2:1
divine law, 118, 142 (note), 169–70, 187 n4:5
Divine mitzvot, 39
Divine Presence, 67, 69, 81, 134, 136, 138, 141, 198
 Shekhinah, 19, 67, 81, 126 (note)
Divine Principle, 71, 72, 73
divine reason, xviii
divine revelations, 2, 36
divine science, 92
divine word/power/essence *['inyan elohi]*, 67 (note)
divorce, 68, 92, 151
"Doreshei Reshumot," 175
Dunash Ibn Labrat?, 191 n8:6
dunya and din, 57, 57 (note), 63 (note), 196 n16:9, 196 n17:9
Duties of the Heart (Baḥya ben Joseph Ibn Pakudah), 47, 58, 59, 60, 61, 63, 137
 purposes of, 57–58
 see *also* heart, duties of

E

edot [testaments], 149
education and the mitzvot, 32
 pedagogic values of the mitzvot, 155–56
 religious-ethical education, 62, 174
 sociological method, 181–82
Education of Philo (Heinemann), 80 (note), 187 nn4:8,10,17,18
"Eight Chapters" (Maimonides), 97 (note)
Eleazar ben Azariah, 16
elect, the, 63, 162, 162 (note)
Elijah, the Prophet, 182
Elohim, 72, 106 (note), 197
emanations, 136
emotion, religious, 72 (note), 105, 106 (note), 145–46
emotional reasons for the mitzvot, xviii, 6, 10–12, 177
Emunah Ramah (Ibn Daud), 85, 88, 92, 106 (note), 118
emunato [his faith], 74 (note)
enactments, 2, 32, 67, 77, 90, 132, 136, 150, 182
 gezerot [protective enactments], 30 (note)

takkanot [positive enactments], 30 (note)
of Usha, 87 (note)
end/summer *[kayitz/ketz]*, 154 (note)
engraved *[ḥarut]*, 16, 36 (note)
enjoyment *[hana'ah]*, 15
enlightenment, 76, 100, 174–75
"enlightened," 34
intellectual enlightenment, 139, 140
Epicureans, 96
equality, 41
equity, 41, 86
Esau, 155
eschatological intent of mitzvot, 161, 162 (note), 196 n16:8
eschatological eudaemonism, 163
and salvation, 163–64 (note)
essence/matter *[davar]*, 67 (note)
essential mitzvot, 77
Esther, 120
eternal happiness, 63, 132, 133
eternal life, 103 (note), 132–33, 139, 147, 160, 161, 163–64 (note), 171, 175
eternal nature of the mitzvot, 85
eternal reward, 160, 162, 163, 169, 171
eternal salvation, 160–61
ethical reasons for mitzvot, 31–32, 43–44, 46, 55, 77
Hellenists' views on, 41–42
ethical-religious reasons for mitzvot, 156–57
ethical-religious influence of mitzvot, 28–33
and consequences of the mitzvot, 171–75
ethics, 163
autonomous, 36–37
ethical actions, 105 (note)
ethical improvements, 101
ethical mitzvot, 11, 87, 91, 173
ethical content of mitzvot, 118, 119, 170
ethical norms *[derekh eretz]*, 186 n3:5
ethical obligations, 68
ethical perfection, 160
ethical virtues, 43, 100, 118, 137, 162 (note)
philosophical ethics, 173
religious-ethical education, 62, 63
scientific ethics, 52
and value of the mitzvot, 162
Ethics (Aristotle), 105–6 (note)
Ethiopians, 65
etrog, 108, 152 (note), 197, 198
etymological homilies, 154 (note)
Eucharist, 143
eudaemonism, 161, 161 (note), 163, 164, 182 (note), 197
European Conservative Judaism, xv
Eve, 26, 130
evil, 5, 46, 81, 95, 105 (note), 131, 149, 151 (note), 155 (note), 164
evil influences (impulses), 58, 121, 123, 154, 156, 186 n3:16
evil urges and actions, 3, 6, 9, 11, 20, 21–22, 96, 108 (note), 136
exalted faith, 92
exile as a penalty, 180
existence, goal of, 91
Exodus from Egypt, xvi–xvii, 12, 86, 122, 135, 152, 154, 156, 157, 170
explaining the mitzvot
learning from classic Jewish thinkers, 176–83
value of explanations, 178–79
externalization, 144 (note), 146 (note)
"eye for an eye," 170, 187 n3:22

F

fabrics *see* mixed fabrics *[sha'atnez]*
face to face *[lex talionis]*, 41 (note), 109 (note)
faith, 25, 45, 48, 84, 87, 88, 92, 93, 94, 116, 155, 168 (note), 189 n5:4
of Abraham, 91, 91 (note)
in ancient cultures, 37, 46, 73, 164
breaking faith with, 10, 112
and deeds, 17, 91 (note), 92, 116
emunato [his faith], 74 (note)
exalted faith, 92
in God, 42, 68, 71, 85, 130, 168
in immortality of the soul, 161
Jewish faith, 34, 118, 119, 143, 147
of Jews to the Torah, 36, 45, 96, 106, 177, 188 n4:12
lack of, 6
love of God as axis of, 130

as pillar of the Torah, 87, 90, 92
of rabbis, 25–26, 31, 32, 35
of Ruth the Moabite, 6
scientific faith, 82, 93, 130, 138, 168
Falaquera, Shem Tov ibn, 164 (note)
family purity, 103, 172
fear
of God, 86, 106, 133–34, 137, 142, 144, 145–46, 162, 174
of heaven, 111
internalized fear, 144 (note)
yir'ah [fear/reverenance], 144 (note)
Feast of Booths, 199
Feast of Weeks, 135, 198
feelings, tensions in regard to, 105–7
Feldman, Seymour, 125 (note)
festivals, 40, 54, 63, 71, 85, 86, 86 (note), 110, 122, 132, 154, 157, 172, 183, 194 n12:3
law of the festivals, 80, 104
see also individual festivals
"finger of God," 3, 163
fiqh [Talmud], 109 (note), 199
First Cause, 107
first fruits, 39, 135
Fishman, Y. L., xiii
Five Elements, The, 133 (note)
forbidden *[orlah]*, 39, 78, 112, 135
forms, 123 (note)
seventh form, 123
Foundation of Faith, The [Yesod Mora] (Ibn Ezra) *see Yesod Mora [The Foundation of Faith]* (Ibn Ezra)
Foundation [Yesod], 141
Foundations of the Torah (Maimonides), 107
four goods, 131–32
Four Species, 26
Frankel, Zechariah, xv
free will, 129
freedom *[ḥerut]*, 16, 36 (note), 178
frenetic spirits, 20
fruit of love, 106, 193 n11:13
fulfillment, 65
of the commandments, 17, 19, 30, 45, 55, 58, 62, 67, 95, 104, 106, 130, 139, 140, 144–46, 157, 160, 162, 163, 174, 175
personal fulfillment, 164
of uncommanded good deed, 18

G

gannav, 29
Gaon, Saadia, xiii
garment fringe *[tzitzit]*, 9, 26, 31 (note), 71, 86, 105, 155 (note), 158, 174, 187 n3:26
symbolism of, 122
garments
golden garments, 150
of the High Priest, 155–56
gazlan, 29
Geiger, Abraham, xv, 97, 115, 167
Gemara, 25
generation of the wilderness, 127, 136
gentiles, 3, 6, 17, 35, 83, 168, 181
and circumcision, 44 (note)
Gersonides, 120–26, 161, 170, 171, 172, 173
and Abravanel, 151 (note), 153, 155 (note)
and Baḥya ben Joseph Ibn Pakudah, 137 (note)
books by, 121, 124, 125 (note)
commentaries on Deuteronomy, 123 (note)
commentaries on Genesis, 120 (note)
commentaries on Leviticus, 123 (note)
commentaries on Numbers, 122, 123 (note), 194 n12:3
commentaries on *Shemini*, 121, 126, 126 (note)
commentaries on the Torah, 121, 125
and Crescas, 139
and Ibn Ezra, 120 (note), 120–21, 122–23
and Maimonides, 120 (note), 123–24, 127, 147
Gesammelte Aufs (Grunwald), 67 (note)
Geschichte der Gemeinde Halberstadt (Auerbach), 178 (note)
gezerot [protective enactments], 30 (note)
Ghazali, Abu Ha-med Mohammad ibn Mohammad al-, 72 (note), 192 n10:4,7
Gnostics, 187 n3:25
goals
of existence, 91
initial goals, 131–32

goat-satyrs, 113, 124
God
  Adonai [Lord], 106 (note), 197
  attributes seen as mercies, 23
  being given physical attributes, 117
  bringing suffering, 95
  "Cause of Causes," 50
  commanded by God rather than listening to conscience, 17
  Commander and the commanded, 134, 160, 162, 167
  Creator-Legislator, 56, 160
  as creator of commandments, xviii–xix, 5, 37, 42–43, 55
  Creator's wisdom, 54, 66, 71, 89, 161–62, 168–69, 173
  Elohim, 197
  Elohim [God], 72, 106 (note)
  fear of, 86, 106, 133–34, 137, 142, 144, 145–46, 162, 174
  "finger of God," 3, 163
  gift of reason, 49
  God-concept of Maimonides, 193 n11:21
  God of religion vs. metaphysical God, 72–73
  God's deeds, 71, 102
  governing astral powers, 80
  Holy Blessed One, 23
  image of, 31 (note)
  importance of God authoring the Torah, 37, 37 (note)
  imposing decrees on Israel, 23–24
  Indwelling God, 198
  issuing divine commands, 66–67
  judges as partners of, 16
  justice of, 13, 32, 130, 161
  kindness of, 86, 134, 136, 170
  knowledge of, 66, 72, 90, 106, 122, 128, 150, 173, 174
  love of, 105–6 (note), 105–6, 130, 133–34, 136, 136 (note), 137, 138, 139, 140, 145–46, 150, 162, 163, 174, 175
  man as servant of God, 16, 29, 36
    servants of God *[therapeutai theou]*, 160 (note)
  obedience to, 5, 55, 85, 98 (note)
  "partners to God," 183
  power and sovereignty of, 12–13
  and prayers of the righteous, 70 (note)
  as Prime Mover, 66
  and the reasons for the commandments *[ta'amei ha-mitzvot]*, xvi–xvii, xviii
  redeeming the Jews, 10
  remembrance of God, 63, 78, 86, 111, 173
  as righteous and compassionate, 3, 7, 32
  as the "seventh form," 123, 123 (note)
  sovereignty of, 154
  Torah's conception of, 3–4
  unity of the Holy and Blessed God, 108, 117
  way of God is pure, 19
  what is rational to God, xviii
  will of, 2, 5–6, 7, 13, 25, 36, 133, 143, 149, 160, 161, 166, 171, 175, 186 n3:16
Goethe, Johann Wolfgang von, 176
Golden Calf, 81
golden garments, 150
"golden mean," 171
Golden Rule, 31 (note)
Gomorrah, 5
good deeds, 27, 116, 134
goods, four, 131–32
grammar, laws of, 166
gratitude, 54, 86, 133, 170
Greek culture, 34, 45–46
    see also Hellenistic philosophers
Guide of the Perplexed (Maimonides), xvii–xviii, 2, 95–96 (note), 97, 99, 100, 103, 104, 106, 107, 108, 109, 109 (note), 110, 110 (note), 112, 115, 115 (note), 116, 117, 118, 119, 120, 123, 124, 136, 137, 139, 150, 151 (note), 160, 170 (note), 175, 193 n11:7
guilt-offering, 153
Gundel, W., 129 (note)
Gunkel, Hermann, 82 (note)
Guttmann, Jacob, 192 n10:1
Guttmann, Michael, 185–86 n3:9, 187 n3:22

H

Ha-tzedakah be-Yisrael (Bergman), 164 (note)
hadar [citron] tree as symbol, 26–27
Hagar, 6
Haggadah, 22
hair, cutting of, 112
  see also beards, removing of
halakhah, 197
Halakhah, 199
Halevi, Judah, xiii, 62 (note), 65–75, 160, 162 (note), 163, 163 (note), 164 (note), 166, 167 (note), 168, 169, 170, 172, 174, 175, 179, 182, 191–92 n10:8, 197, 190 n8:3, 191 n9:13, 196 nn16:5,8
  and Abravanel, 157
  and Albo, 141, 143
  and Baḥya ben Joseph Ibn Pakudah, 74, 162 (note), 164 (note)
  books by, 47, 65, 65 (note), 70 (note), 72, 90, 91, 92–93, 105, 171, 175, 191–92 n10:8
  compared to Ghazali, 72 (note)
  and Crescas, 137, 138, 139, 167 (note)
  and Gersonides, 126
  and Ibn Daud, 90, 93–94, 191–98
  and Ibn Ezra, 84
  and Maimonides, 105, 106, 106 (note), 115, 118
  personality of, 74–75
  and Philo, 170
  poems by, 192 n10:8
  and Saadia ben Joseph, gaon, 70
Hammurabi's Code, 179
hana'ah [enjoyment], 15
Hananiah ben Akashya, Rabbi, 18–19, 103 (note), 167
Hanina, Rabbi, 17–18
Hanukkah, 30 (note), 86 (note)
happiness, 71, 85, 139, 161, 163, 164, 197
  eternal happiness, 63, 132, 133
harmony, 196 n17:5
harness of intellect, 189 n5:4
ḥarut [engraved], 16, 36 (note)
Hasidism, xii
Hasmonean period, 34, 35, 182
head-tax ransom, 81
hearing *[hören]*, 53 (note)
heart
  commandments of the heart, 60–62
  duties of the heart, 57, 59, 63, 92, 179
    see also Duties of the Heart (Baḥya ben Joseph Ibn Pakudah)
  evil thoughts of, 136
  heart's blood, 130
  heart's knowledge, 189 n5:4
  intentions of, 142–43, 146 (note), 169
  piety of, 62
  purity of the heart, 58, 141
  religiosity of, 58, 162, 174
  religious mitzvot, 62
  service of the heart, 114, 115, 143
  speak unto our hearts, 144
  wisdom of, 92
heaven, fear of, 111
heifers
  broken-necked, 122
  red heifer ceremony, 20, 26, 83 (note), 96, 98, 147 (note), 155
Heine, Heinrich, 73 (note)
Heinemann, Isaac, xv–xvi
Hellenistic period, 34–46
Hellenistic philosophers, 163, 164, 170, 172, 173, 174 (note), 181, 188 n4:8
  assimilation and religious intermingling during, 22
  attacked by Luzzatto, 163
  differences between Hellenistic and Medieval thinking, 159–62, 166, 171
  Greek ethics, 173
  Greeks on science, 115 (note)
  Hellenistic School, 47
  Hellenists' views on the Temple, 56 (note)
  impact on Ibn Daud, 87
  impact on Ibn Ezra, 84
  views on astrology, 83
heretics, 22, 49, 117
Hermetic tradition, 67, 190 n8:2
ḥerut [freedom], 16, 36 (note), 178
Heschel, Abraham J., xv, 71 (note)
heteronomy, xvi
  autonomous reasons vs. heteronomous reasons, 159–61, 166–67, 197
  heteronomic explanations, 175, 180–81
  heteronomous obedience, 24, 36
  mitzvot as heteronomous, xix, 16, 18, 24, 36, 55, 97

Philo and, 47
of religious discipline, 62
Talmudic School and, 48
theonomy, 38
unworthy of a free person, 178 (note)
Hezekiah, 186 n3:5
hidden reasons and *ḥukkim* [not rational commandments], 19–21, 157
hierarchy of purposes, 194 n13:8
High Court, 135 (note)
High Holy Days, 173
High Priest, 17, 110, 113 (note), 124, 126, 150
garments of, 81, 155–56
Hilkhot Avodah Zarah (Pseudo-Empedocles), 99
Hilkhot Yesodei Ha-Torah (Maimonides), 175
Hillel the Elder, 30–31, 31 (note), 38, 105, 132, 137, 170, 173, 191 n8:5
Hippocrates, 69 (note)
Hirsch, Samson Raphael, xv, 27, 71, 158, 173, 177, 179 (note), 182
commentary on Deuteronomy, 187 n3:17
Ḥisda, Rabbi, 27, 67 (note)
"historic" method, 170
historical facts, commemoration of, 110–11
History of the Romans (Mommsen), 182 (note)
Hoffman, David, 153 (note)
holiness, 11, 45, 53, 72
Holiness Code, 21, 156
Holy Blessed One, 23
Holy of Holies, 81, 124
Homer, 178 (note)
homilies, 27, 154 (note), 173, 186 n3:13, 186 n3:14, 194 n13:9
honoring parents, 40, 43, 86, 96, 147 (note)
hören [hearing], 53 (note)
horoscopes, 191 n9:18
see also astrology
hortative *[shim'iyot]* mitzvot, 53 (note), 60, 60 (note), 79, 83, 84, 120, 157, 160, 171, 172, 197
denigration of, 93
explanations of, 54–55, 114
ranking of, 87–88
and rational mitzvot, 52–54, 85, 90
two kinds of, 88–89
weakness of, 88–90, 93, 115
household management, 85, 85 (note), 87, 132
ḥukkim [not rational commandments], xvi, 25–26, 32, 96–97, 98, 100, 166, 198
distinguishing from rational commandments, 21–22, 95
Hellenists' views on, 35–36, 37, 38
reasons for are hidden, 19–21
statutes *[ḥukkim]*, 149
Torah not distinguishing from rational commandments, 21
see also irrational commands
ḥukkot laws, 79
humanism, 37, 187 n4:7
humanitarianism, 79
humans, 39, 65
authoring the commandments, xviii–xix, 5
in God's image, 31 (note)
human reason, xviii, 34, 51, 53 (note)
awakening of, 59, 59 (note)
cannot understand all the mitzvot, 68
different tasks of, 51–52
as gift of God, 49
and the law, 76
pretensions of, 66 (note)
and rational mitzvot, 53
requiring acknowledgment of mitzvot, 98
unable to define religious obligations, 60
humanity, 7, 8, 31, 37, 41 (note), 44, 66, 128 (note), 166
perfection of humankind, 125
hybrids (mixed species), 11, 40, 136, 150 (note), 157
hygiene *see* cleanliness and cleansing rituals
hypocrisy, 190 n7:6
hyssop, 194 n13:9

I

I and Thou (Buber), 71 (note)
"I" vs. a national "you," 22

Ibn Daud, Abraham, 84, 85–94, 106, 117, 120, 126, 141, 159, 162 (note), 166, 167, 169, 173, 174, 192 nn10:1,8,9
  and Baḥya ben Joseph Ibn Pakudah, 92–93
  books by, 85, 88, 92, 106 (note), 118
  commentaries on *Vayikra*, 126
  and Halevi, 90, 93–94, 191–92 n10:8
  and Ibn Ezra, 93–94, 98
  and Maimonides, 114–16
  and Philo, 174
  and Saadia ben Joseph gaon, 88–90
Ibn Ezra, Abraham, 76–84, 161, 169, 170, 171, 172, 173, 174, 177, 181, 191 n9:1, 191 n9:14, 192 n10:9
  and Albo, 141
  and Baḥya ben Joseph Ibn Pakudah, 76 (note), 77, 87, 91
  books by, 76, 77, 78, 80, 83
  commentary to Exodus, 56 (note)
  cosmological explanations, 56 (note), 83, 111
  and Crescas, 139
  and Gersonides, 120 (note), 120–21, 122–23
  and Ibn Daud, 93–94, 98
  and Maimonides, 108, 109, 111, 117
  and Philo, 83, 174
Ibn Gabirol, Solomon, 196 n16:5
Ibn Tibbon, Judah, 57 (note), 164 (note)
Ibn Tibbon, Samuel, 109 (note), 164 (note)
Idea of the Holy, The (Otto), 148
idealization, 188 n4:27
idolatry, 3, 20, 21, 22, 30, 34, 99, 101, 103, 128, 135, 190 n7:6
  distancing people from, 111–12, 114, 123, 136, 138, 141, 152, 157, 157 (note), 172
  forbidding of, 53, 112, 157 (note)
  idolatrous customs, 170 (note)
  importance of prohibiting, 89 (note), 105, 123
  sacrifices and, 112–13, 114–15, 123–24, 170 (note), 172
  worship of the golden calf, 37
image of God, 31 (note)
immersion, 135 (note), 136, 187 n3:26
immortality, 59 (note)
  of the intellect, 122
  of the soul, 161
impurity, 11, 20, 48, 70, 72, 121, 136, 149
  laws of impurity, 103, 109, 113, 114, 124, 131–32, 135 (note)
  see also purity
inanimate beings, 65
incantations, 129
incest, 54, 93
"inclination to materiality," 130
individualism, 22, 63, 163–64, 181, 182, 182 (note)
initial goals, 131–32
injustice, 85, 95
  see also justice
inner purity, 153
intellect, 51, 62, 66, 131, 155, 189 n5:4
  Active Intellect, 123 (note), 125, 125 (note)
  immortality of, 122
  intellectual actualization, 100 (note), 105
  intellectual awakening, 59, 92
  intellectual clarity, 177
  intellectual creativity, 165
  intellectual enlightenment, 139, 140
  intellectual perfection, 101, 110 (note), 132–33, 137, 160
  intellectualism, 107, 116, 168
  medabber [logikos] [intellect], 90 (note)
  as messenger between man and God, 76, 106
  and the mitzvot
    explaining the mitzvot, 52
    intellectual mitzvot, 92
    intellectual reasons for the mitzvot, xviii, 23–24, 176, 177
    intellectual value of mitzvot, 110–13
    and rational mitzvot, 52–54
    spiritual-intellectual reasons for mitzvot, 122
  non-intellectuals and precepts of the Torah, 101–4
  perfecting of, 91, 101, 102
  pure intellect, 153
  and salvation, 57
  Separate Intellects, 123, 123 (note), 125 (note), 143 (note)
  see also humans, human reason
intentions, heart's, 142–43, 146 (note), 169
intermarriage, 44, 83, 183

internalization, 146 (note)
internalized fear, 144 (note)
intrinsic value of mitzvot, 149–50
intuition, 51, 72
'inyan elohi [divine word/power/essence], 67 (note)
irrational commands, 6–7, 20–21, 25–26, 32
distinguishing from rational commandments, 21–22, 95
irrationality of heteronomous explanations, 167
Torah not distinguishing from rational commandments, 21
see also ḥukkim [not rational commandments]
irrational obedience, 5
irrational reasons for the mitzvot, 38
Hellenists' views on, 35–36, 37, 38
Isaac, 26, 58, 83, 128 (note), 128–29
binding of, 6, 97, 143, 155
Isaac, Rabbi, 2
Isaiah the prophet, 85
Ishmael, 6, 7
Israel, 74, 81 (note), 128 (note), 153, 156, 157
called holy, 72
love between Heavenly Father and Israel, 175
People of Israel and the commandments, 8, 23, 57, 62, 70, 87, 98
relationship with God, 29, 45, 152
and the Torah, 7, 19, 163, 173
tribes of, 155

J
Jacob, 26, 82, 155
Jacob ben Asher, 107, 170
Jaffe, Mordecai, Rabbi, 49 (note)
Jason of Kyreine, 44 (note)
jealousy, divine, 185 n2:1
Jerusalem (Palestinian) Talmud, 199
Jeshurun (journal), 30 (note), 113 (note)
Jesus, 128 (note), 129, 143
Jewish Diaspora, 47, 182
Jewish Theological Seminary (Breslau), xiii, xv
Joel, Manuel, 138 (note)
Johanan ben Zakkai, Rabbi, 20, 29
Jonah, xix
Joseph, 26, 39, 39 (note)
Joseph, Rabbi, 18
Joseph (the blind), Rabbi, 17
Josephus, Flavius, xvi, 35, 37, 37 (note), 39, 84, 155, 159, 188 n4:27, 195 n15:9
books by, 40, 41, 83
on Moses, 36
and Philo, 39, 40, 43, 84, 159
on theocracy, 42–43
joy of mitzvah, 104, 138, 145–46, 148, 171, 172
Jubilee year, 43, 135, 154
"Judah ben Halevi" (poem), 73 (note)
Judah Ben Tema, 107
Judah, Rabbi, 17, 25
Judah the Patriarch, 16–17
Judaism, 57 (note), 73, 74, 164, 166, 178, 178 (note), 179–80, 181, 192
and astrology, 82
and Christianity, 27–28, 92, 127, 128 (note), 143, 147 (note), 180
and intentions, 143
"legalistic Judaism," 89
prophetic Judaism, 89, 115
Schools of *see* Hellenistic School; Mystical School; Philosophical School; Talmudic School
and science, 34–35, 41–42, 43, 57, 74, 94
ultra-Orthodox Judaism, 178 (note)
judges as partners of God, 16
justice, 3, 38, 41–42, 43, 51, 53, 90 (note), 109, 164
God's justice, 13, 32, 130, 161
see also injustice

K
kabbalah, 47, 63, 67 (note), 84, 141, 172, 174, 176, 181, 198, 195 nn15:3,13
Kadushin, Max, xvi
Kalir, 194 n13:9
Kant, Immanuel, 6, 16, 18, 63, 163, 178 (note), 197, 186 n3:5
Kaplan, Mordecai, xv–xvi
kappot [branches], 26, 154 (note)
Karaites, 67, 92
Kaufamann, D., 192 n10:8
Kaufmann, D., 133 (note)
kayitz/ketz [summer/end], 154 (note)
kebhes [sheep], 154

Kedoshim, 123, 156
Portion *Kedoshim*, 150 (note), 157 (note)
Kenesset (journal), 163 (note)
Kerem Ḥemed (Luzzatto), 196 n16:5
Khazars, king of, 71
kindness of God, 86, 134, 136, 170
kingdom of heaven, yoke of, 16, 17, 29, 36
kings, conduct of, 2 (note), 9, 25, 98, 147 (note)
kiyyum [preservation/ performance], 183
Klatzkin, Jacob, 164 (note)
Kneset (journal), xiii
knowledge, 115 (note), 162 (note), 193 n11:13
of God, 66, 72, 90, 106, 122, 128, 150, 173, 174
heart's knowledge, 189 n5:4
Tree of Knowledge, 185 n2:1
Kobak, Joseph, 113 (note)
kobeshim ["overtake"], 154
kofer [ransom], 81 (note)
Kook, Abraham, 177
Koraḥ, 125
kosher and non-kosher, 16, 153 (note), 198
see also dietary laws
Kuzari: A Book of Proof and Arguement in Defense of a Despised Religion (Halevi), 192 n10:8
Kuzari: A Book of Proof and Argument in Defense of a Despised Religion (Halevi), 47, 65, 65 (note), 70 (note), 72, 90, 91, 92–93, 105, 171, 175, 191–92 n10:8

L
Landauer edition of *Book of Beliefs and Opinions*, 53 (note), 189 n6:3
laws, 34–35, 76, 89, 101, 127, 141–42, 142 (note), 153, 166–67, 176, 193 n11:7
civil laws *[mishpatim]*, 149
divine law, 118, 142 (note), 169–70, 187 n4:5
ḥukkot laws, 79
Judaism as "religion of the law," 181
law of love, 127
laws of Pesaḥ, 156
laws of purity and impurity, 53, 103, 109, 113, 114, 124, 131–32, 135, 135 (note)
laws of sacrilege, 96–97
"Laws of the Lulav," 104
laws of the universe, 40–41
of Mezuzah, 193 n11:14
natural law, 40, 45, 47, 54–55, 79, 80, 142 (note), 160, 178
Hellenistic Jews reverence for, 173
natural law vs. political law, 38–39, 142, 166
similarity of natural law and the mitzvot, 39–41
penal law, 109–10
political laws, 38–39, 42, 85, 85 (note), 123, 142, 166
pre-existing law, 179
rationale for laws, 76 (note)
religious laws, 74, 142, 142 (note), 182 (note)
Ten Commandments as law, 87
revealed law, 187 n4:5
Torahitic law, 193 n11:2
"Laws of Megillah and Hanukkah" (Maimonides), 110
Laws of Repentance (Maimonides), 105 (note), 106, 108
leavening, prohibition against, 156, 170 (note), 173
"legalistic Judaism," 89
lekhaper [to atone], 81
lepers, 20, 77, 78, 121, 172
Letter to Yemen (Maimonides), 101 (note)
Letters (Seneca the Younger), 2
Levi ben Gershon, Rabbi *see* Gersonides
Levi, Rabbi, 153 (note)
Leviathan, 27
levirate marriage, 20, 24, 26, 114 (note)
Levites, 37, 78
Levush (Jaffe), 49 (note)
lex talionis [face to face], 41 (note), 109 (note)
licentiousness, 71, 109
Life of Moses (Philo), 36
Light of the Lord (Crescas), 128, 131, 133 (note), 141
literacy
ability to read Greek, 47
ability to read Hebrew, 45, 47
liturgical poems, 194 n13:9
logikos [medabber] [intellect], 90 (note)

Lord *[Adonai]*, 106 (note)
lore and maxims *[aggadot]*, 179
love, 106, 116, 132, 137 (note), 148, 152, 162, 163, 169, 174 (note), 174–75
- as elevating principle, 162 (note)
- fruit of love, 106, 193 n11:13
- of God, 105–6 (note), 105–6, 122, 130, 133–34, 136, 136 (note), 137, 138, 139, 140, 145–46, 150, 162, 163, 174, 175
  - relationship to fear of God, 106
- law of love, 127
- love your neighbor, 11, 31, 31 (note), 45, 86, 87 (note), 91, 102, 122, 132, 137, 137 (note), 138, 152

lulav, 104, 108, 152 (note), 154 (note), 197, 198
Luther, Martin, 82
Luzzatto, S. D., 163, 182 (note), 196 n16:5

M

ma'alot [ascensions, virtues], 61 (note)
macrocosm, 56 (note), 81
magical approach, 67
Mahzor, 158
"Maimoni" the philosopher, 104
Maimonides, Moses, xiii, xvii–xviii, 2, 48, 95–119, 104, 111, 121, 150, 159, 160, 163, 164 (note), 166, 167, 168, 169, 170, 171, 172, 173, 174, 175, 176, 177, 178, 179, 180, 182 (note), 193 n11:3,20,21, 196 n16:5
- and Abravanel, 151 (note), 152–53, 154, 157
- and Albo, 141, 142
- and Baḥya ben Joseph Ibn Pakudah, 106, 115, 118, 119, 170
- books by, xvii–xviii, 95–96 (note), 96–97, 97 (note), 98, 99, 100, 101 (note), 103, 104, 105, 106–7, 108, 109, 110, 112, 115, 116, 118, 119, 120, 123, 124, 137, 145, 170 (note), 175
- commentaries on *Behar*, 121
- commentaries on *Shemini*, 121
- commentaries on the Mishnah, 30 (note), 97 (note), 103 (note), 104, 105, 110, 137, 156, 162
- and Crescas, 129, 137, 138, 139
- and Gersonides, 120 (note), 123–24, 127, 147
- and Halevi, 105, 106 (note), 115, 118
- and Ibn Daud, 114–16
- and Ibn Ezra, 108, 109, 111, 117
- and Neuberger, 193 n11:7
- on *Pesaḥim* 119a, 23
- and Saadia ben Joseph, gaon, 162 (note)

Man Is Not Alone (Heschel), 71 (note)
man-made laws, 101
manna, 154
marriage
- to beautiful captive woman, 173
- discouraging intermarriage, 44, 83, 183
- levirate marriage, 26, 114 (note)
- of relatives, 54, 93, 172
- restrictions on marital relations, 27, 82

masters and servants, 10, 13, 55, 86, 186 n3:2
- man as servant of God, 16, 29, 36, 171
  - servants of God *[therapeutai theou]*, 160 (note)
- obligation to serve, 190 n6:10
- serving only to receive reward, 55, 59, 162, 171

"materiality, inclination to," 130
mathematics, 76, 84, 90, 92, 120, 166
matzah and maror, 77, 198
maxims and lore *[aggadot]*, 179
mazal, 129 (note), 171
meal-offering, laws of, 153
"measure for measure," 170, 187 n3:22
medabber [logikos] [intellect], 90 (note)
medical science, 44 (note), 74 (note), 90, 151, 160, 172
Medieval philosophers, 47–50, 109 (note), 125 (note), 129 (note), 143 (note), 174 (note), 182, 182 (note)
- differences between Hellenistic and Medieval thinking, 159–62, 166, 171
- on Separate Intellects, 123 (note)
- summary of Medieval thinking, 159–64
- *see also* Abravanel, Isaac; Albo, Joseph; Baḥya ben Joseph Ibn

Pakudah; Crescas, Ḥasdai; Gersonides; Halevi, Judah; Ibn Daud, Abraham; Ibn Ezra, Abraham; Maimonides, Moses; Saadia ben Joseph, gaon
mefursamot [commonly held], 85
Meir, Rabbi, 17, 133
Melanchthon, Philipp, 82
Mendelssohn, Moses, xv
menstrual purity, 26 (note), 121
mercies
  vs. decrees, 23
  God's attributes seen as, 23, 154 (note)
Meribah, 7
metaphysical God, 72–73
metaphysics, 52, 103, 103 (note)
Metaphysics (Aristotle), 105–6 (note)
mezuzah, 30, 61, 77, 86, 108, 111, 113, 179, 198
  laws of mezuzah, 193 n11:14
microcosm, 56 (note), 81
Middle Ages *see* Medieval philosophers
middle cosmos, 56 (note), 81
Midianites, 26
Midrash, 15, 28, 29, 31, 35, 39, 48, 55, 111, 143, 147, 153 (note), 159, 170, 198
mind, colloquy with soul, 191 n9:3
"minor to major" principle, 110
Minos of Crete, 36
miracles, 28, 51, 58, 65, 88, 128, 132, 136, 181
Miriam, 7, 109
mishma'at [discipline], 53
Mishnah, 23, 48 (note), 105, 106, 198, 199, 185 n1:1
Mishneh Torah (Maimonides), 47, 95, 95–96 (note), 96–97, 98, 104, 107, 109 (note), 110, 112, 116, 169, 179
  Book of Knowledge, 137
  "Laws of Ethical Qualities," 145
Mishpatim, 1, 15, 27, 29, 149, 151, 156
  Portion *Mishpatim*, 151
mishpatim [rational commandments], xvi, 96–97, 166, 198
  civil laws *[mishpatim]*, 149
  distinguishing from non-rational commandments, 21–22, 95
  Torah not distinguishing from irrational commandments, 21
mitzvah performers, 58–59
mitzvot, 21–22, 27–28, 78–79, 102–4, 107–9, 118, 131, 152, 198
  categorized as "light" and "heavy," 89–90
  consequences of, 171–75
  difference between Divine and human mitzvot, 39
  duality of nuance in, 95
  ethical mitzvot, 11
  ethical-religious influence, 28–33
  fulfillment of, 17, 19, 30, 45, 55, 58, 62, 67, 95, 104, 106, 130, 139, 140, 144–46, 157, 160, 162, 163, 174, 175
  and the intellect, 110–13
    explaining the mitzvot, 52
    intellectual mitzvot, 92
    intellectual reasons for the mitzvot, xviii, 23–24, 176, 177
    intellectual value of mitzvot, 110–13
    and rational mitzvot, 52–53
    spiritual-intellectual reasons for mitzvot, 122
  kinds of, 85, 85 (note), 87, 104–5
  see also hortative *[shim'iyot]* mitzvot; rational commandments *[mishpatim]*
  love of, 163, 169
  mystical power of, 27, 129–30, 175, 176, 177
  "negative mitzvot," 142
  neglect of mitzvot, 167
  not given for enjoyment, 172 (note)
  obedience to the mitzvot, 4, 62, 161
  and pedagogic values, 155–56, 161–62, 164, 171–75, 179, 187 n3:25
  psychological explanations of, 70–72
  psychological explanations of mitzvot, 70–72, 148, 152
  rabbincal views on, 28–33
  "rabbinic mitzvot," 30 (note)
  ranking of, 89 (note), 89–90, 91–93
  religious mitzvot, 11
    ethical-religious reasons, 156–57
    religious influence of the mitzvot, 157

religious-theoretical reasons for the mitzvot *see* theoretical-religious reasons
Torah and the religious value of mitzvot, 12–14
religious value of, 12–14
revealed status of, xvi, 45, 166
serving as "Book of Memories" and "Book of Principles," 173
systematic arrangement of problem, 166–75
unified explanation of, 138
yoke of the mitzvot, 16, 18, 22, 58, 76
see also reasons for the commandments *[ta'amei ha-mitzvot]*
mitzvot shim'iyot, 53 (note)
mitzvot sikhliyot, 53 (note)
see also shim'iyot [hortative] mitzvot
mixed fabrics *[sha'atnez]*, 112, 123, 147 (note)
mixed species, 11, 40, 136, 150 (note), 157
Mizraḥi, xv
modern rationalists, 88–90, 114–16
molad, 78
Mommsen, Theodor, 182 (note)
moral influence, 30
morality, 63, 100, 139
mitzvot acting upon, 121–22
moral awareness, 173
moral explanations are social, 109–10
moral perfection, 91, 173
non-moral considerations, 185 n2:1
objective morality, 6–7
and piety, 14, 42–43, 160
mortality, 125
Mosad Ha-Rav Kook (publisher), xiii
Moses, xvii, xix, 7, 36, 36–37, 37, 42–43, 48 (note), 76, 77, 80, 81, 106, 110, 125, 126, 139, 170, 173
Moses ben Maimon *see* Maimonides, Moses
Mount Sinai *see* Sinai
mourning, national, 183
murder, 9, 20, 110, 185 n1:1
forbidding of, 6, 7, 53, 142
not forbidden until age of Noah, 5
myrtle trees as symbols, 26–27
mystical power of mitzvot, 27, 129–30, 175, 176, 177
Mystical School, 47–50
mystics, 191 n9:3

N

Naḥmanides, 152, 153, 170
commentaries on Leviticus, 170 (note)
naive masses, 182 (note)
national conservatism, 37
national mourning, 183
nationalism, 22
naturalism, xviii
nature, 65, 83–84
forces of nature, 78–79
natural law, 40, 47, 54–55, 79, 80, 142 (note), 160, 178
Hellenistic Jews reverence for, 45, 173
vs. law of the legislators (political law), 38–39, 142, 166
similarity of natural law and the mitzvot, 39–41
Ten Commandments as, 87
observation of nature *[tzipiyah]*, 190 n7:12
and science, 66, 69, 122
Nazirite vow, 11, 28–29, 171, 198
"negative mitzvot," 142
neglect of mitzvot, 167
Ne'ilah prayer, 70 (note)
Neo-Platonic school, 67
Neuburger, Chaim, 101 (note), 110 (note), 193 n11:20
and Maimonides, 193 n11:7
neurochemistry of the brain, 70 (note)
niddaf [persecuted], 29
Nietzsche, Friedrich, 163, 178, 178 (note)
nikhbashim [subdued], 154
Nineveh, 6, 17–18
Noah, 5, 66, 80, 153, 186 n3:5, 187 n3:21
non-intellectuals and precepts of the Torah, 101–4
non-Orthodox Jews, 36 (note)
non-rational commandments *see ḥukkim* [not rational commandments]

numerology, 41, 78, 79, 82 (note), 84, 99, 123, 135, 154, 173, 191 n9:10
nutritive soul, 125, 125 (note)

O
oaths, 27
Obadiah, Abraham, xiii
Obadiah of Bertinuro, Rabbi, 48, 48 (note)
obedience, 16, 47, 53, 53 (note), 55, 58, 85, 88, 98 (note), 161 (note), 167, 168 (note), 174, 177
  of Abraham, 97, 167 (note), 178
  absolute obedience, 178 (note)
  blind obedience, 97
  to God, 5, 55, 85, 98 (note)
  heteronomous obedience, 18, 24, 31, 36
  to the mitzvot, 4, 62, 161
  obligation of, 166
  perfect obedience, 41
  rational obedience, 5
  as thanks to our Creator, 170
objectification, 146 (note)
objective laws, 176
objective morality, 6–7
obligations, religious, 60, 71, 86, 87, 92, 110 (note), 160, 166, 190 n6:10
observance, 74–75, 96
observation of nature *[tzipiyah]*, 190 n7:12
Odyssey (Homer), 178 (note)
offerings, 82, 113 (note), 124, 135, 135 (note), 170 (note), 172
  burnt offerings, 81, 113, 130, 136, 153
  daily offering, 154, 154 (note), 155
  guilt-offering, 153
  meal-offerings, 153
  paschal offerings, 78, 154
  peace offerings, 153
  public offerings, 154
  sacrificial offerings, 89
  sin offering, 28, 81, 87, 99, 111, 112, 153
  see also sacrifices
olah [something that goes up], 153
olam [world] and the Torah, 57 (note)
Old Testament Pseudepigrapha, The (Charlesworth), 35 (note)
Omer, 135
omniscience, 85
On Air, Water, and Places (Hippocrates), 69 (note)
On Foods (Hippocrates), 69 (note)
On Joseph (Philo), 39
On Philanthropy (Philo), 45
On the Decalogue (Philo), 35 (note), 40
On the Soul . . . (Aristotle), 125
On the Special Commandments (Philo), 35 (note), 40, 43, 44
On the Virtues (Philo), 35 (note), 43
Onan, 5–6
optimism, 176
optional sacrifices, 11
original sin, 127, 128–29, 130, 135, 156, 168
orlah [forbidden], 39, 78, 112, 135, 198
Otto, Rudolph, 72 (note), 148
oved [to serve], 160 (note)
"overtake" *[kobeshim]*, 154

P
pagans, 20, 21, 32, 96, 112, 173, 179, 180, 1014, 186 n3:16
palm trees as symbols, 26–27
Panaetius of Rhodes, 187 n4:7
parables, 61, 114, 151, 153 (note), 188 n4:13, 193 n11:7
Parah, 122
pardons, 110
parents, honoring of, 11, 40, 43, 86, 96, 147 (note)
"partners to God," 183
Paschal lamb, 28, 142 (note), 154, 192 n10:11
Passover, 9, 28, 39, 40, 78, 135, 198
  Second Passover, 78
Paul the Apostle, 91 (note), 128 (note)
peace offerings, 153
pedagogic values and the mitzvot, 155–56, 161–62, 164, 171–75, 179, 187 n3:25
penal law, 109–10
"people of God," 65–66, 69
perfect obedience, 41
perfection
  of humankind, 69, 91, 102, 125, 134, 146 (note)
    ethical perfection, 160
    eudaemonism, 161

intellectual perfection, 110 (note), 132–33, 137, 160
is perfection of intellectual knowledge, 101
moral perfection, 173
self-actualization, 100 (note)
of soul and body, 100–101, 132, 139
ultimate perfection, 100, 101, 105
of the world, 164
performance/preservation *[kiyyum]*, 183
"performed deed," 142
perpetual commandments, 5
persecuted *[nirdaf]*, 29
personal fulfillment, 164
personal virtue, 85, 87, 87 (note)
Pesaḥ, 70 (note), 77, 102, 157, 158, 173, 198
laws of, 156
petitions, 68, 71 (note)
Philo, xii, xiii, xv, xvi, 36, 41, 41 (note), 43 (note), 43–44, 154 (note), 160 (note), 161, 168, 171, 177, 188 n4:10
and Abravanel, 173
and Albo, 170
and Baḥya ben Joseph Ibn Pakudah, 118, 174
books by, 35, 35 (note), 36, 39, 40, 43, 45, 80 (note), 167 (note)
and Halevi, 170
as a Hellenistic Jew, 35, 37, 39, 44, 45–46, 47, 84, 176
and Ibn Daud, 174
and Ibn Ezra, 83, 174
and Josephus, 39, 40, 43, 84, 159
On Reward and Punishment, 187 n4:2
and Saadia ben Joseph, gaon, 54–55, 55, 72, 118, 174
On the Special Commandments (Philo), 188 n4:18
on Stoic doctrine, 36 (note)
"philosophical" commandments *see* "spiritual" commandments
philosophical ethics, 173
philosophical reasons for the mitzvot, 93
Philosophical School, 47–50
Phinehas, Rabbi, 153 (note)
Phinehas (son of Eleazar), 26
phylacteries, 172, 199
physical attributes of God, 117
piety, 42, 58, 72, 91, 106, 164, 192 n10:6
of Abraham, 167 (note)
of the heart, 62
and morality, 14, 42–43, 160
Pinḥas, Portion, 154
Plato, 2, 37, 42, 93, 151 (note), 161, 163, 176
pleasure, 161 (note)
pledges and widows, 24–25
Poems of Ibn Ezra (Rosin), 191 n9:3
poetry and religion, 72, 73, 73 (note), 191–92 n10:8, 194 n13:9, 196 n16:5
political laws, 38–39, 42, 85, 85 (note), 87, 142
importance of the Sabbath, 123
pollution, 130
poor, 49
poor, treatment of, 30
portion, 156
Portion *Aḥarei Mot*, 150
Portion *Kedoshim*, 150 (note), 157 (note)
Portion *Mishpatim*, 151
Portion *Pinḥas*, 154
Portion *Shoftim*, 149–50
Portion *Terumah*, 152 (note)
Poseidonions metaphysische Schriften (Heinemann), 115 (note), 161 (note)
positive commandments, 142
positive enactments *[takkanot]*, 30 (note)
poverty, remembering, 49
"practical philosophy," 85, 86
practical reasons for the mitzvot, xviii, 6, 143–44, 169, 176, 177
practical-religious man, 107
practical-religious reasons for the mitzvot, xviii, 4
"practical religious" value in Halevi, 73–74
pragmatists, 177, 178
prayers, 18, 30 (note), 67, 68, 69, 71, 73, 80, 86, 111, 113, 114, 115, 124, 134–35, 143, 152, 153, 174, 191 n9:13
communal prayer, 163 (note)
confessional prayer, 16
formulation of, 97, 169
Ne'ilah prayer, 70 (note)
as petitions, 71 (note)
of the righteous, 70 (note)

Rosh Hashanah prayer, 32
symbols of, 26
Yom Kippur prayer, 19
pre-existing law, 179
preservation/performance *[kiyyum]*, 183
prevailing wisdom, 168
Priestly Code, 89
priests
appointment of, 124
High Priest, 17, 110, 113 (note), 124, 126, 150
garments of, 81, 155–56
reasons for the priesthood, 126
Prime Mover, 66
primitive life, 188 n4:27
"Princess Sabbath" (poem), 73 (note)
Principles (Albo), 89 (note)
privations, 125
Probleme des Spätjudentums (Kittel), 31 (note)
propadeutic value of the Torah, 59–60
prophets and prophecies, 74, 88, 89, 90 (note), 94, 126
prophetic inspiration, 70 (note)
"Prophetic Judaism," 115
prostitution, 112, 123 (note)
protective enactments *[gezerot]*, 30 (note)
Proverbs, 151 (note)
"Pseudo-Empedocles," 133 (note)
psychology, 148
psychological explanations of mitzvot, 70–72, 148, 152
value of mitzvot, 173
public offerings, 154
punishment, 5–6, 7, 8, 24, 29, 43, 59, 80, 104, 109–10, 112, 129, 135, 144 (note), 170, 185–86 n3:9
not before age 14, 156–57
reward and punishment, 8, 36, 55–56, 59, 135, 144, 162
pure *[tzerufah]*, 19
purification
of the leper, 20, 78
of mankind, 30, 98 (note)
purification ritual, 12, 40, 109, 134, 154
Purim, 86 (note), 110, 169
purity, 11, 62, 63, 149, 152, 153, 172, 174
family purity, 103, 172
of the heart, 58, 141
inner purity, 153
laws of, 20, 72, 103, 114, 124, 135
menstrual purity, 26 (note)
of the race, 82–83
ritual purity, 44
see also impurity
purposes
and actions, 131–32
purpose of the world and the Torah, 138 (note)
ultimate purpose of the Torah, 132–34
Pythagorean school, 41, 84, 196 n17:5
Pythagorean theorem, 176

R
"R. Judah Halevi's Historical Outlook" (Levin), 66 (note)
Rabbi Judah Halevi (Fishman), 65 (note)
Rabbi Moshe ben Naḥman (Uno), 170 (note)
"rabbinic mitzvot," 30 (note)
rabbis
commands of, 193 n11:2
compared to a child, 32
differences between Hellenistic Jews and rabbis, 45
enactments of Usha, 87 (note)
faith of, 25–26, 31, 32, 35
rabbinic exegeses, 177
and reasons for the commandments, 25–33, 28 (note)
use of parables, 188 n4:13
see also Sages
"Rambam" the Legislator, 104
rankings of mitzvot, 87–88, 89 (note), 91–93, 102–4
ransoms, 81, 136
kofer [ransom], 81 (note)
rape, 9, 12
Rashbam (grandson of Rashi), 48–49, 50, 168 (note), 172
Rashi, 15, 23–24, 48, 50, 168 (note)
rational commandments *[mishpatim]*, xvi, xvii–xviii, xviii, 3, 6, 53 (note), 55, 60, 68, 93, 110 (note), 166–67, 176
distinguishing from non-rational commandments, 21–22, 95
and hortative *[shim'iyot]* mitzvot, 52–53, 85, 90

mefursamot [commonly held], 85
Torah not distinguishing from irrational commandments, 21
rational obedience, 5
rational reasons for mitzvot, 31, 45
Hellenists' views on, 38
rational *[sikhliyot]* vs. hortative *[shim'iyot]* mitzvot, 52–54
rationalism, 51, 52, 60
acting in a rational way, 74–75
of Maimonides, 116–17
Medieval philosophers, 167
modern rationalists, 88–90, 114–16, 167
rational side of Judaism, 73
rationalization, 167
Rava, 103
reason *see* humans, human reason
reasons for the commandments *[ta'amei ha-mitzvot]*, xvi, 8, 12, 45, 97–98, 122
according to the rabbis, 25–33
caution required in investigating reasons, 98–99
Crescas' interpretation of, 134–40
different views concerning, 169–71
and God, xvi–xvii, xviii
hidden reasons, 3, 157, 162–63
learning from classic Jewish thinkers, 176–83
reasons not to ask about, 1–3
reasons to ask about, 3–4
revealed reasons, 21
see also apologetic reasons for the mitzvot; authoritative reasons for the mitzvot; Divine reason; emotional reasons for the mitzvot; ethical reasons for mitzvot; hidden reasons; humans, human reason; intellect, and the mitzvot; irrational commands; mitzvot; philosophical reasons for the mitzvot; practical reasons for the mitzvot; practical-religious reasons for the mitzvot; rational reasons for mitzvot; scientific reasons for the mitzvot; symbolic reasons; teleological reason for the mitzvot; theoretical-religious reasons; utilitarian reasons for the mitzvot
rebellion, 8, 50, 186 n3:14, 189 n5:4
rebellious son, 28
red heifer ceremony, 20, 26, 54, 83 (note), 96, 98, 122, 147 (note), 155
redemption, 127, 135, 168
Re'eh, 152
Reform Judaism, xv
Refutation of Christian Principles (Crescas), 128, 128 (note), 129, 131, 135 (note), 139
religion and the world, 57, 57 (note)
religiosity, 145–46, 182
of the heart, 58, 62, 174
and immortality, 59 (note)
religious commandments *see mitzvot shim'iyot*
religious emotion, 72 (note), 105, 106 (note), 145–46
religious laws, 74, 142, 142 (note), 182 (note)
religious mitzvot, 11
ethical-religious reasons, 156–57
religious influence of the mitzvot, 157
religious-theoretical reasons for the mitzvot *see* theoretical-religious reasons
Torah and the religious value of mitzvot, 12–14
religious obligations, 60, 71, 86, 87, 92, 110 (note), 160
remembering poverty, 49
remembrance of God, 63, 78, 86, 111, 173
repentance, 32, 68, 73, 111, 126, 134, 139, 143, 154, 155, 173, 187 n3:26
return *[teshuvah]*, 182
revealed law, 187 n4:5
revealed status of the mitzvot, xvi, 45, 166
revealed Torah, xvi, 2, 36, 45, 89, 161, 180
revelations, 2, 36, 74, 86, 135, 187 n4:5
reverence, 45, 54, 109, 144, 145, 146–47, 147 (note), 148, 150, 157, 171
reverence/fear *[yir'ah]*, 144 (note)
Revue des Études Juives, 59 (note)
rewards, 17, 25–26, 52, 59, 97, 117, 119, 132, 134, 142, 145, 192 n10:11
eternal reward, 160, 162, 163, 169, 171

for performing the mitzvot, 171
reward and punishment, 8, 36, 55–56, 59, 135, 144, 162
serving only to receive reward, 4, 28, 55, 59, 162, 171
in the World to Come, 55, 58, 133, 170, 171
Rhetoric (Aristotle), 105–6 (note)
righteous, 8, 14, 16, 19, 23, 26, 29, 30, 70 (note), 90 (note), 95, 98, 143
God as, 3, 7, 32
rites and rituals, 20, 38, 40–41, 61, 70 (note), 93, 99, 115, 134, 157
King's ritual, 37
opposition to religious ritual, 168
prevention of idolatry, 112–13
ritual purity and impurity, 12, 40, 44, 70, 109, 121, 134, 154
ritual slaughter, 110
of Sukkot, 135
as thanks to our Creator, 170
and the Torah, 61, 112, 114
of Yom Kippur, 12, 126
robbery *see* theft and stealing
Romantic school, 73, 73 (note)
Romanzero (Heine), 73 (note)
roof covering *[sekhakh]*, 136
Rosenzweig, Franz, xv, xix, 177
Rosh Hashanah, 32, 80, 108, 154, 198
Rosin, David, 81 (note), 191 n9:3, 191 n9:10
Rousseau, Jean Jacques, 38
Ruth the Moabite, 6

S

Saadia ben Joseph, gaon, xvii, 49–50, 51–56, 60, 70 (note), 74 (note), 83 (note), 91, 160, 162, 162 (note), 164 (note), 166, 170, 170 (note), 171, 172, 174, 176, 197
and Baḥya ben Joseph Ibn Pakudah, 62–64, 74
books by, 49, 57
commentaries on *Sefer Yetzirah*, 53–54, 56 (note)
and Crescas, 139
and Halevi, 70
and Ibn Daud, 85, 87, 88–90, 93
and Maimonides, 118, 162 (note)
and Philo, 54–55, 55, 72, 118, 174
Sabbath, 11, 16, 30, 39, 43, 68, 69–70, 86, 94, 102, 135, 141, 174, 180
as commemoration of creation, 9, 28, 61, 71, 77, 110, 122, 152, 154, 156, 172, 186 n3:3
importance of, 73, 89 (note), 90, 91
lighting Sabbath candles, 26 (note)
mitzvot relating to the Sabbath, 8, 9, 43, 44, 53, 71, 80, 89, 103, 122–23, 139
observance of, 89, 181
in other places, 85
Philo's views on, 39, 43 (note), 43–44
rest for body and soul, 69, 71, 77
Sabbath poems, 47, 73 (note), 191 n8:6
sabbatical year, 121
and Saturn/Chronos, 80, 80 (note)
zemirot, 47
Sachs, Jehiel Michael, 158
Sacred Canopy, The (Berger), 146 (note)
sacrifices, 81, 81 (note), 88, 89, 90 (note), 92, 93, 99, 103, 104, 114, 119, 123–24, 126, 128–29, 136, 136 (note), 170, 173–74, 174, 180, 194 n12:3
commandments of the sacrifices, 54, 91, 136
and idolatry, 112–13, 114–15, 123–24, 170 (note), 172
optional, 11
reasons and rules for, 49, 141, 152–54, 170, 172
see also offerings
sacrilege, laws of, 96–97
saeculum, 196 n16:9
safwa *see segullah* [treasure]
safwa [elect], 162 (note)
Sages, 2, 22, 24, 25, 29, 30, 31, 32, 58, 96, 130, 132, 149, 150, 152, 172, 180, 187 n3:17
of the Aggadah, xii
Greek sages, 101
see also rabbis
salt and sacrifices, 126
salvation, 52, 57, 59, 103, 127, 128, 129, 130, 163–64 (note), 164
Christian doctrine of, 180
eternal salvation, 160–61
sanctification, 132, 175

Sanctuary, implements of, 125
Sarah, 6
Satan, 3, 108, 108 (note), 154, 186 n3:14
Saturnalia, 80 (note)
Saul (king), 16
scapegoat, 20, 96, 109, 113 (note), 135
Schleiermacher, Friedrich Daniel Ernst, 72 (note)
Schocken (publisher), xiii
Schöpfung und Chaos (Gunkel), 82 (note)
sciatic nerve, prohibition, xvii, 82, 83
science, 40–41, 68, 69, 116, 162
  Abravanel's interpretation of, 151 (note), 152 (note)
  classification of, 92
  Crescas' interpretation of, 130, 133, 137, 138, 139–40
  divine science, 92
  Greeks on, 115 (note), 159
  Ibn Daud's interpretation of, 86–87, 93–94
  Ibn Ezra as a mystic of science, 83–84
  and Maimonides, 102, 117, 170
  medical science, 44 (note), 74 (note), 90, 151, 160, 172
  and nature, 66, 69, 78–79, 122
  neurochemistry of the brain, 70 (note)
  psychology, 148
  scientific ethics, 52
  scientific idealism, 164
  scientific mystics, 84
  see also cosmological explanations
scientific reasons for the mitzvot, xvii, xviii, 3, 32, 39, 45, 50, 93
  laws of the universe, 40–41
Second Book of the Maccabees, 44 (note)
Second Passover, 78
Second Temple, 89
secondary intention of the Torah, 114
Sefarad, xii
Sefer Ha-Ikkarim [Book of Principles] (Albo), 141, 142 (note)
Sefer ha-Kabbalah [Book of Tradition] (Ibn Daud), 92
Sefer Ha-Mitzvot (Maimonides), 98
Sefer Yetzirah, 41 (note), 53–54, 56 (note)
Sefirah, 141
segullah [treasure], 66 (note)
sekhakh [roof covering], 136
self-actualization, 100, 100 (note), 105
self-esteem, 35
semukhim, 123 (note)
Seneca the Younger, 2, 38
sense perception, 52
Separate Intellects, 123, 123 (note), 125 (note), 143 (note)
servants and masters, 10, 13, 55, 86, 186 n3:2
  man as servant of God, 16, 29, 36, 171
    servants of God *[therapeutai theou]*, 160 (note)
  obligation to serve, 190 n6:10
  serving only to receive reward, 55, 59, 162, 171
serve *[oved]*, 160 (note)
service *[avodah]*, 160 (note)
service of the heart, 114, 115, 143
seven, importance of the number, 41, 78, 79, 99, 123, 135, 141, 154, 173
Seven Nations, 9
sexual relations, 27, 43, 135
sha'atnez [mixed fabrics], 112, 123, 147 (note), 198
Shabbat *see* Sabbath
Shabbat Parah, 194 n13:9
shaked/shoked [almond/take care], 154 (note)
shar'iya, 57 (note)
Shavuot, 28, 135, 173, 198
sheep *[kebhes]*, 154
Shekhinah, 19, 67, 81, 198
  see also Divine Presence
Shema, 17, 111, 122, 134
Shemini, 121, 126, 126 (note)
shim'iyot [hortative] mitzvot, 53 (note), 60, 60 (note), 197
  vs. *sikhliyot* [rational] mitzvot, 52–54
Shir HaYiḥud (poem), 47
Shofar, 108, 158, 173, 198
  reasons for, 154–55
Shoftim, Portion, 149–50
Shor, Joseph ben Isaac Bekor, 49 (note)
Shulḥan Arukh (Caro), 47
Siegel, Seymour, xv
Sifra Vayikra (Eleazar ben Azariah), 16
sikhliyot [rational] mitzvot vs. *shim'iyot* [hortative] mitzvot, 52–54

silluk, 194 n13:9
Simeon, Rabbi, 25
Sinai, 16, 29, 48 (note), 77, 86, 104, 130, 155, 178 (note)
 behavior after, 7–8
 behavior prior to, 5–6
sins and sinners, 54, 110, 173–74, 196 n17:4
 no punishment for until age 14, 156–57
 original sin, 127, 128–29, 130, 135, 156, 168
 sin of Adam, 174
 sin offering, 81, 87, 99, 111, 112, 153
 transgressions, 7, 43, 109, 153
slaves and slavery, 10–11, 16, 29, 43, 77, 121, 132, 154
social content of mitzvot, 118, 119
social motives vs. social ideas, 164, 164 (note)
social value of mitzvot, 174
sociological method, 180–83, 182 (note)
Socrates, 37, 66
Sodom, 5
Solomon ibn Gabirol, 50, 80 (note), 189 n5:4, 196 n16:5
Solomon (king), 2 (note), 98, 144, 154
Solon, xvi
Song of Songs, 175
sorcery, 112, 135
soul, 26, 57, 60, 62, 63, 72, 77, 81, 90, 92, 130, 136, 137, 145, 149, 153, 162 (note)
 "added soul" active on Sabbath, 174
 of an animal, 23
 body and soul, 50, 60, 61, 69–70, 71, 91, 135, 136, 145, 191 n9:3
  heart and soul, 146
  perfection of the soul, 100–101
 as a candle, 26, 156
 and certain foods, 38, 131, 156
 colloquy with mind, 191 n9:3
 eternal or immortal nature of, 103 (note), 132, 133, 161
 functions of, 125 (note)
 harming of, 149
 health of, 162 (note)
 nutritive soul, 125, 125 (note)
 rational soul, 125
 and sacrifices, 54
sovereignty of God, 154
"Special Commandments," 40
Special Commandments, The (Philo), 154 (note)
species, mixing of *see* animals
spirit of community, 182
"spiritual" commandments, 68
spiritual-intellectual reasons for mitzvot, 122
spiritual virtures, 61
statutes *[ḥukkim]*, 149
stealing *see* theft and stealing
Stein, quoted in *Jeshurun* (Wohlgemuth), 30 (note)
Sterne und Sternbilder (Gundel), 129 (note)
Stoic doctrine, 36 (note), 37, 176
strangers, treatment of, 10–11
Strauss, Leo, 193 n11:20
Studien über Ibn Gaibirol (Kaufmann), 133 (note)
subdued *[nikhbashim]*, 154
subjective factors in explaining the mitzvot, 176–78
submission, 71, 136, 137, 139, 155, 171
sukkah, 9, 31 (note), 49, 77, 136, 199
Sukkot, 40, 135, 173, 199
Summa (Thomas Aquinas), 168 (note)
summer/end *[kayitz/ketz]*, 154 (note)
supernaturalism, xvi, xviii, 94
superstition, 20, 22, 95, 98, 107, 108, 115, 164, 169
survival, 172, 181
symbolic reasons, 26–27
symbols, 56 (note), 77–78, 105 (note), 109, 122, 135–36, 155, 170, 173, 176, 194 n13:9
 astrology and religious symbolism, 192 n9:20
 and mitzvot, 157–58
 of Passover, 28
 Philo's perceptions of, 44
 seven, importance of the number, 41
 symbolic method, 179, 179 (note)
 symbolistic commentaries of Abravanel, 195 n15:14
 in the Temple, 125
 Tent of Meeting, 192 n9:24
 trees as symbols, 26–27, 39

T
ta'am [taste/reason], 126
Ta'amei Ha-Mitzvot (Heinemann), xv
ta'amei ha-mitzvot [reasons for the commandments], xvi
Tabernacle, 69, 155
take care/almond *[shaked/shoked]*, 154 (note)
takkanot [positive enactments], 30 (note)
talismans, 129
tallit, 107, 175
Talmud *[fiqh]*, 109 (note), 199
Talmudic School, 47–50
tamtzit see segullah [treasure]
Tannaim, 15, 160, 199
Tänzer, Aaron, 147 (note)
Targum Pseudo-Jonathan, 23
Tchernowitz, H., 49 (note)
tefillin, 9, 30, 61, 71, 77, 86, 91, 102, 105, 113, 172, 175
teleological reason for the mitzvot, 50
Temple, 54, 69, 70, 70 (note), 94, 103, 109
  destruction of, 27, 67
  implements of the Sanctuary, 125
  limiting access to, 113, 124
  preventing worship in other high places, 113
  Second Temple, 89
  service in, 11, 67, 93, 94, 134–35
  structure of, 81–82
  symbolism of, 40, 56 (note), 70, 81–82, 83
  worship in, 74, 113, 114, 115
temporary commandments, 5, 6–7
Ten Commandments, 9, 21, 40, 122, 156
  Ibn Daud's interpretation of, 86–87
tensions
  with regard to actions, 104–5
  with regard to feelings, 105–7
Tent of Meeting, 69, 84, 113, 125, 131, 173, 192 n9:24
Terumah, 125
  Portion *Terumah*, 152 (note)
teshuvah [return], 182
thankfulness, 87, 194 n12:3
thanksgiving, 111, 153, 155
theft and stealing, 19, 48, 53, 105, 109, 142
  penalties for those who rob directly vs. those who steal in secret, 29
theocracy, 42–43
theonomy, 38, 166
  theonomic reasons for the mitzvoh, 160
theoretical reasons for the mitzvot, 164, 168–69, 179
theoretical-religious reasons
  for the mitzvot, xviii, 3, 32, 45, 50, 95
  relationship between theoretical and practical man, 107
therapeutai theou [servants of God], 160 (note)
Thesaurus of Hebrew Philosophical Terms (Klatzkin), 164 (note)
Thomas Aquinas, Saint, 168 (note)
Three Jewish Philosophers (Heinemann), 65 (note), 66 (note)
Thummim, 136
Thus Spoke Zarathustra (Nietzsche) *see Also sprach Zarathustra* (Nietzsche)
tithing, 110
Toledot Ha-Posekim (Tchernowitz), 49 (note)
Torah, xii, 18–19, 58, 61, 132–34, 138 (note), 170, 199, 186 n3:8
  authority of, 59, 60
  authorship of, xviii–xix
  awakening of, 59, 59 (note), 60, 62, 92
  defense of Torah against Christian attacks, 127
  as divine law, 118–19, 169
  divine origin of, 6, 37, 42–43, 55, 101, 102, 130, 139, 161, 168, 170
  faith as pillar of, 87, 90, 92
  narratives and precepts of, 101–4
  not distinguishing between rational and irrational commandments, 21
  and *olam* [world], 57 (note)
  propadeutic value of the Torah, 59–60
  revealed status of, xvi, 2, 36, 45, 89, 161, 180, 187 n4:5
  and rites and rituals, 61, 112, 114
  secondary intention of the Torah, 114
  shar'iya, 57 (note)
  those who loathe, 58

unified explanation of, 138
unity of, 138, 150, 156, 157–58
value of, 32, 37, 39, 59–60, 102
Torahitic law, 193 n11:2
traditionalists, xviii, 52
tranquility, 161 (note)
transgressions, 7, 43, 109, 153
see also sins and sinners
treasure *[segullah]*, 66 (note)
trees as symbols, 26–27, 39, 62
triangulation
externalization, objectification, internalization, 146 (note)
love, fear, and joy, 145–46
"triple cord," 78
truth, 45, 51, 53, 93, 117, 133, 162
Tur, The (Jacob ben Asher), 2, 48 (note), 107, 170, 175, 176
Tur Yoreh Deah, 112
Tzav, 123, 126
tzedakah , 110, 164 (note)
tzerufah [pure], 19
tzipiyah [observation of nature], 190 n7:12
tzitzit [garment fringe], 9, 26, 31 (note), 71, 105, 122, 155 (note), 158, 174, 199, 187 n3:26
Tziyon (journal), 66 (note), 67 (note)

U
ultimate perfection, 100, 101, 103, 105, 116, 119, 142
ultimate purpose of the Torah, 132–34
ultra-Orthodox Judaism, 178 (note)
uncircumcised *[arel]*, 78
unified explanation of mitzvot, 138
unity
of the Holy and Blessed God, 108, 117
of Jewry, 74 (note)
of the Torah, 138, 150, 156, 157–58
universal standards of common propriety *[derekh eretz]*, 49
universe, laws of, 40–41
Uno, R. Y., 170 (note)
"unwritten" laws, 38
Urbach, Ephraim, 113 (note)
Urim, 136
Usha, enactments of, 87 (note)
utilitarian-practical value, 143
utilitarian reasons for the mitzvot, 10, 44, 55–56, 63, 71, 77, 109, 139, 151 (note), 151–52, 160, 172, 176
and consequences of the mitzvot, 171–75

V
Vajda, 59 (note)
value
of customs, 37, 38
of deeds, 92
hierarchy, 56
of the mitzvot, 34–35, 58, 149–50
of the Torah, 32, 37, 39, 59–60, 102
Vayikra, 126
violence, 9, 34, 42, 90, 100
virtue, 42, 61 (note), 77, 92, 96, 105 (note), 132, 134, 137, 156
actions vs. virtues, 103
benefits of, 63 (note)
ethical virtues, 43, 100, 118, 137, 162 (note)
four cardinal virtue of Greek ethics, 40, 42, 45, 173
ma'alot [ascensions, virtues], 61 (note)
personal virtue, 85, 87, 87 (note)
spiritual virtures, 61
vows, 11, 15, 28, 171

W
Wajab, 190 n8:3
Wars of the Lord (Gersonides), 125 (note)
Ways of the Aggadah, The [Darkhei Ha-Aggadah] (Heinemann), xv, 71 (note)
weak-mindedness of Israel, 59, 60 (note)
Wellhausen, Julius, 89, 181
"wicked son," 22
widows, 1, 10, 24–25
Wiener, A., 49 (note), 189 n5:4
will, free, 129
will of God, 2, 5–6, 7, 13, 25, 36, 133, 143, 149, 160, 161, 166, 171, 175, 186 n3:16
willow trees as symbols, 26–27
wisdom, 42, 54, 88, 99
Creator's wisdom, 71, 161–62, 168–69
neglect of, 50
pillar of wisdom, 107
prevailing wisdom, 168
witches and witchcraft, 20

Wohlgemuth, Joseph, 30 (note), 31 (note), 89 (note)
women, 26, 112, 121, 213
  adulterous women, 28–29
  maidens, 185 n1:1
  and marriage, 24, 25, 28, 53–54, 68, 173
  men wearing women's clothing, 79, 112, 123
  rape of a young betrothed, 9, 12
  referred to in Proverbs, 151 (note)
  value, 24
wordplay of Heinemann, 74 (note)
"work of the divine Chariot," 103, 103 (note)
World of Rest, 59
World to Come, 55, 58, 63, 63 (note), 81, 81 (note), 97, 98 (note), 103 (note), 105, 106, 108, 133, 134, 137, 144, 147, 170 (note), 199
world-view, 49
  world-view of the Greeks, 36, 37
worship, 19, 32, 66, 80, 100, 103, 104, 108, 114, 134, 136 (note), 145, 146, 151
  sacrificial worhip, 96, 141
  and Shofar, 125
  Temple worship, 69, 74, 81, 113, 114, 115, 124, 125
  value of, 58, 152

Y
Yesod [Foundation], 141
Yesod Mora [The Foundation of Faith] (Ibn Ezra), 76, 77, 78, 80, 83
YHWH, 66, 68, 72, 197
Yigdal (poem), 47
yir'ah [fear/reverence], 144 (note)
Yitzḥaki, Shlomo *see* Rashi
yoke, 8, 16, 29, 122, 163
  of divine authority, xvi, 13
  of the kingdom of heaven, 16, 17, 29, 36
  of the mitzvot, 16, 18, 22, 58, 76
Yom Kippur, 12, 16, 19, 43, 78, 123, 124, 126, 139, 150, 155, 173, 199
"Yosef ben Gorion," 195 n15:9

Z
Zipporah, 88, 192 n10:9
Zohar, 198

Printed in the United States
215904BV00002B/6/P

9 781934 843536